3

Life

SECOND EDITION

NATIONAL GEOGRAPHIC
LEARNING

JOHN HUGHES
HELEN STEPHENSON
PAUL DUMMETT

Australia · Brazil · Mexico · Singapore · United Kingdom · United States

Contents

Unit	Grammar	Vocabulary	Real life (functions)	Pronunciation
1 Lifestyle pages 9–20	simple present adverbs and expressions of frequency simple present and present continuous	everyday routines wordbuilding: collocations with *do*, *play*, and *go* word focus: *feel* medical problems	talking about illness	/s/, /z/, or /ɪz/ one or two syllables?
VIDEO: Laughter yoga page 18 ▶ REVIEW page 20				
2 Competitions pages 21–32	modal verbs for rules *-ing* form	sports wordbuilding: suffixes word focus: *like*	talking about interests	/ŋ/ silent letters
VIDEO: Mongolian horse racing page 30 ▶ REVIEW page 32				
3 Transportation pages 33–44	comparatives and superlatives *as … as* comparative modifiers	ways of traveling transportation nouns wordbuilding: compound nouns transportation adjectives transportation verbs taking transportation	going on a trip	*than* sentence stress intonation
VIDEO: Indian Railways page 42 ▶ REVIEW page 44				
4 Challenges pages 45–56	simple past past continuous and simple past	risks and challenges personal qualities wordbuilding: verbs and nouns	telling a story	/d/, /t/, or /ɪd/ *was / were* intonation for responding
VIDEO: A microadventure page 54 ▶ REVIEW page 56				
5 The environment pages 57–68	quantifiers articles: *a / an*, *the*, or no article	materials recycling results and figures word focus: *take*	calling about an order	/ðə/ or /ðiː/ sounding friendly
VIDEO: Recycling Cairo page 66 ▶ REVIEW page 68				
6 Stages of life pages 69–80	infinitive forms future forms: *going to*, *will*, and present continuous	life events describing age celebrations word focus: *get* wordbuilding: synonyms	inviting, accepting, and declining	/tə/ contractions emphasizing words
VIDEO: Steel drums page 78 ▶ REVIEW page 80				

Listening	Reading	Critical thinking	Speaking	Writing
someone talking about a national park near a city a radio interview about long life	a quiz about how well you sleep an article about centenarians an article about how nature is good for you	giving examples	finding out about lifestyle your current life making a town healthier	text type: filling out a form writing skill: information on forms
someone describing an Ironman competition three people talking about competitive sports in schools	an article about crazy competitions an article about female wrestlers in Bolivia	reading between the lines	explaining the rules of a sport or competition talking about your sports preferences your opinions about Olympic sports	text type: an ad writing skill: checking your writing
someone describing a photo two people discussing the pros and cons of different types of transportation a documentary about animal transportation	an article about solutions to transportation problems an article about the fate of the rickshaw in Kolkata, India	opinions for and against	talking about and comparing commutes advice on transportation a presentation about a pedicab company	text type: notes and messages writing skill: writing in note form
a caver talking about his hobby a climber makes an impossible decision	an article about two adventurers an article about different types of challenges	looking for evidence	talking about your past events you remember giving tips or advice on the best ways to learn English	text type: a short story writing skill: structure your writing
an excerpt from a documentary about a house made from recycled materials a news report about environmental projects	an article about e-waste an article about a boat made of plastic bottles	reading closely (part 1)	talking about recycling a general knowledge quiz changing attitudes and behaviors	a quiz text type: emails writing skill: formal words
differences between the generations a news item about Mardi Gras	an article about how a couple changed their lives an article about how Mardi Gras is celebrated around the world an article about coming-of-age ceremonies	analyzing the writer's view	plan the trip of a lifetime planning a celebration describing annual events	text type: a description writing skill: descriptive adjectives

Unit	Grammar	Vocabulary	Real life (functions)	Pronunciation
7 Work pages 81–92	present perfect and simple past present perfect with *for* and *since* prepositions of place and movement	language to describe jobs jobs wordbuilding: suffixes in job words parts of a building word focus: *make* or *do* job ads	a job interview	intrusive /w/
VIDEO: My working life page 90 ▶ REVIEW page 92				
8 Technology pages 93–104	zero and first conditionals defining relative clauses	internet verbs wordbuilding: dependent prepositions instructions	finding out how something works	linking
VIDEO: Ancient languages, modern technology page 102 ▶ REVIEW page 104				
9 Vacations pages 105–116	past perfect subject questions	vacation collocations wordbuilding: *-ed* / *-ing* adjectives word focus: *place*	requesting and suggesting	*'d* number of syllables /ʤə/
VIDEO: Living in Venice page 114 ▶ REVIEW page 116				
10 Products pages 117–128	the passive (simple present and simple past) *used to*	wordbuilding: word forms describing design websites	discussing opinions	stress in different word forms /s/ or /z/
VIDEO: Wind turbines page 126 ▶ REVIEW page 128				
11 History pages 129–140	reported speech reporting verbs (*say* and *tell*)	wordbuilding: verb + preposition communication ancient history word focus: *one*	giving a short presentation	pausing
VIDEO: The Golden Record page 138 ▶ REVIEW page 140				
12 Nature pages 141–152	second conditional *anywhere, everyone, nobody, something*, etc.	extreme weather nature word focus: *start*	finding a solution	*would / wouldn't / 'd*
VIDEO: Cambodia animal rescue page 150 ▶ REVIEW page 152				

COMMUNICATION ACTIVITIES page 153 ▶ GRAMMAR SUMMARY page 156 ▶ AUDIOSCRIPT page 181

Listening	Reading	Critical thinking	Speaking	Writing
a woman talks about her job in a steel mill an interview with a scientist two people giving instructions	an article about new jobs in an area an article about modern-day cowboys	analyzing comparisons in a text	describing past experiences giving directions job satisfaction a job interview	text type: a résumé writing skill: leaving out words in résumés
a documentary about the importance of technology a science program about an invention	an explorer's blog an article about biomimetics	the writer's sources	planning a trip important inventions design an invention for everyday life favorite technology	text type: a paragraph writing skill: connecting words
three people talk about their vacations an interview with a tour guide	a vacation story an article about the two sides of Paris	the author's purpose	a story about a vacation planning a group vacation a presentation about a place you know well	text type: an email requesting information writing skill: formal expressions
a description of a producer and his products a radio program about a famous product from the past	an article about some famous logos an article about having less "stuff"	fact or opinion?	some famous products or brands talk about things you used to do in the past a presentation on having less "stuff" planning a new website	text type: a review writing skill: giving your opinion
a historian talking about Robert Falcon Scott's hut in Antarctica a news story about a message in a bottle	a timeline of video gaming an article about stealing historical objects	emotion words	planning a time capsule opinions about games reporting a message a museum in your town or city	a message in a bottle text type: a biography writing skill: punctuation in direct speech
a description of the life of a storm chaser a documentary about a photographer	an article about a science blog an article about chimpanzee expert Jane Goodall	reading closely (part 2)	hopes and dreams questions with *any*-interview questions	text type: an article writing skill: planning an article

Life around the world—in 12 videos

Unit 10 Wind turbines

Learn about an innovative product and how it can change lives.

Unit 11 The Golden Record

Voyager 1 carries a message for other life forms in the universe.

USA

UK

Unit 1 Laughter yoga

Find out why laughing is good for you.

Unit 6 Steel drums

Steelband music, or pan, is an important part of the culture in these Caribbean islands.

Trinidad & Tobago

Unit 7 My working life

Some people talk about their working lives.

Unit 9 Living in Venice

Learn what it's like to live in Venice.

Unit 2 Mongolian horse racing

Horse racing at a Mongolian festival.

Unit 8 Ancient languages, modern technology

Find out how technology is being used to record and preserve disappearing languages.

Unit 4 A microadventure

Two friends spend 24 hours in Croatia on a microadventure.

India

Unit 5 Recycling Cairo

Find out how recycled objects are used in Cairo.

Cambodia

Unit 12 Cambodia animal rescue

Rescuing victims of illegal animal poaching in Cambodia.

Unit 3 Indian Railways

Learn more about the Indian railway system.

Australia

UNIT 1
LIFESTYLE

UNIT 2
COMPETITIONS

UNIT 3
TRANSPORTATION

UNIT 4
CHALLENGES

UNIT 5
THE ENVIRONMENT

UNIT 6
STAGES OF LIFE

UNIT 7
WORK

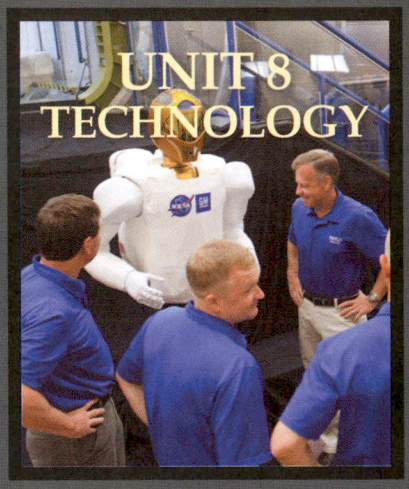
UNIT 8
TECHNOLOGY

UNIT 9
VACATIONS

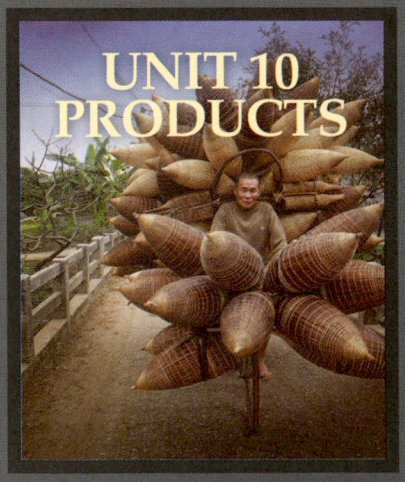
UNIT 10
PRODUCTS

UNIT 11
HISTORY

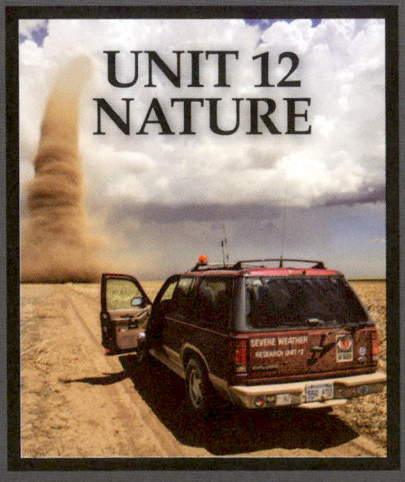
UNIT 12
NATURE

Unit 1 Lifestyle

Bukhansan National Park, South Korea

FEATURES

10 How well do you sleep?
Complete a questionnaire about sleep

12 The secrets of a long life
How can you live to be one hundred?

14 Nature is good for you
Nature and health

18 Laughter yoga
A video about why laughing is good for you

1 Work in pairs. Describe the place in the photo. How do you think the person feels?

2 ▶1 Work in pairs. Listen to a description of the place in the photo. Answer the questions.

1 Where is Bukhansan National Park?
2 How many people visit it every year?
3 Why do they go there?

3 Look at the activities in the box. Which activities do you often do? When do you do them? Tell your partner.

take a bike ride	cook a meal
chat on social media	play sports and exercise
go for long walks	go fishing
play video games	play a musical instrument
read books	watch movies

I often go for long walks in the evening.

1a How well do you sleep?

Vocabulary everyday routines

1 Work in pairs. Match the two parts of the expressions for everyday routines. Then describe your typical day using some of the expressions.

1 get	○	○	asleep
2 fall	○	○	home late
3 take a	○	○	TV
4 watch	○	○	break
5 work long	○	○	until midnight
6 wake up	○	○	eight
7 get up about	○	○	early
8 stay up	○	○	hours

I often get home late from work …

Reading

2 Answer the questionnaire below. Then work in pairs and compare your answers.

3 Turn to page 153 and find out what your answers say about your lifestyle.

Grammar simple present and adverbs of frequency

4 Match the sentences (1–2) with their uses (a–b).

1 I work long hours and get home late.
2 The average human needs around eight hours of sleep per night.

a to talk about things that are always true ____
b to talk about habits and routines ____

▶ SIMPLE PRESENT

I/you/we/they ***sleep***.	*He/she/it* ***sleeps***.
I/you/we/they ***don't sleep***.	*He/she/it* ***doesn't sleep***.
Do *I/you/we/they* ***sleep***?	***Does*** *he/she/it* ***sleep***?

For more information and practice, see page 156.

▶ 2

How well *do* you sleep?

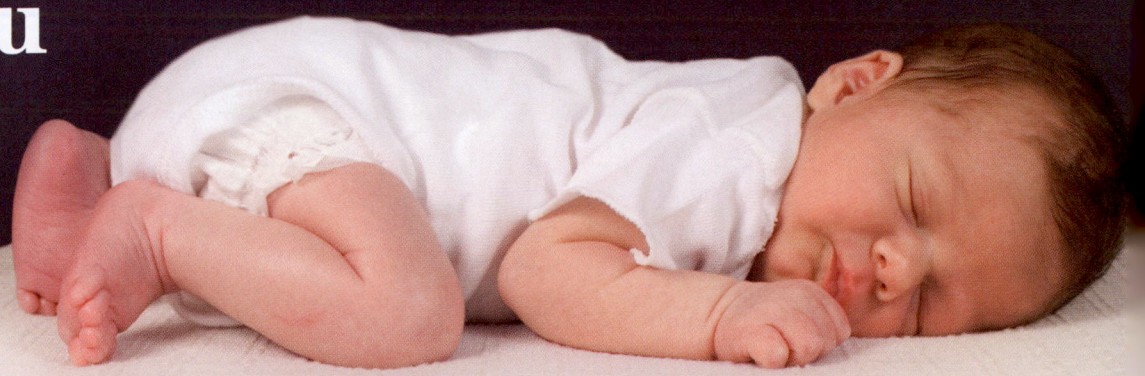

1 Do you often feel tired?
A No, I never feel tired during the day.
B I sometimes feel tired after a long day at work.
C All the time! I'm always ready for bed.

2 How many hours do you usually sleep at night?
A Between seven and eight hours.
B More than nine. I rarely stay up late.
C Fewer than six.

3 What do you usually do before you go to bed?
A I watch TV or read a book.
B I exercise.
C I do some work.

4 How long do you usually sleep on the weekends?
A I usually sleep the same amount as any other day.
B I sometimes sleep for an extra hour or two.
C I always sleep until noon! I never get up early.

5 How often do you wake up in the middle of the night?
A I never wake up before morning.
B I rarely wake up more than once.
C Two or three times a night.

5 Look at the grammar box on page 10. Complete the article about sleep with the simple present form of the verbs in parentheses.

The secrets of sleep

Why [1] *do we sleep* **(we / sleep)?**
From birth, we [2] _____ (spend) a third of our lives asleep, but scientists still [3] _____ (not / know) exactly why.

Why [4] _____ **(we / have) problems sleeping?**
In modern society, many adults [5] _____ (not / get) the seven or eight hours' sleep they need every night. We [6] _____ (work) long hours, and we rarely [7] _____ (go) to bed at sunset.

Why [8] _____ **(we / sleep) differently?**
It [9] _____ (depend) on the time of year and also our age. Teenagers usually [10] _____ (need) more sleep than adults. Lots of elderly people [11] _____ (not / sleep) longer than four or five hours at night, but they often [12] _____ (take) naps during the day.

6 Pronunciation /s/, /z/, or /ɪz/

3 Listen to the endings of these verbs. Is the sound /s/, /z/, or /ɪz/? Circle your answers. Then listen again and repeat.

1	feels	/s/ /z/ /ɪz/		5	goes	/s/ /z/ /ɪz/	
2	needs	/s/ /z/ /ɪz/		6	dances	/s/ /z/ /ɪz/	
3	watches	/s/ /z/ /ɪz/		7	does	/s/ /z/ /ɪz/	
4	sleeps	/s/ /z/ /ɪz/		8	works	/s/ /z/ /ɪz/	

7 Work in pairs. Discuss these questions.

1 What time do you and your friends usually get up? How late do you stay up?
2 Does anyone in your family ever take a nap in the afternoon?
3 Do people sleep longer in the summer or in the winter?

8 Look at the list below. Then underline the adverbs of frequency in the questionnaire on page 10 and write the missing adverbs in the list.

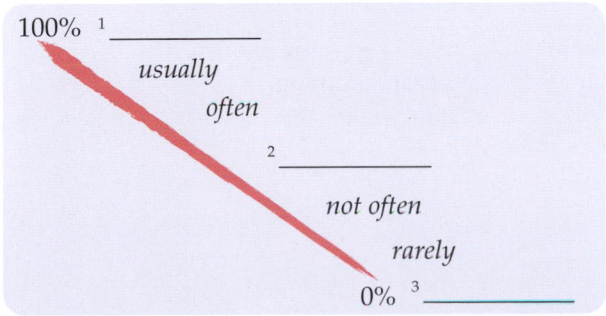

ADVERBS and EXPRESSIONS OF FREQUENCY

*She's **usually** late for work.*
*I **often wake up** at seven.*
*Do you **often** wake up in the middle of the night?*
*She wakes up **two or three times a night**.*
***Every month,** I visit my grandparents.*

For more information and practice, see page 156.

9 Look at the grammar box above. Circle the correct options to complete the rules (1–2).

1 An adverb of frequency usually goes *after / before* the main verb, but it goes *after / before* the verb *be*.
2 An expression of frequency (e.g., *twice a week*) usually goes *at the beginning / in the middle* or at the end of a sentence.

10 Show the correct place in the sentence for the adverb or expression in parentheses. Sometimes there is more than one correct answer.

1 My brother plays tennis on Saturday mornings. (always)
2 We eat at a restaurant. (about once a month)
3 I take a bus to school. (every day)
4 She is at home during the day. (rarely)
5 They go on vacation. (twice a year)
6 Are you late for work? (often)

Speaking myLife

11 Work in pairs. Find out about your partner's habits. Take turns asking questions with *How often …?* and the ideas in the box. Answer using an adverb or expression of frequency.

*A: **How often do** you **eat** out?*
*B: About **once a month**.*

go on vacation	be late for work/school
check your email	check your phone for messages
play board games	take public transportation
eat at a restaurant	feel stressed

12 Work in groups. Prepare a questionnaire about lifestyle for another group. Start each question with *How often …?, Are you often …?,* or *Do you often …?,* and offer three choices of answer (A, B, or C). Then ask your questions to the other group. Can you tell them what their answers say about their lifestyle?

1b The secrets of a long life

Reading

1 Work in pairs. Who is the oldest person you know? How old is he or she? How healthy is their lifestyle?

My grandfather is the oldest person I know. He's 83 and still plays golf.

2 Work in pairs. Read the article *The Secrets of a Long Life*. Answer the questions.

1 Why is Okinawa famous?
2 What kind of food do the people eat there?
3 Which of their activities do you do?
I don't go fishing, but I do some gardening.

Wordbuilding collocations with *do, play,* and *go*

▶ WORDBUILDING collocations with *do, play,* and *go*

We use certain nouns with certain verbs. These are called collocations.
go fishing NOT ~~*do fishing*~~ or ~~*play fishing*~~

For more practice, see Workbook page 11.

3 Look at the wordbuilding box. Complete the chart below with activities from the article.

Do	Go	Play
	fishing	

4 Add these activities to the chart in Exercise 3. Use a dictionary if necessary.

cards	hiking	homework	nothing
running	shopping	tennis	the piano
yoga	soccer	karate	surfing

5 Work in pairs. Tell your partner about people you know using the collocations in the chart.

*My brother **does** karate. He's a black belt.*

▶ 4

The Secrets of a
Long Life

Okinawa in Japan has some of the oldest people in the world. It's famous for its high number of centenarians—men and women who live beyond one hundred years of age. Some of the reasons for their good health are that they:

- go fishing and eat what they catch.
- do a lot of gardening and grow their own fruit and vegetables.
- go cycling, and rarely drive when they can walk.
- often spend time with friends. They meet at people's houses and play games.
- exercise regularly, go swimming, and lead active lives.

An 89-year-old woman from Okinawa picks seaweed. It's part of her everyday food.

Listening

6 ▶ 5 Listen to a radio interview with photographer David McLain. Check (✓) the topics the speakers talk about.

- ☐ the age of men and women
- ☐ family life
- ☐ sleep
- ☐ food
- ☐ exercise

7 ▶ 5 Listen again. Are the sentences true (T) or false (F)?

1	David McLain is traveling to different countries.	T	F
2	He's talking to the radio announcer in the studio.	T	F
3	In Sardinia, men live to the same age as women.	T	F
4	Sardinian families rarely eat together.	T	F
5	Younger people are eating more unhealthy food, and they aren't exercising enough.	T	F

8 Work in pairs. Think about the lifestyle of people in your country. Is it similar to the lifestyle in Sardinia? How traditional is your country?

Grammar simple present and present continuous

9 Look at the grammar box and the sentences below from the interview. Which sentences use the simple present (S)? Which use the present continuous (C)?

1	Well, one man is trying to answer these questions—photographer David McLain.	S	C
2	He's speaking to us right now on the phone.	S	C
3	Men live to the same age as women.	S	C
4	Every Sunday, the whole family eats a big meal together.	S	C
5	Also, young people are moving to the city, so they are exercising less because of their lifestyle.	S	C

10 We use the present continuous to talk about something happening now or around now. Match the three present continuous sentences in Exercise 9 with the uses (a–c).

a to talk about a changing situation ____
b to talk about something happening around now, but not necessarily at this exact moment ____
c to talk about something actually in progress now ____

▶ PRESENT CONTINUOUS

*I'**m** speak**ing**.*
*You/we/they'**re** speak**ing**.*
*He/she/it's speak**ing**.*

*I'**m** not trave**ling**.*
*You/we/they **aren't** trave**ling**.*
*He/she/it **isn't** trave**ling**.*

***Am** I work**ing**?*
***Are** you/we/they work**ing**?*
***Is** he/she/it work**ing**?*

For more information and practice, see page 156.

11 Complete the sentences with the simple present or present continuous form of these verbs.

reply	go	~~learn~~
read	spend	

1 We *'re learning* _____ a new language at the moment.
2 My friends and I often _____ time at each other's houses.
3 Can you wait a minute? I _____ to an email.
4 How often _____ you _____ to the gym?
5 I _____ a really interesting book at the moment.

Speaking myLife

12 Write pairs of questions. Use the simple present in one question and the present continuous in the other. Then work in pairs. Take turns asking and answering the questions.

1 a How / usually spend your free time?
How do you usually spend your free time?
b / you / play / many sports these days?
Are you playing many sports these days?
2 a / often / read novels?
_____
b / read / any good books at the moment?
_____
3 a Where / usually go on vacation?
_____
b Where / plan to go this year?
_____
4 a / speak / any other languages?
_____
b / learn / any new languages?
_____

1c Nature is good for you

Reading

1 Work in pairs. Look at the photo. Where do you think this woman is?

2 Read the article. Match the topics (a–c) with the paragraphs in the article (1–3).

a how much time we spend outdoors ____
b making nature part of city life ____
c studies by doctors ____

3 Work in pairs. Read the article again. Answer the questions.

1 What is the main change in how people spend their time?
2 What is happening at national parks in Canada?
3 After the math test, where did some people look at pictures of nature?
4 What are they going to build in Dubai?
5 In South Korea, how many people visit the new forests every year?

Word focus *feel*

4 Work in pairs. Underline four phrases with *feel* in the first paragraph of the article. Match the phrases to the uses (1–3).

1 to talk about your emotions or health
2 to talk about wanting to do something
3 to talk about an opinion

5 Complete the questions with the words in the box.

about	better	like	that

1 What do you usually feel _____ doing after a long day at work?
2 Do you feel _____ nature is good for us? Why or why not?
3 After a difficult day, what makes you feel _____ in the evening?
4 How do you feel _____ nature?

6 Work in pairs. Take turns asking and answering the questions from Exercise 5.

A: What do you usually feel like doing after a long day at work?
B: Going for a run in my local park and then eating dinner. Sometimes I go out and meet friends.

Critical thinking giving examples

7 When writers give an opinion, they often support the idea with examples. Look at these sentences. Which sentence has the main idea (M)? Which sentences give examples (E)?

a	For example, the number of visitors to Canada's national parks is going down every year.	M	E
b	Humans are spending more time inside and less time outside.	M	E
c	And in countries such as the USA, only 10% of teenagers spend time outside every day.	M	E

8 Work in pairs. Read paragraphs 2 and 3 of the article. Find the sentence with the main idea and sentences with examples. Underline the phrases for giving examples.

For example, the number of visitors to Canada's national parks is going down every year.

9 Complete these sentences in your own words. Use examples from your own life. Then share your sentences with a partner.

1 I relax in my free time in different ways. For example, …
2 My hometown has some places with trees and nature, such as …
3 There are some beautiful national parks in my country. A good example is …

Speaking myLife

10 Work in groups of four. Imagine your town has some money to make people's lives healthier. Look at the ideas below and think of one more.

- plant one hundred new trees in the town
- build a new park with a children's play area
- increase the number of bike paths across the town

11 Discuss the ideas in your group and choose the best one. Give reasons and examples.

I think increasing the number of bike paths is a good idea because cycling is good for your health and good for the environment.

NATURE
is good for you

▶ 6

1 How do you feel about nature? After spending hours indoors, do you often feel like going outside for a walk? Or if you work for hours at your desk, do you feel better when you take a break and visit your local park? Most people think that nature is good for us; it's good for our bodies and good for our brains. However, humans are spending more time inside and less time outside. For example, the number of visitors to Canada's national parks is going down every year. And in countries such as the USA, only 10% of teenagers spend time outside every day. Many doctors feel that this is a problem in the twenty-first century, and that it is making our physical health worse.

2 As a result, some doctors are studying the connection between nature and health; one example of this is the work of Dr. Matilda van den Bosch in Sweden. The doctor gave two groups of people a math test. During the test, the heart rate[1] of people in both groups increased. After the test, one group of people sat in a 3D-virtual-reality room with pictures and sounds of nature for fifteen minutes. Later, their heart rates were slower than the heart rates of people in the other group. The virtual contact with nature helped these people feel more relaxed. Another good example of how nature is good for health comes from Canada. In Toronto, researchers studied 31,000 people living in cities. Overall, they found that people who lived near parks were healthier.

3 Because of studies like these, some countries and cities want nature to be part of people's everyday life. In Dubai, for example, there are plans for a new shopping mall with a large garden, so shoppers can relax outside with trees, plants, and water. In some countries—such as Switzerland—"forest schools" are popular; schoolchildren study their subjects in the forest and do lots of exercise outside. And South Korea is another good example: It has new forests near its cities, and around 13 million people visit these forests every year. So after building cities for so long, perhaps it's now time to start rebuilding nature.

[1] **heart rate** (n) /hɑrt reɪt/ the speed at which the heart beats (number of heartbeats per minute)

1d At the doctor's

Vocabulary medical problems

1 Look at the pictures. Match the people (1–8) with the medical problems (a–h).

a I have a headache.
b I have a backache.
c I have a runny nose.
d I have an earache.
e I have a stomachache.
f I have a temperature.
g I have a sore throat.
h I have a bad cough.

2 What do you do when you have the problems in Exercise 1? Discuss with a partner. Choose the best option (1–3) for each problem.

1 I go to bed.
2 I take medicine.
3 I go to the pharmacy or see my doctor.

3 Pronunciation one or two syllables?

▶ 7 Listen to these words. Which words have one syllable? Which words have two? Underline the stressed syllable in the two-syllable words. Then listen again and repeat.

ache	headache	ear	earache
stomach	throat	cough	backache

Real life talking about illness

4 ▶ 8 Work in pairs. Listen to two conversations, one at a pharmacy and one at a doctor's office. What medical problems does each person have?

5 ▶ 8 Listen again and write the number of the conversation (1 or 2) next to each piece of medical advice (a–e).

a Take this medicine three times a day. 1
b Get some rest. ___
c Drink hot water with honey and lemon. ___
d Take one tablet twice a day. ___
e Buy cough drops. ___

6 Match the beginnings of the sentences (1–6) with their endings. Use the expressions for talking about illness to help you.

1 Do you have	○	○	this medicine.
2 You should take	○	○	see a doctor?
3 It's good for	○	○	a sore throat.
4 Why don't you	○	○	a headache?
5 I don't feel	○	○	well.
6 You need to	○	○	take these tablets.

▶ TALKING ABOUT ILLNESS

Asking and talking about illness
I don't feel very well.
I feel sick/ill.
Do you feel sick/ill?
Do you have a temperature?
How do you feel?

Giving advice
You need to / You should take this medicine.
Why don't you buy some cough drops?
It's good for a stomachache.
Try drinking hot tea.
If you still feel sick, then come back and see me again.

7 Work in pairs.

Student A: You have a medical problem. Choose one of the problems from Exercise 1 and tell Student B what your problem is.

Student B: You are a pharmacist. Ask how Student A feels and give advice.

Then change roles and have a new conversation.

1e Personal information

Writing filling out a form

1 Work in pairs. Discuss these questions.

- What kinds of forms do you sometimes fill out?
- Think of a form you filled out recently. What information did you write?

2 Work in pairs. Look at these forms. What is each form for?

A

Title		Current occupation	
First name			
Middle initial			
Last name			
Address		Do you smoke?	
Zip code		Yes	No
Gender		Current medications	
DOB			
No. of dependents			
Country of origin			
First language			

Details of past surgery or operations

B

PLEASE USE CAPITAL LETTERS

PASSPORT NO. _____ PLACE OF BIRTH _____

NATIONALITY _____ MARITAL STATUS _____

EDUCATION (DEGREE, ETC.) _____

Have you visited this country before? (If yes, give details)

_____

Contact details of person in case of emergency (e.g., spouse, next of kin)

_____

3 Writing skill information on forms

a Work in pairs. Match the questions (1–6) with the headings on the forms in Exercise 2 where you write the information.

1 Are you married, single, or divorced? *marital status*
2 Do you take any medicine?
3 How many children do you have?
4 What country were you born in?
5 Who can we call in your family if you need help?
6 What is the first letter of your middle name?

b Look at the forms again. Discuss these questions with your partner. Then check your answers on page 155.

1 How many abbreviations can you find in the forms? What do they mean?
DOB = Date of birth
2 Under the heading *Title* on forms, we use the abbreviations *Mr.*, *Mrs.*, *Ms.*, and *Dr.* What do they mean?
3 Which form doesn't want you to write in lowercase letters?

4 Work in pairs. Design a form for new students at a language school.

- List all the information you need about the students.
- Then prepare the form.

5 Exchange your form with another pair. Use these questions to check their form.

- Is their form easy to fill out?
- Do you know what to write in each part?
- Would you change anything on the form?

1f Laughter yoga

Members of a laughter club meet by the seaside in Laguna Beach, California.

Before you watch

1 Work in pairs and answer these questions.

1 Think of someone you know who laughs a lot. Describe that person.
2 Do you laugh often? What makes you laugh?
3 Look at the photo and the caption. Why do you think people join this laughter club?

2 Key vocabulary

Read the sentences (1–6). The words and phrases in **bold** are used in the video. Write these words and phrases next to their definitions (a–f).

1 I heard a funny **joke** yesterday.
2 Exercise is a good **way** to relieve stress.
3 The doctors performed an operation to clear a blockage in the **blood vessels** that supply his heart.
4 One of the **benefits** of yoga is increased muscle strength and tone.
5 There are about 50 **calories** in an apple.
6 If you take in 2,500 calories a day, and **burn** 2,500 calories a day, you'll stay at about the same weight.

a good or helpful results or effects _____
b a method, style, or manner of doing something _____
c units used to measure the amount of energy that food provides _____
d the narrow tubes through which your blood flows _____
e use up _____
f something said to cause laughter _____

3 You are going to watch members of a laughter club doing laughter yoga. What do you think the members do during their laughter yoga session? Check (✓) the items you think are true.

☐ They walk around and greet one another.
☐ They watch a funny movie.
☐ They make eye contact with other members.
☐ They chant and clap their hands.
☐ They take funny photos on their cell phones.
☐ They all do the same body movements while laughing.

While you watch

4 1.1 Watch the video. Were your predictions in Exercise 3 correct?

5 1.1 Watch the video again. Are these sentences true (T) or false (F)?

1 The people in the video are laughing because someone told a joke.	T	F
2 Laughter yoga helps people feel happier through laughing.	T	F
3 When you laugh, changes happen in your body.	T	F
4 Laughing can help you lose weight.	T	F

6 1.1 Watch the video again. Choose the correct option (a or b) to complete each sentence.

1 Laughing can make your blood vessels _____ .
a cleaner b wider
2 Laughing can reduce the risk of _____ .
a heart disease b certain cancers
3 You can burn _____ calories when you laugh for five to ten minutes.
a 40 b 400
4 We start laughing when we are around _____ .
a one month old b three months old

After you watch

7 Vocabulary in context

1.2 Watch the clips from the video. Choose the correct meaning of the words and phrases.

8 Work in pairs and answer these questions.

1 Would you join a laughter club? Why or why not?
2 Do you think laughter is better than other forms of exercise? Give examples to support your answer.

UNIT 1 REVIEW AND MEMORY BOOSTER

Grammar

1 Circle the correct options to complete the text about a man named Nazroo.

Every day, Nazroo [1] *works / is working* with elephants. In this photo, [2] *he takes / he's taking* his favorite elephant, Rajan, for a swim. [3] *They swim / They're swimming* in the ocean around the Andaman Islands. Sometimes they [4] *like / are liking* to relax this way after a hard day. Rajan [5] *doesn't seem / isn't seeming* worried about being underwater. I suppose [6] *it feels / it is feeling* good after a long, hot day at work.

2 Show the correct place in the sentence for the expression in parentheses. In three sentences, there is more than one correct answer.

1 I play video games. (rarely)
2 We're studying Spanish. (at the moment)
3 My family plays sports. (every weekend)
4 All my friends are working. (these days)

3 >> MB Rewrite the sentences in Exercise 2 so they are true for you.

I CAN	
talk about everyday routines	☐
use adverbs and expressions of frequency	☐

Vocabulary

4 Match the verbs in A with the words in B. Then complete the sentences with the expressions.

A	fall	take	work
B	long hours	asleep	a break

1 I can't _____ _____ because of all the noise outside my bedroom.
2 At work, we always _____ _____ at 11 and have coffee.
3 We all _____ _____ these days because there is a lot to do.

5 Which words can follow the verb in **bold**? Cross out the incorrect word.

1 **do** homework, housework, ~~relaxing~~, yoga
2 **go** asleep, surfing, jogging, home
3 **play** golf, swimming, games, tennis
4 **feel** tired, happy, ache, sick

6 >> MB Work in pairs. Write four sentences using verbs from Exercises 4 and 5, but leave out the verb.

We often _____ yoga when we wake up.

Then work with another pair. Take turns reading your sentences and guessing the missing word.

I CAN	
describe daily routines	☐
talk about free-time activities	☐

Real life

7 Circle the correct options to complete the conversation between two friends.

A: [1] *How do / Do* you feel?
B: Not very [2] *well / ill*. I have a [3] *pain / sore* throat.
A: [4] *Do you feel / Do you have* a temperature?
B: I don't know. I feel a little hot.
A: [5] *Try / You need* drinking some honey and lemon in hot water.
B: Good idea.
A: But you [6] *should / it's a good idea* also see your doctor.

8 >> MB Work in pairs. Look at the pictures and answer the questions.

1 What medical problems do these people have?
2 What advice can you give them?
You should go to bed.

I CAN	
talk about medical problems and illness	☐
give advice	☐

Unit 2 Competitions

Athletes in Cozumel, Mexico, compete for a place in the Ironman championship.

FEATURES

22 Crazy competitions!
Making rules for new competitions

24 Winning and losing
Is competition important in sports?

26 Bolivian wrestlers
Women competing in a national sport

30 Mongolian horse racing
A video about horse racing at a Mongolian festival

1 Work in pairs. Look at the photo and the caption. What do you know about this kind of competition?

2 ▶ 9 Listen to someone talking about the Ironman competition. Work in pairs. Answer the questions.

1 How many races are there in the Ironman competition?
2 How many kilometers do the competitors swim and cycle?
3 How many people compete in Hawaii every year?

3 The words in the box are from the same family. Which word is:

1 a verb?
2 an adjective?
3 a noun (thing)?
4 a noun (person)?

competitor	competitive	competition	compete

4 Complete the questions with the words from the box above. Then ask and answer the questions with a partner.

1 In sports, are you normally a _____ or a spectator?
2 Do you ever _____ in sports?
3 What types of _____ do you like?
4 Are you a _____ person? Why or why not?

2a Crazy competitions!

Reading

1 Work in pairs. Look at the title of the article and the two photos. Why do you think these competitions are "crazy"?

2 Read the article and match the sentences (1–6) with the competitions (A or B). Two sentences are true for both competitions.

1 Competitors start and end at the same place. A
2 The rules are similar to those of another real sport. ____
3 The competition is held once a year. ____
4 It involves a type of transportation. ____
5 It's for teams. ____
6 There is a time limit. ____

3 Which of the two competitions would you like to watch or take part in? Do you have any crazy competitions in your country? Discuss with a partner.

Vocabulary sports

4 Look at the highlighted words in the article. Use these words to complete the sentences below.

1 Runners at the Olympic Games get a gold medal when they win a _____ .
2 In soccer, there are eleven _____ on each side.
3 A baseball _____ is played between two _____ .
4 How many _____ did you score?
5 After two hours of running, the _____ was finally in sight.
6 The _____ received a gold medal.

5 Work in pairs. Answer these questions.

1 How many different kinds of races can you think of?
2 What is your favorite team sport? How many players are there in a team?
3 What are the names of the sports teams in your town or city?
4 In what games do you score goals and in what games do you score points?

▶ 10

CRAZY COMPETITIONS!

There are lots of competitions in the USA, and some of them are a bit crazy!

A The Idiotarod

The Idiotarod is an annual race in twenty different US cities. Each team must have five people and a shopping cart. One person usually rides in the cart, and four people pull it. Teams can decorate the shopping cart, but they can't change the wheels. All the teams have to start and finish at the same place, but they don't have to run on the same roads. The members of each team must cross the finish line together, and they can't finish without the cart!

B The Mud Bowl Championship

Mud Bowl football—played every September in North Conway, New Hampshire, USA—is similar to regular American football, in that players can pick up the ball and run with it. There are also two teams, but the game is shorter. The winner is the team with the most points at the end of sixty minutes. The really big difference is that the players have to play in a field with half a meter of mud!

Grammar modal verbs for rules

▶ MODAL VERBS FOR RULES

*Each team **must** have five people and a shopping cart.*
*They **can't** change the wheels.*
*All the teams **have to** start and finish at the same place.*
*They **don't have to** run on the same roads.*
*Players **can** pick up the ball and run with it.*

For more information and practice, see page 158.

6 Look at the sentences in the grammar box. Complete the explanations (a–d) with the modal verbs in **bold** in the grammar box.

a We use _____ or _____ when the rules say it's necessary.
b We use _____ when it's allowed by the rules.
c We use _____ when something isn't necessary but is allowed by the rules.
d We use _____ when it isn't allowed by the rules.

7 Circle the correct options to complete the sentences about different sports.

1 Do you *have to / must* wear a helmet when you play ice hockey?
2 In tennis, players *don't have to / can* use video replay technology if they want to see where the ball landed. This technology has transformed the game of tennis.
3 In bowling, you can bring your own ball, but you *have to / don't have to* if you don't want to.
4 Soccer players *must / don't have to* follow the rules, or the referee will send them off the field. They *have to / can't* argue with the referee.

8 Complete the description of another competition with these modal verbs. Use each modal verb only once.

~~must~~ have to don't have to can't can

Every two years, people from all over the globe enter the World Beard and Moustache Championships. The rules are simple. You [1] *must* be over eighteen years old, and you [2] _____ have a moustache or a beard, or both. Also, you [3] _____ put on false hair! In total, there are eighteen different categories, but competitors [4] _____ only enter one category. There are categories for short beards and different moustaches, so you [5] _____ have the longest moustache or the biggest beard to win a prize.

Speaking myLife

9 Work in pairs. You are going to explain the rules of a sport or competition. Choose one of the following. Make a list of six to seven rules. Then explain your rules to another pair.

- a popular sport in your country
- a popular TV quiz show or TV competition
- an annual national or international competition

*Baseball is a popular sport in my country. You **have to** play with two teams, a ball, and a bat.*

2b Winning and losing

Wordbuilding suffixes

1 Are any of the athletes in the photos famous in your country? Match the people (A–C) with these words.

tennis player ____ runner ____
soccer player ____

▶ WORDBUILDING suffixes

You can add *-er* to some sports to describe the person who plays the sport:
ski → skier, golf → golfer
You can add *player* to some sports:
tennis → tennis player, baseball → baseball player
Some sports don't use the suffix *-er* or *player*:
athletics → athlete, cycle → cyclist

For more practice, see Workbook page 19.

2 Work in pairs. Look at the wordbuilding box. What is the word for a person who:

1 boxes? *boxer*
2 motorcycles?
3 plays basketball?
4 swims?
5 plays chess?
6 drives a racing car?
7 does gymnastics?
8 goes surfing?

3 Work in pairs. Who are the most famous athletes in your country? What type of athlete are they? (e.g., *a swimmer, a golfer, a skateboarder*)

Lionel Messi is very famous in my country. He's a soccer player.

Listening

4 Read the quotes with the photos. Do you think winning is always important in sports? Why or why not? Discuss with a partner.

5 ▶ 11 Listen to three people talking about competitive sports in schools. Match the speakers (1–3) with their opinions (a–c).

a Speaker _____ thinks non-competitive sports are a good idea.
b Speaker _____ thinks competitive sports are a good idea in schools.
c Speaker _____ thinks sports in schools are a good idea, but there can be problems.

6 Look at these opinions for and against competitive sports in schools. Which are the opinions for (F) and which are the opinions against (A)?

1	Winning and losing teaches students about life.	(F)	A
2	A lot of successful schools don't have competitive sports.	F	A
3	Children get more exercise when they try to win.	F	A
4	Winning isn't important as long as you do your best.	F	A
5	Children learn to work well in teams when they play against other teams.	F	A
6	Students learn to work hard by doing competitive sports.	F	A
7	Some parents don't like losing and get angry with their children.	F	A
8	All children are different, and some aren't good at sports.	F	A
9	Competitive sports are fun.	F	A

7 ▶ 11 Which opinions (1–9) from Exercise 6 does each speaker give? Listen again and check.

Speaker 1 ___1,___
Speaker 2 _____
Speaker 3 _____

8 Work in groups. Discuss the opinions in Exercise 6. Answer these questions.

1 Which opinions do you agree with?
2 Which do you disagree with?
3 Are there any other reasons for or against competitive sports in schools?

Grammar *-ing* form

▶ *-ING* FORM

1 ***Learning*** *to win and lose is important in a child's education.*
2 *Competitive sports in schools are good for* ***teaching*** *children the value of teamwork.*
3 *Some parents hate* ***losing****.*

For more information and practice, see page 158.

9 Look at the grammar box. The verbs in the *-ing* form are in **bold**. Match these verbs (1–3) with the uses of the *-ing* form (a–c).

a It is the subject of the sentence. ___
b It comes after a verb (e.g., *like*). ___
c It comes after a preposition (e.g., *of*). ___

10 Work in pairs. Put the words in the correct order to make quotes by famous athletes. Then match the *-ing* forms with the uses (a–c) in Exercise 9.

1 never / thought / losing / of / I
(Muhammad Ali, boxer)
2 love / I just / winning
(Ayrton Senna, race car driver)
3 a champion / afraid / losing / isn't / of
(Billie Jean King, tennis player)
4 hate / I / losing
(Sachin Tendulkar, cricket player)
5 I'm / more worried about / a good person / being / than being the best soccer player
(Lionel Messi, soccer player)

11 ▶ 12 Circle the correct options to complete this conversation. Then listen and check.

A: What's on TV?
B: [1] *Cycle / Cycling*. It's the Tour de France. I love [2] *watch / watching* it.
A: Oh, no! I [3] *think / thinking* it's boring!
B: I disagree. I really enjoy [4] *watch / watching* the cyclists ride through the mountains.
A: [5] *Sit / Sitting* in front of the TV all day isn't exciting. I'm tired of [6] *do / doing* nothing. Are you any good at tennis? We could [7] *play / playing* this afternoon.
B: But I want to [8] *watch / watching* this.
A: What's wrong? Are you afraid of [9] *lose / losing*?

12 Pronunciation /ŋ/

a ▶ 13 Listen to six words. Circle the word you hear.

1	thin	think	thing
2	win	wink	wing
3	ban	bank	bang
4	sin	sink	sing
5	ran	rank	rang
6	pin	pink	ping

b ▶ 12 Listen again to the conversation from Exercise 11. Notice the pronunciation of the *-ing* forms. Then work in pairs and practice the conversation.

Speaking myLife

13 Work in pairs. Ask questions to find out what sports or activities your partner likes. Then complete the sentences.

A: What sports do you ***love watching****?*
B: Tennis. What about you?

1 I love watching _____, but my partner doesn't.
2 I think _____ is boring, but my partner loves it!
3 We both enjoy _____, but we hate _____.
4 I'm good at _____, but my partner isn't.

2c Bolivian wrestlers

Reading

1 Work in pairs. Discuss the questions.

1 Do many people watch boxing or wrestling in your country?
2 Why do some people dislike these types of sports?
3 What do you think about these sports?

2 Read the article about wrestling in Bolivia. Which paragraph (1–5) describes:

a the two wrestlers before the fight? 2
b the popularity of male and female wrestling in Bolivia? ___
c Yolanda's family life? ___
d the reason why a fan watches it? ___
e the fight between the two wrestlers? ___

3 Find words in the article for these definitions.

1 something people watch for pleasure
e*ntertainment*
2 a large group of people
c_____
3 the person who describes the action in a sport
c_____
4 get very excited, shout, and jump up and down
g_____ c_____
5 people who like a famous athlete
f_____
6 the money you earn for work done
s_____

Critical thinking reading between the lines

4 An article doesn't always tell us about how people feel, but we can often guess. Match the people from the article (1–3) with the sentences (a–c).

1 Yolanda
2 Yolanda's daughter
3 Esperanza

a "I don't understand why wrestling is so popular." ___
b "I feel wonderful every time I step into the ring." ___
c "Life is very hard for people like me." ___

5 Work in pairs. Discuss these questions.

1 How do you feel about the women wrestlers?
2 Would you like to see this sport? Why or why not?

Word focus *like*

6 The word *like* has a number of meanings and uses. Match the sentences (1–4) with the uses (a–d).

a We use *like* + noun to talk about things we enjoy.
b We use *like* + *-ing* to talk about activities we enjoy doing.
c We use *be/look like* to talk about similarities between people/things/actions.
d We use *would like to* + base form of a verb to talk about future plans or ambitions.

1 Most people **like** soccer. ___
2 Yolanda and Claudina **are like** famous pop stars. ___
3 **Would** your daughters **like to** become wrestlers one day? ___
4 Esperanza **likes** watching wrestling. ___

7 Match the questions with *like* (1–5) with their answers (a–e).

1 What do you like doing on the weekend?
2 What kind of music do you like?
3 Are you like anyone in your family?
4 Where would you like to go on your next vacation?
5 What does your dad look like?

a Yeah, I'm really similar to my mom. ___
b Spain. Or Portugal, maybe. ___
c Anything. Rock, classical—I don't mind. ___
d Going to the movies. ___
e He's tall and has brown hair. ___

8 Work in pairs. Take turns asking the questions from Exercise 7 and giving your own answers.

Speaking myLife

9 Work in groups. Can you name ten sports in the Olympic Games?

10 These six sports are not in the Olympic Games. Discuss the questions in your group and give reasons for your answers.

American football	bowling	cricket
mixed martial arts	darts	squash

1 Which of the six sports do you think is the most popular?
2 Which three sports would your group like to have at the next Olympics?

BOLIVIAN WRESTLERS

1 In Bolivia, soccer is the national sport, but the country is also famous for another sport—wrestling. Local people like watching wrestling, and it's popular with tourists, too. It's an exciting mixture of sport, drama, and entertainment. When modern wrestling started in Bolivia in the 1950s, the competitors were all men, but nowadays women are also competing in the ring.

2 The city of El Alto is a good place to watch wrestling. Hundreds of spectators go to the fights in the evening. This evening, the crowd is sitting around a huge wrestling ring and shouting, "Bring them on! Bring them on!" Suddenly, the commentator is speaking into a microphone, "Ladies and gentlemen. It's time for Yolanda and Claudina!" The crowd is screaming with excitement as two women in colorful clothes enter the ring.

3 Yolanda and Claudina are like famous pop stars. They smile and wave to their fans. The music stops, and the referee starts the fight. Claudina jumps on Yolanda. Then Yolanda throws Claudina on the floor. As Claudina lies on the floor, Yolanda smiles and waves to the crowd. Then Claudina gets up and pushes Yolanda onto the ground. One minute, Yolanda is winning. The next minute, Claudina is winning. The spectators go crazy!

4 Away from the ring, many wrestlers are women with families. At home, Yolanda has a normal, quiet family life. She has two daughters, and she makes clothes for a living. Her father was also a wrestler, so it's a family tradition. In answer to the question "Would your daughters like to become wrestlers one day?", Yolanda says they wouldn't. She answers, "My daughters ask me why I do this. It's dangerous, and they complain that wrestling doesn't bring any money into the house." So why does she do it?

5 Yolanda loves wrestling because of her fans—and she has lots of them. One of her fans is named Esperanza Cancina. Esperanza pays $1.50 (a large part of her salary) to sit near the ring. She likes watching wrestling because, she says, "We laugh and we forget our problems for three or four hours."

2d Joining a group

Speaking

1 Work as a class or in groups. Interview different people. Find someone who:

1 is a member of a team or club.
2 has to go to regular meetings (e.g., every week).
3 competes with their team or club.

Real life talking about interests

2 Work in pairs. Look at the ads below. Would you like to join one of these clubs? Why or why not?

A

Would you like to **get fit** and **make new friends?**

Join our running groups for beginners and for more experienced runners. It's non-competitive and fun.

7 p.m. every Wednesday.

Call Mike for details at 415-555-2671.

B

Join us and WIN a new camera!

The Barton Photography Club welcomes new members. We are a busy club with regular speakers. Join before March 1st and enter our summer photography competition. First prize is a new XP8ii camera! The entry fee is $15 (including membership).

Visit **www.bartonphotoclub.com** to join.

C

Theater group

Have fun with a local theater group. We are looking for actors to be in a musical comedy this summer. You must be available twice a week starting April 2nd. Enthusiasm is more important than talent!

Write to Mandy Giles at mandy76@gmail.com

3 ▶ 15 Two people are looking at the ads (from Exercise 2) in their local newspaper. Listen to their conversation. Number the ads (A–C) in the order they are discussed (1–3).

A ___ B ___ C ___

4 ▶ 15 Listen again and complete these sentences with the words you hear.

1 You're really _____ taking photos.
2 Well, _____ joining something else?
3 Are you _____ acting?
4 I _____ standing up in front of people.
5 I'm _____ good at singing.
6 You should _____. I think you'd enjoy it.
7 I think I'd _____ join this one on Wednesday evenings.
8 It _____ like fun. _____ you come, too?

5 Work in pairs. Match the sentences in Exercise 4 with the three categories in the box below.

▶ TALKING ABOUT INTERESTS

Talking about interests and abilities
Do you like taking photos?
I'm good at acting.
I'm (not) interested in photography.

Talking about plans
I'd like/prefer to join a running club.
I wouldn't like to do it.

Recommending and encouraging
It looks interesting.
Go on.
I think you'd enjoy it.
You should do it with me.

6 Pronunciation silent letters

▶ 16 Some letters in English words are not pronounced. Listen to these words from the conversation and cross out the silent letters. Then listen again and repeat.

1 interested
2 should
3 friends
4 could
5 what
6 whole

7 Work in pairs. What other clubs would you like to join? Why would you like to join them?

2e Advertising for members

Writing an ad

1 Work in small groups. What makes a good ad and a bad ad? Think about ads you like and don't like in magazines, on TV, or online.

2 Read the advice about how to write effective ads. Then look at the ads on page 28. Discuss these questions as a group.

1 Which ad follows most of the advice?
2 How could you improve the ads?

How to WRITE EFFECTIVE ADS

- Start with a good headline. You could ask a question or solve a problem.
- The ad should explain the reasons for buying something or joining a club.
- If possible, offer something for free or a prize.
- Include any other important information (dates, times, location, contact information, etc.).
- Photos, pictures, or images always help.

3 Work in pairs. You are going to plan a new club. Discuss these questions.

1 What type of club is it?
2 Who is the club for?
3 Are there any rules for members?
4 Is there a membership fee? How much is it?
5 Where and how often will it meet?

4 Plan and write an ad for your club.

5 Writing skill checking your writing

a It is important to check your writing for mistakes before people read it. Read these sentences (1–8) from ads and find one mistake in each sentence. Circle the mistake and write the correct symbol from the correction key. Each key is used once.

1 Would you like to learn a musical instrument? P
2 Enter our exciteing competition! ___
3 Are you good at play tennis? ___
4 We meet at Tuesdays and Thursdays. ___
5 It's fun way to get fit. ___
6 Join this club new! ___
7 Get healthy and play yoga. ___
8 Call peter at 077 237 5980. ___

Writing correction key

Sp	=	spelling mistake
MW	=	missing word
P	=	punctuation mistake
Prep	=	preposition mistake
Gr	=	grammar mistake
WO	=	word order mistake
C	=	capital letter mistake
WW	=	wrong word

b Read your ad from Exercise 4 again. Are there any mistakes?

6 Display your ads around the classroom. Walk around and read about each other's new clubs. Think about these questions.

- Which clubs would you like to join?
- Which ads are effective? Why?

2f Mongolian horse racing

Children compete in a horse race at the Naadam festival, Mongolia.

Before you watch

1 Work in pairs. Look at the photo of horse racing in Mongolia. Answer these questions.

1 Do you have horse racing in your country?
2 How popular is it as a sport?

2 Key vocabulary

Read the sentences (1–7). The words and phrases in **bold** are used in the video. Write these words and phrases next to their definitions (a–g).

1 In the Olympic Games, each winner receives a gold **medal**.
2 I got 100% on the exam, so I feel very **proud** of myself.
3 A religious man **blesses** people.
4 My horse can run **like the wind**.
5 At the festival, there were **displays** by actors and performers.
6 A typical **rodeo** includes events such as bull riding and catching cows with ropes.
7 In this competition, I have one main **rival** who always tries to beat me.

a asks a god (or gods) to protect something or someone _____
b pleased because you've done something well _____
c shows or presentations _____
d a metal disc given for an achievement _____
e very quickly _____
f a competition where cowboys show different skills _____
g a person who is as good or almost as good as you at doing something _____

While you watch

3 2.1 Watch the video. Number these actions in the order you see them (1–6).

___ Mukhdalai's horse wins the race.
___ The riders leave the starting point.
_1_ A religious woman blesses the horses.
___ Mukhdalai receives first prize.
___ A horse rider picks up poles.
___ Two men wrestle.

4 2.1 Watch the video again. Choose the correct option (a or b) to complete each sentence.

1 The Naadam is a Mongolian _____ festival.
a spring
b summer
2 Mukhdalai and Namjin are horse _____ who compete against each other.
a riders
b trainers
3 Mukhdalai and Namjin _____ each other.
a like
b don't like
4 There are about _____ horses competing in the race.
a twenty
b eighty
5 The starting point is at the _____ .
a top of a hill
b bottom of a valley
6 _____ is wearing green and white.
a Mukhdalai's son
b Namjin's son
7 Mukhdalai's horse is in first place for _____ race.
a the whole
b part of the
8 It is Namjin's horse's _____ race.
a first
b fifth

After you watch

5 Vocabulary in context

a 2.2 Watch the clips from the video. Choose the correct meaning of the words and phrases.

b Work in pairs. Ask and answer these questions.

1 What are some annual celebrations in your country?
2 Imagine you and your classmates are competing in a 100-meter race. Who do you think will take the lead and win? Do you think this person will finish a long way ahead of the rest?

6 Work in pairs. Write five questions about the Naadam festival in the video.

What is the Naadam festival famous for?

7 Work with a new partner. Take turns asking and answering your questions from Exercise 6 about the Naadam.

UNIT 2 REVIEW AND MEMORY BOOSTER

Grammar

1 Circle the correct options to complete the text about an unusual competition.

The first bed race was in Knaresborough, UK, in 1966. The rules are simple. Each team [1] *can / has to* race with one bed on wheels. There are six people to a team and one passenger. The team [2] *must / doesn't have to* have either six men or six women, or you [3] *can / can't* also race with a team of three men and three women. The passenger [4] *has to / doesn't have to* be an adult, but he or she [5] *doesn't have to / can't* be younger than twelve years old. The time limit for the race is thirty minutes, and you [6] *can't / have to* take longer.

2 >> MB Work in pairs. What sports do these people play? Describe two rules for each sport.

Venus Williams	Lionel Messi	Usain Bolt

3 Complete the sentences with the *-ing* form of these verbs.

go	learn	lose	watch	win

1 _____ to speak another language is very useful.
2 Peter is very competitive—he hates _____ .
3 Trying is more important than _____ .
4 I think _____ to a basketball game is more fun than _____ it on TV.

4 >> MB Complete the sentences in your own words using the *-ing* form. Then tell a partner.

1 _____ is very good for you.
2 I'm really interested in _____ .
3 I don't like _____ .

I CAN	
use modal verbs for rules	☐
use the *-ing* form	☐

Vocabulary

5 Write the missing vowels in these words related to sports. Race with a partner to see who can finish first.

1 r__c__
2 g__ __ls
3 cr__wd
4 g__me
5 f__n__sh l__n__
6 b__s__b__ll
7 w__nn__r
8 f__ns
9 t__ __m
10 b__x__r

6 Work in pairs. Answer these questions with four of the words from Exercise 5.

1 What do you have to cross in a race?
2 What is the opposite of *a loser*?
3 What type of competition is Formula One?
4 What do you call a group of people who like an athlete or a sports team?

7 >> MB Work in pairs. Choose three more words from Exercise 5 and write three questions for them. Then work with another pair and take turns asking and answering your questions.

I CAN	
talk about sports and athletes	☐

Real life

8 Complete the conversation. Write one word in each blank.

A: Are you interested [1] _____ painting? There's a new evening class at my college.
B: But I'm not very good [2] _____ art.
A: I'm not either, but I'd like [3] _____ learn. Come on. You should do it [4] _____ me.
B: Sorry. What about doing something else?
A: [5] _____ you like taking photos? There's also a class for that.
B: Actually, that sounds interesting.

9 >> MB Complete these sentences in your own words. Then share your sentences with a partner.

1 I'm good at …
2 I think I'd enjoy learning …
3 I'm also interested in …
4 I wouldn't like to …

I CAN	
talk about my interests	☐

Unit 3 Transportation

Taking the train in Dhaka, Bangladesh

FEATURES

34 Transportation solutions

Find out about some new transportation ideas

36 Transportation around the world

Comparing different types of transportation

38 The end of the road

How much longer can the rickshaw survive?

42 Indian Railways

A video about one of the world's largest transportation networks

1 Work in pairs. Look at the photo. Where is the woman? Why do you think she is traveling like this?

2 ▶ 17 Listen to someone talking about the photo. Why isn't the woman inside the train?

3 Work in pairs. Which ways of traveling would you prefer for the activities (1–7)? Give your reasons.

by bicycle	by bus	by truck	by plane
by train	in my car	in a taxi	on a ferry
on foot	on a motorcycle	on a ship	

1 visit relatives
*I'd prefer to **visit** my **relatives by bicycle** or **on foot** because they only live five minutes from my house.*
2 move house and furniture
3 get to the airport
4 cross an ocean
5 go out in the evening to a party or restaurant
6 commute to school or work
7 go shopping

3a Transportation solutions

Reading

1 Read the article about three solutions to transportation problems. Match the paragraphs with the photos (1–3).

Paragraph A ____
Paragraph B ____
Paragraph C ____

2 Look at the photos and read the article again. Which types of transportation do the sentences (1–4) describe? Match the sentences to a–c below. Some sentences describe more than one type.

1 It moves over people's heads.
2 It's a faster way to commute.
3 It's environmentally friendly.
4 It's good for long distances.

a driverless cars _____
b monorail __1,__
c Hyperloop __1,__

Vocabulary transportation nouns

▶ WORDBUILDING compound nouns

We can join two words to make a new noun: *bus + stop = bus stop, air + port = airport , down + town = downtown*
A compound noun can be two words (*bus stop*) or one word (*airport*).

For more practice, see Workbook page 27.

3 Find the compound nouns in **bold** in the article. Match them with their definitions (1–6).

1 the maximum speed you can legally drive __*speed limit*__
2 a long line of vehicles moving slowly on the road _____
3 the time of day when lots of people travel to/from work _____
4 the money you spend on gas for transportation _____
5 the amount of CO_2 that a type of transportation produces _____
6 the main or central part of a city _____

4 Work in pairs. Discuss these questions.

1 Which of the three transportation solutions in the article do you think are a good idea?
2 Which traffic problems could they solve in your area?

TRANSPORTATION SOLUTIONS

▶ 18

A BMW, Volvo, General Motors, and Google are all currently working on driverless cars. Some driverless cars use solar energy, which reduces **fuel costs** and lowers **carbon emissions**. They are also safer because the computer controls the speed, so they can't go faster than the **speed limit**.

B This monorail in New Zealand is a new solution for commuters in a **traffic jam** during **rush hour**. The passenger sits in a pod and can cycle over people's heads. Google has already invested over $1 million in this idea.

C In the future, the Hyperloop could be a common type of public transportation. It's a long tube with no air inside, and passengers sit inside pods that travel at 1,200 kilometers per hour. It would reduce air and noise pollution. There are already plans for the first Hyperloop between **downtown** San Francisco and Los Angeles. The distance is around 600 kilometers, and it would only take 30 minutes of travel time.

Grammar comparatives and superlatives

5 ▶ 19 Work in pairs. Listen to a conversation between two colleagues at work. Which types of transportation do they talk about? What advantages and disadvantages do they mention?

6 ▶ 19 Look at the grammar box below and circle the correct options in these sentences. Listen again and check.

1 Eight-thirty in the morning is the *bad / worst* time for traffic.
2 My bicycle is *faster / fastest* than your car during rush hour!
3 I travel *far / farther* than you.
4 They're better, but they're also *more / most* expensive.
5 The *most fast / fastest* bus takes over an hour.

▶ COMPARATIVES and SUPERLATIVES

Regular adjectives	Comparative	Superlative
fast	*faster*	*fastest*
big	*bigger*	*biggest*
expensive	*more expensive*	*most expensive*
Irregular adjectives		
far	*farther*	*farthest*
good	*better*	*best*
bad	*worse*	*worst*

For more information and practice, see page 160.

7 Work in pairs. Look at the grammar box. Answer these questions.

1 What letters do we add to short adjectives (*fast*, *cheap*, etc.) to form comparative and superlative adjectives?
2 We use *more* before longer adjectives to make the comparative. What word do we use to make the superlative?
3 Which word often comes after a comparative adjective? Which word normally comes before a superlative adjective?

8 Pronunciation *than*

a ▶ 20 Listen to the pronunciation of *than* in these sentences. Listen again and repeat.

1 Cars are faster than bicycles.
2 Bicycles are better for the environment than cars.

b Work in pairs. Practice saying these sentences.

1 I travel farther than you.
2 A train is more expensive than a bus.

9 Complete this report about a transportation survey. Write the correct comparative or superlative form of the adjectives in parentheses.

Report on local transportation

For commuting and daytime travel in our town, the [1] _____ (popular) form of transportation is the bus because it's [2] _____ (cheap) than going by car or taxi. However, some people in the survey prefer to cycle because the bus is [3] _____ (slow) than a bicycle during rush hour. Everyone said that parking downtown is the [4] _____ (big) problem, so people don't often use their cars. As a result, taxis are [5] _____ (popular) than private cars.

Speaking myLife

10 Work in pairs. Form comparative and superlative sentences with these transportation words and adjectives. How many sentences can you make in three minutes?

trains	cars	fast	cheap	bad
taxis	buses	slow	popular	
planes	ships	expensive	safe	
bicycles	motorcycles	quick	good	

*Trains are **quicker than** cars, but planes are **the fastest** type of transportation.*

11 Work in pairs. Find out about your partner's commute to work or school. Take turns asking and answering these questions.

1 How far do you travel to work or school?
2 What type of transportation do you use?
3 How long does it take?
4 How much does it cost every week?

12 With your partner, form sentences comparing your commutes.

*My home is **farther** from school **than** yours. / Your home is **closer than** mine.*

13 Work with another pair. Compare your information. Find out:

1 who lives the closest to / farthest away from work or school
*Mario lives **the closest to** work, and Ahmed lives **the farthest away**.*
2 who has the shortest / longest commute
3 who has the cheapest / most expensive commute each week
4 which type of transportation is the least / most popular in the group

3b Transportation around the world

Listening

1 Work in pairs. Look at the photos. Where do you think they were taken? What are the advantages of using animals for transportation in these places?

2 ▶ 21 Work in pairs. Listen to a documentary about animal transportation. Why does the speaker say camels and huskies are better than cars?

3 ▶ 21 Listen to the documentary again. What do these numbers describe? Make notes and compare your answers with a partner.

Camels	Huskies
50 degrees	-50 degrees
40 kilometers	6 and 8 huskies
3 to 5 days	1,600 kilometers

Grammar *as … as*

▶ *AS … AS*

1 *In some parts of the world, animal transportation is **as** popular **as** these modern vehicles.*
2 *In winter, northern Alaska can be **as** cold **as** the North Pole.*
3 *For long distances, modern vehicles are **not as** good **as** camels.*
4 *A camel **isn't as** comfortable **as** a car.*

For more information and practice, see page 160.

4 Work in pairs. Look at the grammar box and answer these questions.

a Which two sentences say two things are the same or equal?
b Which two sentences say two things are different, and one thing is less than the other?

5 Work in pairs and rewrite these sentences. Use *as … as* or *not as … as* and the adjective in parentheses.

1 The subway from Hong Kong airport to Kowloon costs $100, and a taxi costs $210. (not / expensive)
The subway from Hong Kong airport to Kowloon isn't as expensive as a taxi.
2 The ferry from Jordan to Egypt takes one hour. A bus ride over land takes two hours. (not / slow)
3 During rush hour in New York, riding a bike to work and taking a bus take the same amount of time. (fast)
4 In Colombia and Greece, 9% of households own motorcycles. (popular)

6 Pronunciation sentence stress

▶ 22 Listen to these sentences. Underline the stressed word in each sentence. Then listen again and repeat.

1 Riding a bike is as popular as jogging.
2 Trains aren't as expensive as taxis.
3 Los Angeles airport is as busy as London Heathrow.
4 A car isn't as fast as a bicycle in a traffic jam.

7 Work in pairs. Ask questions to find out how similar or different you and your partner are. Then write sentences.

Carlos is as tall as me. / He isn't as old as me.

His family isn't as big as mine.

Vocabulary transportation adjectives

8 Read part of a news article about taxis in London. What does it compare?

BATTLE OF THE TAXIS

When you travel in London, the city's famous black taxis or black cabs are a **convenient** type of transportation. On any main road, there are plenty of cabs, and even with four or five people, they're **comfortable** to ride in. But now the **traditional** black cab has competition from private taxis such as Addison Lee. Using your cell phone, you can book a private taxi for a certain time—they are very **punctual**. Sometimes these private taxis are also a bit cheaper and a little faster. However, in bad traffic, black-cab drivers say their cabs are much faster. They have to learn all the roads around London, so they don't use GPS, and they know the best routes around the city. They think that private taxis are a lot less **reliable** in rush-hour traffic.

9 Find the words in **bold** in the article. Then match them with their definitions (1–5).

1 It's always on time. _____
2 It has existed for a long time. _____
3 It's nice to sit in. _____
4 It's nearby or easy to use. _____
5 It does what you need it to. _____

Grammar comparative modifiers

▶ COMPARATIVE MODIFIERS

*Sometimes these private taxis are **a bit** cheaper and **a little** faster.*
*Black-cab drivers are **much** faster because they know the best routes.*
*They think that private taxis are **a lot** less reliable.*

For more information and practice, see page 160.

10 Look at the grammar box. Complete these rules (1–2) with the comparative modifiers in **bold** in the grammar box.

1 To talk about a small difference, we use _____ or _____ before a comparative adjective.
2 To talk about a big difference, we use _____ or _____ before a comparative adjective.

11 Work in pairs. Look at the information about transportation for visitors to Tokyo. Form sentences using these ideas and comparative modifiers.

1 A taxi is / expensive than …
*Taking a taxi is **a lot more** expensive than taking a bus.*
2 The subway is / frequent than …
3 Taxis are / quick than …

	Subway Train	Taxi	Bus
Prices	¥800 for unlimited use of all subway lines for 24 hours	Around ¥300 for every kilometer traveled	¥500 for unlimited travel anywhere in the main areas of the city for one day
Frequency	About every 3 minutes during peak hours	All the time at taxi stands and on busy streets	A bus comes about every 5 minutes
Other information	13 subway lines cover every part of Tokyo	Red shows the taxi is vacant; a green plate means it's occupied	Buses are slower than taxis and subways; buses don't run at night

Speaking myLife

12 What advice would you give a visitor arriving in your country for the first time? What are the best ways to get around? Tell your partner.

3c The end of the road

Reading

1 You are going to read an article about a city in India. Write one thing you know about India. Then tell the class.

2 Read the article. Which paragraph (1–3) talks about:

a why people like rickshaws in Kolkata? ____
b modern transportation in Kolkata? ____
c the end of the old rickshaws in Kolkata? ____

3 Work in pairs. Read the article again and answer these questions.

1 What is the population of Kolkata?
2 What are streets like in Kolkata?
3 Where is it safer for pedestrians to walk? Why?
4 Why do local housewives and tourists like taking rickshaws?
5 Some politicians want a new type of rickshaw. How is it different?
6 How many people pull the old rickshaws in Kolkata?
7 Why don't these drivers use the new rickshaws?

Vocabulary transportation verbs

4 Read paragraphs 1 and 2 of the article again. Find verbs or verb phrases that can replace the verbs in **bold** below.

1 I'd prefer to **travel by** taxi to the airport. It's much quicker.
go___ by___

2 I can **collect** the children from school on my way home from work.
p___ u___

3 I need to go now if I want to **get** the next train.
c____

4 You'd better leave now or you will **not make** your flight.
m____

5 Tell the driver to **leave you** outside the restaurant.
d____ you o____

Critical thinking opinions for and against

5 Work in pairs. There are five different groups of people mentioned in the article: shoppers, tourists, politicians, children (and parents), and rickshaw drivers. Which groups:

1 are for hand-pulled rickshaws in Kolkata?
2 are against the hand-pulled rickshaws?

Give reasons for your answers.

6 Work in pairs. Do you think the writer gives a balanced view of the opinions on both sides? Why or why not?

Speaking myLife

7 Look at the photo above of a pedicab. Then work in groups. You want to start a pedicab company in your town or city. Discuss these questions and make notes.

1 Who are your main customers? (commuters, tourists, etc.)
2 Why are pedicabs better than other types of transportation (buses, taxis, etc.)?
3 How much do you charge? Are you cheaper or more expensive than other transportation?
4 What is the name of your business? How can you advertise your business? (on the internet, on TV, etc.)

8 As a group, give a presentation about your pedicab company to the class. Listen to other groups and compare your ideas. Which group has the best ideas?

The end *of the* road

▶ 23

1 Kolkata is the capital of West Bengal in India. It has a population of around 15 million people, and rush hour starts early in the morning. All day there are traffic jams with cars, public buses, taxis, motorcycles, and pedicabs,[1] and drivers honk their horns[2] from morning to night. You can also catch the train or get on the subway, but those are busy, too. For pedestrians, Kolkata can be dangerous—crossing the road is especially difficult. Fortunately, the old parts of the city have smaller streets that are better for pedestrians. Cars can't drive down them, so they are much quieter and a lot safer.

2 In these old streets, you'll see men pulling rickshaws. Rickshaws are a traditional type of transportation in the city, and local people still like using them. In the morning, the drivers pick up children and take them to school. And if you miss your bus to work, a hand-pulled rickshaw is much cheaper than taking a taxi. Later on in the day, housewives often prefer to go by rickshaw to the local markets. The drivers drop the women off with their shopping outside their houses; no other type of public transportation can do that! So rickshaws are popular with many local people. When the traffic is very bad, you can go anywhere by rickshaw. Kolkata is one of the last cities in the world with hand-pulled rickshaws, so the drivers also make money from tourists. Visitors to the city often want to get a photograph of themselves sitting on a rickshaw because it's a famous symbol of Kolkata.

3 However, not everyone thinks the famous rickshaws are a good idea. Some local politicians don't like this old type of transportation because they think it's wrong for one human to pull another. Instead, they want more rickshaw drivers to use pedicabs or modern electric rickshaws, which are clean and fast. The problem is that Kolkata has around 2,000 traditional rickshaw drivers. They are often men from villages in the countryside, and they don't have any other job. The new electric rickshaws are very expensive, so these drivers can't afford them. For these men, it's probably the end of the road for the traditional rickshaw and their way of life.

[1] **pedicab** (n) /ˈpedɪkæb/ a type of taxi with no engine. The driver pedals.
[2] **honk your horn** (exp) /hɒŋk jɔː hɔːrn/ make a loud noise in a car to tell people you are there

3d Getting around town

Vocabulary taking transportation

1 Look at these pairs of words (1–5). Match the words with their definitions (a or b).

1 stop __b__ / stand __a__
   a the place you get a taxi
   b the place you get a bus
2 fare ___ / price ___
   a the money you pay for a trip by bus, train, or taxi
   b the amount of money something costs
3 change ___ / receipt ___
   a the money you get back when you pay more than the price
   b the piece of paper you receive to show you paid for something
4 gate ___ / platform ___
   a the place you get on a train
   b the place you get on a plane
5 book ___ / check in ___
   a when you buy a ticket in advance
   b when you arrive at an airport and register for a flight

Real life going on a trip

2 ▶ 24 Work in pairs. Listen to five conversations. Javier and Shelley are going to the airport, but they take different transportation. Answer the questions.

1 Where does Javier ask the taxi driver to take him?
2 How much is the taxi fare?
3 Where does Shelley want to go?
4 How much is Javier's train ticket? Which platform does the train leave from?
5 What does Shelley show the woman? How many bags does she check in?

3 ▶ 24 Look at the expressions for going on a trip. Then listen to the conversations again. Circle the sentences you hear.

▶ GOING ON A TRIP

In a taxi
I'd like to go to the station, please.
You can stop here.
How much is that?
Do you have change?
Do you want a receipt?

On a bus
Do you stop at the airport?
A one-way or round-trip ticket?
Please stop at the next one.
That's two dollars.

At the train station
A round-trip ticket to the airport, please.
First or second class?
One way or round trip?
Which platform is it?

At the airport
Can I see your passport?
How many bags are you checking in?
I only have this carry-on.
Window or aisle seat?
Can I get a seat next to my friend?

4 **Pronunciation intonation**

▶ 25 In everyday English, people don't always use full questions. For example, they can say *One way or round trip?* instead of *Do you want a one-way or round-trip ticket?* Listen to these questions. Mark the intonation ↗ or ↘.

1 One way or round trip?
2 Window or aisle seat?
3 Credit card or cash?
4 Bus or train?
5 North or south?
6 First or second class?

5 Work in pairs. Look at the four situations (a–d) with people going to an airport. Act out conversations using the expressions for going on a trip to help you.

Student A: You are the passenger.

Student B: Take the other role in the conversations (e.g., the taxi driver).

Then change roles and repeat.

a In a taxi. You have two $20 bills. The fare is $23.50.

b On the bus.

c At the train station.

d At the airport. You have two bags.

3e Quick communication

Writing notes and messages

1 Work in pairs. How do you normally send notes and messages to friends and colleagues? By text or email? What other ways do you use?

2 Read the notes and messages (1–8). Match them with the reasons for writing (a–e).

a thanking
b apologizing
c giving travel information
d suggesting a time and place to meet
e giving a message from someone else

3 Writing skill writing in note form

a Work in pairs. People often leave out words in notes and messages. Look again at the notes and messages in Exercise 2. Find places where the writers have left out these kinds of words.

- articles (e.g., *a, the*)
- pronouns (e.g., *I, me*)
- auxiliary verbs (e.g., *do, are*)
- polite forms (e.g., *Would you like to …? Can we …?*)

(Can we) Meet outside (the) airport at 2? (Is that) OK?

b How would you rewrite these phone messages as shorter text messages? Discuss with a partner.

1 "I'm sorry, but I'm stuck in a traffic jam. I'll see you in half an hour."
Sorry. Stuck in traffic. See you in 30 mins.
2 "Thank you for booking the train tickets. I'll pay you when we meet at the station."
3 "My flight is an hour late. Meet me in the arrivals area at five o'clock."

4 Work in pairs. Write a short note or message for each situation (1–3).

1 You have to work late. Write a text to your friend. Say you will arrive at the restaurant an hour later.
2 You are meeting a friend downtown tonight. Ask your friend to meet you at the taxi stand outside the train station.
3 You cannot travel with your friend on the subway to the airport. Explain that you will take the bus and meet him or her in the check-in area.

5 Think of another situation on your own and write a short message to your partner. Then exchange messages. Can you understand the other person's message? Write a reply if necessary.

1 Meet outside airport at 2? OK?

2 Sorry. Bus late. Will be 15 minutes late.

3 Javier called. Call him back. 213-509-6995.

4 Train leaves platform 6.

5 Thanks for getting tickets. Here's the money.

6 Plane at gate 6.

7 Am in taxi. See you outside in 5?

8 Afraid I was late, so missed meeting. My apologies.

3f Indian Railways

At the Victoria Terminus in Mumbai, India, it always seems to be rush hour.

Before you watch

1 Work in pairs. Look at the photo and the caption. Why do you think trains are a popular type of transportation in India?

2 Key vocabulary

a Work in pairs. Read the sentences (1–5). The words in **bold** are used in the video. Guess the meaning of these words.

1 Don't walk on the railway **track**! A train might come.
2 Some of the trains in India have **impressive** names like *The Himalayan Queen*.
3 I live in a **rural** village about thirty kilometers from the nearest town.
4 This toy train is a **miniature** of the real thing.
5 My company has a large **workforce**. We employ over five hundred people.

b Write the words in **bold** in Exercise 2a next to their definitions (a–e).

a important-sounding _____
b the metal line that a train runs on _____
c the group of people who work for a company _____
d in the countryside _____
e a small copy or model _____

While you watch

3 3.1 Watch the video about Indian Railways with the sound OFF. Number these actions in the order you see them (1–6).

___ A man is checking the railway track with a hammer.
___ A train is traveling in the Indian countryside.
_1_ Hundreds of people are walking on a platform during rush hour.
___ People are playing a game on the train.
___ A man with a white beard is dancing with two swords.
___ A man is serving food on the train.

4 3.1 Watch the video with the sound ON. Circle the correct options.

1 Every day, approximately *two hundred thousand / two million* passengers pass through the Victoria Terminus in Mumbai.
2 There are over *one billion / two billion* people in India.
3 The British built the railways in India in the *eighteenth / nineteenth* century.
4 The first steam train in India was in eighteen *thirty-three / fifty-three.*
5 There are over *thirty-eight thousand / three thousand eight hundred* miles of railway track in India.
6 The Grand Trunk Express has traveled through India since nineteen *twenty-nine / thirty-nine.*
7 India's railways carry *four million / four billion* passengers every year.
8 Indian Railways employs *fifty thousand / one and a half million* staff.

After you watch

5 Vocabulary in context

a 3.2 Watch the clips from the video. Choose the correct meaning of the words and phrases.

b Work in pairs. Ask and answer these questions.

1 Does your country have an enormous public transportation system? Is the transportation system in your country in good condition? Why or why not?
2 What everyday situations do you find most stressful? Why?
3 In your country, which company is one of the largest employers? What do they make or provide?

6 3.3 You are going to prepare a narration for a new version of the Indian Railways video. It's called *A one-minute journey on the Indian Railways*. As you watch, take notes about what you see in each part.

- Rush hour in Mumbai (0:00–0:15)
- On the train (0:16–0:38)
- The workforce (0:39–0:50)
- At the station (0:51–1:00)

7 Now write a script for the new video. Describe what you can see in the video and add any important facts and figures about Indian Railways. Use some of these words and phrases.

checking the track	playing games
cities and rural villages	rush hour
enormous	station
good condition	stressful
passengers	platform
workforce	dancing

8 Work with a partner. Your teacher will play the new video twice. As you watch, take turns reading your script and narrating the video.

UNIT 3 REVIEW AND MEMORY BOOSTER

Grammar

1 Complete the article with the correct form of the adjectives in parentheses.

Santiago is the [1] _____ (large) city in Chile, with a population of five million people. It has some of the [2] _____ (beautiful) buildings in the world, but in the past, it was the [3] _____ (polluted) city in Chile. Its streets weren't as [4] _____ (clean) as they are today. Nowadays, public transportation around the city is also much [5] _____ (good), and the city center isn't as [6] _____ (noisy). Riding bikes is also a lot [7] _____ (popular) these days because there are new bike paths and people can use electric bikes.

2 >> MB Work in pairs. Form three sentences comparing your town or city to Santiago. Talk about:

- size and population
- buildings and streets
- traffic and public transportation

I CAN	
use comparative and superlative adjectives	☐
use *as ... as*	☐

Vocabulary

3 Match words from A with words from B to make compound nouns. Then complete the sentences with the compound nouns.

A	traffic	rush	bus	speed
B	hour	stop	limit	jam

1 There's a _____ _____ on the highway. Nothing's moving.
2 _____ _____ starts at about seven in the morning.
3 Wait at the _____ _____. Another bus should arrive in ten minutes.
4 Slow down! The _____ _____ is only 30 kilometers an hour on this road.

4 Which words can follow the words in **bold**? Cross out the incorrect word or words.

1 **go by** bus, feet, plane, bicycle
2 **go on** a taxi, a ship, foot, a ferry
3 **catch** a train, a plane, a truck, a bus
4 **drop off** your shopping, your children, the subway

5 >> MB Work in pairs. Look at the forms of transportation and answer the questions (1–7). Give reasons for your answers.

taxi	rickshaw	camel
bus	airplane	train

1 Which types of transportation are slow but reliable?
2 Which are comfortable and convenient?
3 Which is the cheapest?
4 Which goes the farthest in a short time?
5 Which lands at a gate?
6 Which stops at a stand?
7 Which are good for sightseeing in a city?

I CAN	
talk about transportation	☐

Real life

6 Complete the conversation at a train station with the words and phrases in the box.

platform	ticket	one way
round trip	receipt	

A: I'd like a train [1] _____ to Boston.
B: [2] _____ or round trip?
A: [3] _____, please.
B: That's twenty-one dollars and fifty cents. Do you want a [4] _____?
A: Yes, please. Which [5] _____ is it?
B: Three.

7 >> MB Work in pairs. Write a similar conversation between two people at an airport. Use these phrases.

see your passport	check in
a carry-on	window or aisle

I CAN	
buy tickets and use different types of transportation	☐

Unit 4 Challenges

Rumbling Falls Cave, Tennessee

FEATURES

46 Adventurers of the year

Profiles of some of the world's top adventurers

48 An impossible decision

The real-life story of two climbers and a difficult decision

50 Challenge yourself

Find out about some challenges for the mind

54 A microadventure

A video about two friends who spend 24 hours in Croatia

1 Work in pairs. Look at the photo. Where is the man? Do you think this activity looks exciting or dangerous? Would you like to do this?

2 ▶ 26 Work in pairs. Listen to a caver talking about his hobby. Answer the questions.

1 Why do his co-workers think he is "a little crazy"?
2 Why do cavers work in teams?
3 How do you get to Rumbling Falls Cave?

3 Look at these sentences from Vic's description. Match the words in **bold** (1–3) with their definitions (a–c).

1 Sometimes you have to **take a risk** when you go caving.
2 Every cave gives you a different **challenge**.
3 Getting to Rumbling Falls Cave is probably my biggest **achievement** as a caver so far.

a do something that can be dangerous ____
b success in something after a lot of hard work and effort (e.g., passing an examination) ____
c something very difficult to do ____

4 Work in groups. Discuss these questions.

1 Are you a person who takes risks or are you usually very careful?
2 What is a big achievement in your life so far?
3 What will be a big challenge for you in the future?

4a Adventurers of the year

Reading

1 Read the article. Are these sentences about Pasang, Marjan, or both of them? Write 1–6 in the diagram.

1 She was born in Nepal.
2 Her father helped her.
3 She started when she was a teenager.
4 She trained for her job.
5 She competed in other countries.
6 She changed other people's lives.

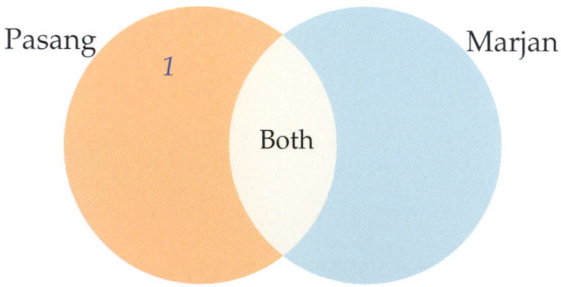

2 Read the article again. Work in pairs and discuss the questions.

1 What do you think was Pasang's biggest challenge?
2 Why is she famous?
3 What was Marjan's ambition?
4 What were her team's achievements?

Grammar simple past

▶ SIMPLE PAST

We use the simple past to talk about finished actions, events, or situations in the past.
*Pasang Lhamu Sherpa Akita **lived** with her younger sister in Lukla.*
*Marjan Sadequi **grew up** in the capital city of Kabul.*
*People **didn't have** homes or food.*
*It **wasn't** easy to practice on the roads of Kabul.*

For more information and practice, see page 162.

▶ 27

ADVENTURERS *of the* YEAR

EVERY YEAR, READERS OF *NATIONAL GEOGRAPHIC* MAGAZINE VOTE FOR THEIR ADVENTURERS OF THE YEAR. HERE ARE TWO OF THEM.

THE MOUNTAINEER

As a child, Pasang Lhamu Sherpa Akita lived with her younger sister in Lukla, a town in northeastern Nepal. Pasang's parents died when she was young. As a teenager, she trained as a mountaineer. She worked as a mountain guide, and she climbed Mount Everest when she was only 22. In 2015, there was a terrible earthquake in Nepal. Many people didn't have homes or food, so Pasang helped them. These days, she also works to improve education in Nepal, and is famous for her volunteer work as well as her mountaineering.

THE CYCLIST

Marjan Sadequi was born in Afghanistan and grew up in the capital city of Kabul. Her father was the national cycling coach for the men's team, and from very early on in life, Marjan's ambition was to become a cyclist. Her father gave Marjan her first bicycle when she was a teenager, and he soon saw how much Marjan loved cycling. As a result, he formed a new women's cycling team with his daughter and ten other women. It wasn't easy to practice on the roads of Kabul, but in 2013, the team went to New Delhi and they had their first international competition against other women's cycling teams. They didn't win, but they entered more races in Pakistan, Kazakhstan, and South Korea. Because of Marjan and her team's achievements, more women are now cycling in Afghanistan.

3 Look at the grammar box on page 46. Then underline the verbs in the past tense in *Adventurers of the Year*. Which are regular? Which are irregular?

4 Work in pairs. Answer these questions.

1 What do we add to regular verbs to form the simple past? What do we add if the verb ends in *-e*? What if the verb ends in *-y*?
2 What is the base form of the irregular verbs you underlined?
grew up—grow up
3 How do we form the negative of most simple past verbs? How do we form the negative of *be*?

5 Pronunciation /d/, /t/, or /ɪd/

▶ 28 Listen to the *-ed* ending of these regular verbs. Is the sound /d/, /t/, or /ɪd/? Circle your answers. Then listen again and repeat.

1	lived	/d/ /t/ /ɪd/		5	waited	/d/ /t/ /ɪd/	
2	finished	/d/ /t/ /ɪd/		6	looked	/d/ /t/ /ɪd/	
3	wanted	/d/ /t/ /ɪd/		7	decided	/d/ /t/ /ɪd/	
4	studied	/d/ /t/ /ɪd/		8	climbed	/d/ /t/ /ɪd/	

6 Complete the text about another adventurer. Use the simple past form of the verbs in parentheses.

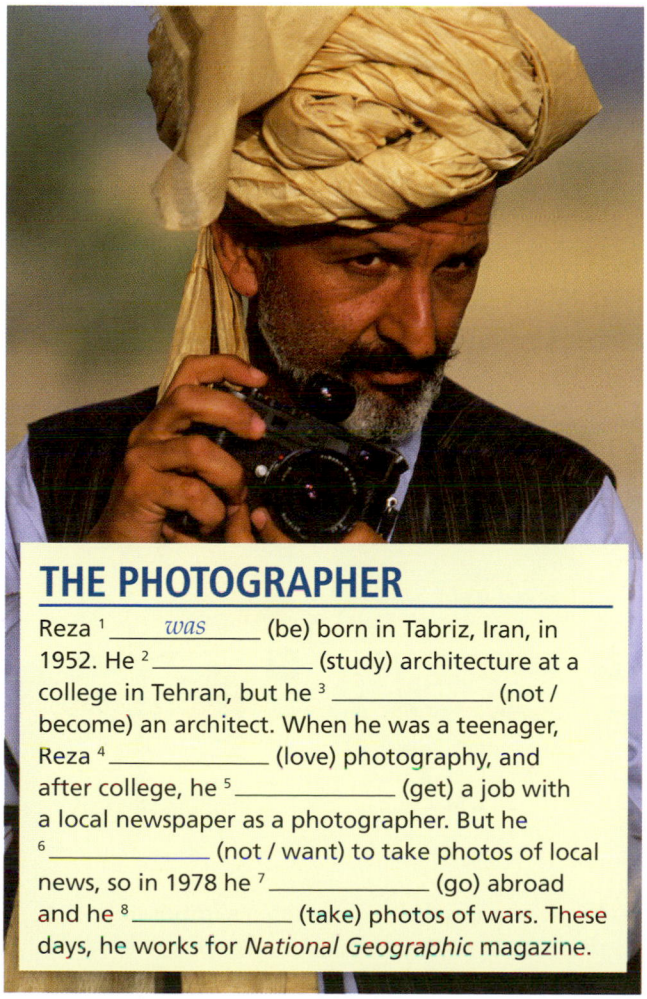

THE PHOTOGRAPHER

Reza [1] ___*was*___ (be) born in Tabriz, Iran, in 1952. He [2] _____ (study) architecture at a college in Tehran, but he [3] _____ (not / become) an architect. When he was a teenager, Reza [4] _____ (love) photography, and after college, he [5] _____ (get) a job with a local newspaper as a photographer. But he [6] _____ (not / want) to take photos of local news, so in 1978 he [7] _____ (go) abroad and he [8] _____ (take) photos of wars. These days, he works for *National Geographic* magazine.

7 Read the text about Reza again. Work in pairs. Answer the questions.

1 When was Reza born?
2 Where did he study architecture?
3 What did he love when he was a teenager?
4 What did he do after college?
5 Did he want to take photos of local news?
6 When did he go abroad?

▶ SIMPLE PAST QUESTIONS

*When **was** Reza born?*
*Where **did** he **study** architecture?*
***Did** he **want** to take photos of local news?*

For more information and practice, see page 162.

8 Look at the grammar box above. Circle the correct option (a or b) to complete these rules.

1 With most regular and irregular verbs, we make questions with _____ .
a the simple past form of the verb
b *did* + base form of the verb
2 With *be*, we make questions with _____ .
a *was* and *were*
b *did* + base form of the verb

9 Read these questions and answers from interviews with Pasang and Marjan. Complete the questions.

1 I: Where ___*did you live*___ as a child?
P: In Lukla, in northeastern Nepal.
2 I: When _____ Mount Everest?
P: When I was 22 years old.
3 I: Who _____ after the earthquake?
P: People with no homes and no food.
4 I: _____ you born?
M: In Afghanistan.
5 I: _____ your first international race?
M: No, we didn't.

Speaking myLife

10 Write six questions to ask your partner about the past. Use some of these ideas.

where / born? where / grow up?
when / learn / to ride a bike?
when / start / studying English?
where / go / vacation / last year?
go / abroad / last year? go / college?
what / be / first job?

11 Work in pairs. Take turns interviewing each other. Make notes about your partner's answers.

12 Work with a new partner. Describe your first partner's life from Exercise 11.

4b An impossible decision

Vocabulary
personal qualities

1 Work in groups. Read this English expression and discuss the questions.

"Two heads are better than one."

1 What do you think the expression means?
2 Do you have a similar expression in your language?
3 What are the advantages and disadvantages of working in teams?
4 What do you think makes a good team member?

2 Read the sentences about what makes a good team member. Write the adjectives in the box next to the matching sentence.

experienced	friendly	hardworking
kind	patient	positive

A good team member:
1 likes meeting people and gets along with everyone. ___*friendly*___
2 is a good listener and thinks about other people. _____
3 gives people the time they need and waits for them. _____
4 is always happy and looks for the good things in life. _____
5 works extra hours when it's necessary. _____
6 knows a lot about his or her area of work. _____

3 Work in pairs. Which qualities in Exercise 2 do these people need? Why?

a close friend	a teacher	a language learner
a manager	a parent	a president

A good teacher is patient because the students need time to learn.

Listening

4 What difficult decisions do people have to make in life? What decisions do you have to make at work or for your studies? Tell your partner.

I left my old company last year. It was difficult because I had a lot of good colleagues there. But I wanted a new challenge.

5 ▶ 29 Listen to the first part of a true story about two climbers named Joe Simpson and Simon Yates. Number these pictures (a–d) in the correct order (1–4).

6 Work in pairs. What was Yates's impossible decision at the end? What do you think he did?

7 ▶ 30 Now listen to the whole story. Work in pairs and answer the questions.

1 What two personal qualities from Exercise 2 did Simpson and Yates have?
2 Why didn't they stay at the top of the mountain for very long?
3 What decision did Yates make in the end?
4 The next day, what did Yates think about Simpson?
5 What did Yates hear in the night?
6 How did the story of Yates and Simpson become famous?

Grammar past continuous and simple past

▶ PAST CONTINUOUS and SIMPLE PAST

*While they **were going** down the mountain, Simpson **fell**. He **wasn't moving**, but he **was** still **breathing**.*
Note: We often use *when* and *while* to talk about one action happening at the same time as another.

For more information and practice, see page 162.

8 Look at the sentences in the grammar box. Work in pairs and answer these questions.

1 Which verb talks about a completed action?
2 Which verbs talk about actions in progress at a moment in the past?
3 We often use the two verb forms together. Which verb form is used for the longer, continuing activity? Which form is used for the shorter, finished action?
4 What is the auxiliary verb in the past continuous? What is the form of the main verb?

9 The sentences below describe the story of Simpson and Yates. Circle the correct options to complete the sentences.

1 The sun *shone* / *was shining* when Simpson and Yates left their tents on the first day.
2 When they reached the top of the mountain, it *snowed* / *was snowing*.
3 While they were going down the mountain, Simpson *broke* / *was breaking* his knee.
4 For an hour, Yates held the rope, but it *pulled* / *was pulling* him off the mountain.
5 Yates was sleeping in his tent, but he suddenly *woke up* / *was waking up*.
6 Finally, Yates *found* / *was finding* Simpson on the ground.

10 Complete each sentence with one verb in the past continuous form and one verb in the simple past form.

1 I ___*was working*___ (work) on my own when a group of people ___*came*___ (come) into my office.
2 We _____ (meet) them when they _____ (live) above our apartment.
3 They _____ (not get along) very well, so the team _____ (agree) to have a meeting.
4 The weather _____ (be) cold this morning, but it _____ (not rain).
5 I saw you across the street, but I _____ (not stop) because I _____ (run) to my job interview!
6 What _____ he _____ (do) when you _____ (call) him?
7 Which cities _____ they _____ (visit) while they _____ (travel)?
8 Why _____ you _____ (answer) that call while we _____ (watch) the movie?

11 Pronunciation *was / were*

a ▶ 31 Work in pairs. Listen to sentences 1 to 4 from Exercise 10. Notice the pronunciation of *was, were, wasn't,* and *weren't*. Which are stressed and which are unstressed?

b ▶ 31 Listen again and repeat the sentences.

Speaking myLife

12 Which of these events happened to you in the past? Write some sentences about them and state when the events happened.

broke a bone
achieved something with a team of other people
got a first job
had an accident
had an argument with a close friend
received really good news
was late for an important meeting

I broke my arm on my sixth birthday.

13 Work in pairs. Tell your partner about the things that happened to you. Take turns asking and answering questions about what you were doing when the events happened.

*A: I **broke** my arm on my sixth birthday.*
*B: What **were** you **doing** when it happened?*
*A: I **was riding** my first bicycle when I **fell off**.*

4c Challenge yourself

Reading

1 Work in pairs. Answer this riddle and solve the matchstick puzzle. Then take the numbers memory challenge on page 51. Turn to page 155 to find the answers.

A riddle: *What is yours, but other people use it more than you?*

A puzzle: Move two matchsticks and make four equal squares.

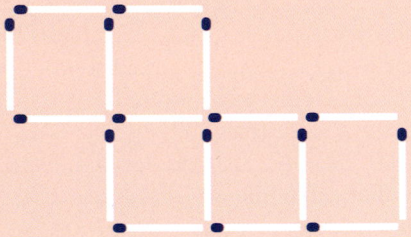

2 Work in pairs. Why do you think people like doing these types of challenges?

3 Read the article on page 51. Are these sentences true (T) or false (F)?

1	Professor Rubik taught students about architecture.	T	F
2	He made the cube to teach his students about puzzles.	T	F
3	Professor Rubik solved the cube right away.	T	F
4	A robot can solve a Rubik's cube faster than a human.	T	F
5	Some scientists think puzzles are good for older people's brains.	T	F
6	A study showed that playing video games has no impact on human memory.	T	F

Critical thinking looking for evidence

4 *Evidence* is factual information to support an idea. Check (✓) the three types of evidence the writer uses in the article. Which does he not use?

- ☐ facts from history
- ☐ data (e.g., numbers and amounts)
- ☐ quotes from people
- ☐ results from a scientific study

5 Read these ideas (a–c) from the article and answer the questions (1–2).

a The Rubik's cube became one of the most popular toys in history.
b Our brain naturally loves solving problems.
c Some scientists think puzzles and games can improve memory in the elderly.

1 Which two ideas have evidence in the article to support them? Underline this evidence. ____
2 Which idea doesn't have much evidence in the article? (It's the writer's opinion.) ____

Wordbuilding verbs and nouns

▶ WORDBUILDING verbs and nouns

Some words have a verb form and a noun form.
Sometimes the verb and noun form is the same:
challenge (v), *challenge* (n)
Sometimes the forms are different:
achieve (v), *achievement* (n)

For more practice, see Workbook page 35.

6 Look at the wordbuilding box below. Complete this chart with words from the article.

Verb	Noun
challenge	challenge
achieve	achievement
1 _____	solution
2 _____	player
3 _____	improvement
memorize	4 _____
test	5 _____
6 _____	score

Writing and speaking myLife

7 Work in pairs. Use the words in Exercise 6 to write a list of tips for someone who is a beginner in English. Take turns giving your partner advice about the best ways to learn.

When you study for a test, you should memorize ...

CHALLENGE YOURSELF

THE NUMBERS MEMORY CHALLENGE

Cover the groups of numbers in this list. Then look at the first group (on the top line), cover it again, and try to say the numbers. Then look at the second group of numbers (on the second line), cover them, and try to say them.

Continue down the list. When do you stop remembering all the numbers in a group?

4 9 2 6
5 7 8 4 3
9 5 3 4 5 6
7 4 3 0 6 7 3
8 9 3 1 4 2 8 9
6 3 9 8 1 8 5 3 1
9 2 7 8 3 6 9 7 0 8

▶ 32

1 In 1974, Professor Erno Rubik was looking for an interesting way to teach his architecture students about 3D[1] geometry.[2] To do this, he made a cube with nine other cubes on each of its sides. The smaller cubes were different colors, and you could turn them in different directions. The challenge was to make each side all one color. The problem was that there are 43 quintillion (43,000,000,000,000,000,000) ways to move the cubes. As a result, it took Professor Rubik over a month to solve his own problem.

2 In the end, the Rubik's cube became one of the most popular toys in history. Over 400 million Rubik's cubes have been sold around the world, and one in seven people have played with one. In 2016, a Dutch man named Mats Valk solved the Rubik's cube in 4.74 seconds—the world record for a human at the time. A robot beat him with a time of 1.019 seconds.

3 So why do humans love challenging themselves with puzzles like the Rubik's cube? It's the same reason we like crosswords and puzzles in newspapers, or why we play games on our cell phones. Our brain naturally loves solving problems.

4 Some scientists also think puzzles and games can improve memory in the elderly. In one study at Illinois University, the researchers studied how video games help older people's mental health. In their study, twenty adults over the age of sixty played a video game for a long period, while another twenty adults over sixty did not. Afterwards, they gave all forty adults a test of memory and mental skill. Overall, the video game players scored higher on the test, which means a challenging video game could be good for our brains.

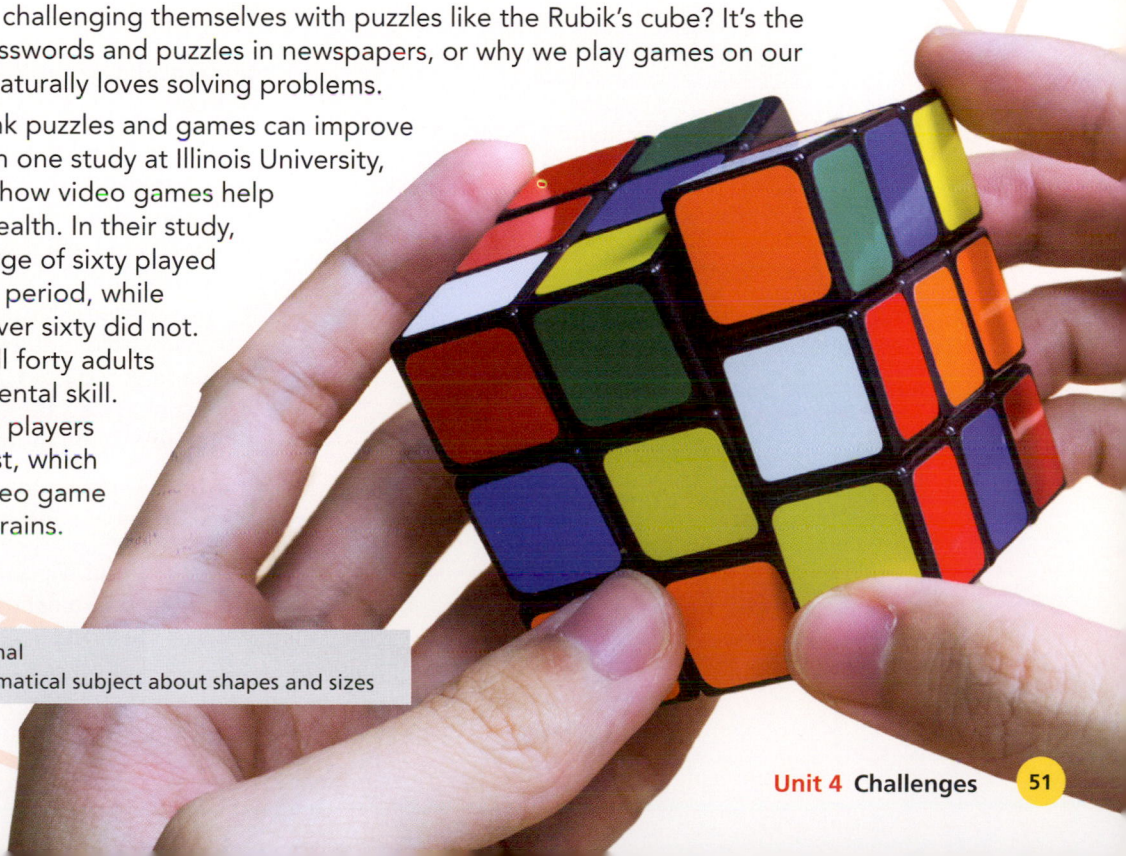

[1]**3D** (adj) /ˌθriːˈdiː/ three-dimensional
[2]**geometry** (n) /dʒiːˈɒmətri/ mathematical subject about shapes and sizes

4d True stories

Real life telling a story

1 ▶ 33 Listen to two friends talking about a camping trip. Work in pairs and answer the questions.

1 Was the start of the weekend good or bad?
2 What happened to the car?
3 Who helped them?
4 What was the problem when they found the campsite?
5 Where did they go instead?

2 ▶ 33 Listen again. Complete the conversation with the words you hear.

A: Hi, Mark. How was your camping trip?
B: It was great in the end, but we had a terrible time at the beginning.
A: Why?
B: [1] _____ , we left the house late, and then after only half an hour, the car broke down.
A: Oh, no! [2] _____ ?
B: [3] _____ , there was a garage nearby and the mechanic fixed the problem. But [4] _____ we arrived at the forest, it was getting dark. [5] _____ we drove around for about an hour, we [6] _____ found the campsite, but it was completely dark by then. And it was raining!
A: Really? So [7] _____ ?
B: We found a nice, warm hotel down the road!
A: That was lucky!
B: Yes, it was a great hotel. [8] _____ , we stayed there for the whole weekend.
A: [9] _____ !

3 Look at the expressions for telling a story. Match the expressions in Exercise 2 (1–9) with the headings (a–d).

▶ TELLING A STORY

a Sequencing the story 1,
At the beginning, … Then … Next, … While …

b Introducing good and bad news _____
Luckily, … But … Unfortunately, …

c Reacting to good and bad news _____
Why?
Really?
That was a good idea!
Oh, no!

d Asking about the next part of the story _____
What did you do?
What happened?

4 Pronunciation intonation for responding

▶ 34 Listen to these expressions for reacting to good and bad news. Notice how the speaker uses intonation to show interest. Listen again and repeat.

1 Why?
2 Really?
3 That was a good idea!
4 Oh, no!

5 Work in pairs. Practice the conversation from Exercise 2. Take turns being person A. Pay attention to your intonation when you are responding.

6 Work in pairs. Practice telling a story and responding.

Student A: Use these ideas to tell a story to your partner.

- You had a terrible commute to work.
- You were cycling, and it started raining.
- A car hit your bike.
- You weren't hurt.
- The driver was very nice. He owns a bicycle store.
- He gave you a new bike! It's much better than your old one!

Student B: Listen to your partner and respond with comments and questions.

7 Now change roles.

Student B: Use these ideas to tell a story to your partner.

- You went hiking in the mountains with a friend.
- It started snowing.
- You went back toward the town, but it was getting dark.
- You passed a large house with the lights on.
- The people in the house invited you in. They made you dinner, and you stayed the night.
- The next day, the sun was shining. You reached the top of the mountain.

Student A: Listen to your partner and respond with comments and questions.

8 Think of a bad trip you had. Did it have a happy ending? Make a list of the events. Then tell your partner the story.

4e A story of survival

Writing a short story

1 Work in pairs. What is an interesting story in the news at the moment? Is it good news or bad news?

2 Stories in the news answer some or all of these questions. Read the short story and answer the questions.

1 Where did it happen?
2 What was the weather like? Who was there? What were they doing?
3 What went wrong?
4 What surprising event happened? Who was there? What were they doing?
5 Did the story have a happy or sad ending?

Boys survive 50 DAYS lost at sea

The islands of Atafu are in the middle of the Pacific Ocean, and the people there go fishing every day. One day, the sun was shining and the ocean was calm, so three teenage boys went fishing in a small boat. In the evening, they didn't arrive home, so the islanders went out and looked for them. After many days, there was no sign of them and everyone thought the boys were dead.

Fifty days later, some fishermen were sailing in the middle of the Pacific Ocean when they saw a small boat in the distance. The three boys were in the boat, over 1,500 kilometers (900 miles) from their home. They were living on fish from the ocean and rainwater. In the end, they returned to their families alive and well.

3 **Writing skill** **structure your writing**

The story has a five-part structure. Number the parts below in the correct order (1–5).

___ The day the story starts, the background events (such as the weather), and what happened first.
___ An important moment when something goes wrong, and what happens next.
___ There is a happy (or sad) ending.
_1_ The place and the typical lives of the people.
___ A surprising (and often positive) change in the story after a long time.

4 Time expressions help the structure of a story. Look at this example and underline the other time expressions in the story.

> The islands of Atafu are in the middle of the Pacific Ocean, and the people there go fishing every day. One day, the sun was shining and the ocean was calm, so three teenage boys went fishing in a small boat.

5 You are going to write a short story. Use a story from your own life or a story in the news. Plan the story using the five-part structure. Make notes to answer the questions in Exercise 2.

6 Write your short story in about 80–100 words. Use some time expressions to help the structure.

7 Work in pairs. Take turns reading your stories. Does your partner use the five-part structure and time expressions?

The islands of Atafu

4f A microadventure

Alastair and Temujin during their microadventure in Croatia

Before you watch

1 Make a list of things you did in the last 24 hours. Write as many things as you can in two minutes. Then work in pairs. Take turns reading your lists. Who wrote the longer list?

I got up, I brushed my teeth, I ate breakfast, …

2 You are going to watch a video about two friends. They are spending 24 hours in Croatia on a "microadventure." Complete these sentences from the video with the simple past form of the verbs in parentheses.

___ We _____ (take) a photo of the city lights below.
___ We _____ (leave) the city.
___ We _____ (wake up) next to this rock.
___ We _____ (buy) some bread, some grapes, some meat.
___ We _____ (go) swimming in the Mediterranean Sea.
1 We *ate* (eat) ice cream.
5 Al _____ (sit) on a wall.
___ We _____ (have) some water and watched the sunset.
7 We _____ (make) a sandwich.
___ We _____ (find) a river.

While you watch

3 4.1 Watch the video. Number the sentences in Exercise 2 in the order they happened (1–10).

4 4.1 Watch the video again. Check (✓) the correct options to complete the sentences.

1 Alastair Humphreys is ___ .
- ☐ a filmmaker
- ☐ an adventurer
- ☐ a writer

2 They rented ___ .
- ☐ a car
- ☐ motorcycles
- ☐ bicycles

3 They drove ___ .
- ☐ through a tunnel
- ☐ over a bridge
- ☐ around a bend

4 At the river, they saw ___ .
- ☐ a fish
- ☐ a dragonfly
- ☐ a frog

5 On the top of the mountain, they could hear ___ .
- ☐ people
- ☐ animals
- ☐ music

6 In the morning, Alastair ___ .
- ☐ ate a banana
- ☐ brushed his teeth
- ☐ called his mother

7 Afterwards, they ___ .
- ☐ took a shower
- ☐ had coffee
- ☐ ate breakfast

After you watch

5 Vocabulary in context

4.2 Watch the clips from the video. Choose the correct meaning of the words and phrases.

6 4.1 Work in pairs. Watch the video again with the sound OFF. Using the simple past tense, describe what happened in the microadventure as you see each action on the screen.

7 Work in pairs. You are going to plan a 24-hour microadventure. Discuss these ideas and make your plans.

- Where will you go?
- What will you do?
- What will you see?

At 9 o'clock, we'll take the train to … and visit …

8 Work with another pair and describe your plans for your microadventure.

A dragonfly

UNIT 4 REVIEW AND MEMORY BOOSTER

Grammar

1 Complete the text with the simple past form of the verbs in parentheses.

In 2013, Aleksander Doba [1] _____ (cross) the Atlantic Ocean in a kayak. He [2] _____ (start) his trip in Lisbon, Portugal, and he [3] _____ (arrive) in Florida six months later. He [4] _____ (travel) 12,427 kilometers (7,722 miles). It [5] _____ (be) a difficult journey. His kayak [6] _____ (break) near the Bahamas, so he [7] _____ (stop) to fix it. He also [8] _____ (have) other challenges—his satellite phone [9] _____ (not work) for 47 days, so he [10] _____ (not have) any communication. Aleksander [11] _____ (be born) in Poland in 1946, and he [12] _____ (not begin) kayaking until the age of 34.

2 >> MB Work in pairs. Answer the questions about the story in Exercise 1.

1 What are the personal qualities of Aleksander Doba?
2 Why do you think people like Aleksander take risks and challenge themselves?

3 Circle the correct options.

The sun [1] *shone / was shining* as the plane turned onto the runway. During take-off, the passengers inside the plane sat quietly. They [2] *took / were taking* their first parachute jump. Everyone [3] *was / was being* nervous, and no one [4] *said / was saying* a word. When the plane [5] *reached / was reaching* the correct height, their teacher shouted, "OK, everyone. It's time to jump!" She [6] *opened / was opening* the door on the side of the plane and, in the next moment, everyone [7] *jumped / was jumping* out of the plane toward the ground.

I CAN
use the simple past and past continuous ☐

Vocabulary

4 Complete the sentences with these words.

challenging	experienced	intelligent
kind	patient	positive

1 Don't get angry when things don't happen as fast as you want. Learn to be _____ .
2 He's a very _____ climber. He started mountaineering when he was a child.
3 It's very _____ of you to help me with my homework.
4 Even when things go wrong, it's important to stay _____ .
5 My friend is the most _____ person in our class. She always gets 100% on tests.
6 Finishing the marathon was very _____ , but I did it in the end.

I CAN
talk about personal qualities and challenges ☐

Real life

5 >> MB Work in pairs. Look at the pictures (1–5).

Student A: Tell the story to your partner using some of these words.

at the beginning	but	luckily	next	while

Student B: Listen to the story and react to good and bad news with some of these phrases.

Oh, no!	Really?	What happened?	Why?

I CAN
tell a story ☐
react to good and bad news ☐

Unit 5 The environment

Uruguayan artist Jaime built this home in Florianapolis, Brazil, from recycled materials.

FEATURES

58 Recycling
The real story behind recycling our trash

60 Managing the environment
Some environmental stories from around the world

62 A boat made of bottles
How one environmentalist is trying to raise awareness

66 Recycling Cairo
A video about how recycled objects are used in Cairo, Egypt

1 Work in pairs. Look at the photo and the caption. What do you think of the home in the photo? Would you like to stay there? Which of these materials did Jaime use?

cardboard glass leather metal paper plastic wood

2 ▶ 35 Work in pairs. Listen to part of a documentary about Jaime and the house in the photo. Answer the questions.

1 What materials does the speaker mention?
2 What did Jaime do with them? Give an example.
3 What does Jaime want people to think about?

3 Work in pairs. Look at the highlighted expressions for talking about objects. Form similar sentences about the everyday objects in the box below.

A dictionary is made of paper. You use it for looking up words.

an envelope a cell phone a wallet a tin can

4 Think of another everyday object. Don't tell your partner what it is, but describe what it's made of and what you use it for. Your partner has to guess the object.

5a Recycling

Vocabulary recycling

1 Work in pairs. What kind of trash do you throw away or recycle every week? What percentage of each type (a–e) is in your trash can?

About 25% of my trash is paper.

a electronics
b glass
c paper and cardboard
d metal
e plastic

2 Match these objects (1–8) to the type of trash (a–e) in Exercise 1. Some items match two categories.

1 computer *a*
2 bottle *b, e*
3 jar ___
4 aluminum foil ___
5 TV ___
6 cereal box ___
7 magazine ___
8 bag ___

Reading

3 Work in pairs. Look at the photos with the article. What do you think *e-waste* is? Why is the boy holding part of an old computer?

4 Read the article and check your ideas from Exercise 3.

5 Work in pairs. Read the article again and answer these questions.

1 What did Peter Essick find in the markets of Ghana?
2 Why do people melt parts of the broken computers?
3 Why is recycling the metal dangerous?
4 What types of electronic products are environmentally friendly?

▶ 36

Electronic waste in Agbogbloshie dump, Accra, Ghana

E-WASTE

Do you ever throw away any electronic waste (or *e-waste*)? Perhaps you have some old technology that doesn't work, like an out-of-date phone or a slow computer. But when you throw away these objects, do you know where they go? The reporter Peter Essick has followed this e-waste to different countries around the world.

Essick found a lot of e-waste in Ghana, with thousands of old computers in the local markets. Here, the sellers resell a few computers, but they can't sell many because a lot of them don't work. Instead, the sellers melt[1] some parts of the computers to recycle the metal. These parts don't have much metal, but sometimes there is a little gold inside.

Unfortunately, recycling the metal can be dangerous because it produces a lot of chemicals that are bad for workers' health. As a result, Essick thinks we shouldn't send any e-waste to other countries. It's bad for the environment, and it's bad for people's health. He believes we need to produce more environmentally-friendly electronics in the future; in other words, electronic products that you can recycle safely and in the country where they were made or sold.

[1] **melt** (v) /melt/ to heat an object until it turns to liquid

Grammar quantifiers

6 Which of these nouns are countable (C)? Which are uncountable (U)? Write C or U.

trash *U*	computer *C*	plastic ___	bag ___
box ___	magazine ___	paper ___	metal ___

▶ QUANTIFIERS

We use *quantifiers* with countable and uncountable nouns to talk about quantity.

*Do you ever throw away **any** electronic waste?*
*Perhaps you have **some** old technology that doesn't work.*
*Essick found **a lot of** e-waste in Ghana.*
*The sellers resell **a few** computers.*
*They can't sell **many** computers in the market.*
*These parts don't have **much** metal.*
*There is **a little** gold inside.*
*We shouldn't send **any** e-waste to other countries.*

For more information and practice, see page 164.

7 Look at the sentences in the grammar box. Then complete these sentences with the correct quantifiers in **bold** in the grammar box.

1 We use ___*some*___ and ___*a lot of*___ in affirmative statements with countable or uncountable nouns.
2 We use _____ in questions and in negative statements with countable or uncountable nouns.
3 We use _____ to talk about small quantities in affirmative statements with countable nouns.
4 We use _____ to talk about small quantities in affirmative statements with uncountable nouns.
5 We use _____ in negative statements and in questions with countable nouns.
6 We use _____ in negative statements and in questions with uncountable nouns.

8 Circle the correct quantifiers to complete the sentences.

1 How *much / many* trash do you recycle?
2 I recycle *a few / a little* things, like glass and plastic bottles.
3 I don't recycle *many / much* glass.
4 I recycle *a few / a little* paper each week.
5 Do you have *much / any* recycling bins?
6 There are *some / any* old TVs for sale.
7 You shouldn't throw away *many / any* paper!
8 How *many / much* times can paper be recycled?
9 Nowadays, *a lot of / a little* cities and towns have special recycling centers.

Speaking myLife

9 Work in pairs. Discuss these sentences (1–4) about recycling. Are they true for you? If necessary, change the words in **bold** so the sentences are true for you.

1 I throw away **a lot of** paper every week.
2 In my area, **a few** places have recycling bins.
3 My school / place of work **doesn't have any** recycling bins for paper.
4 **Some** people in my country think recycling is important.

*A: How **much** paper do you throw away every week?*
*B: I don't throw away **any** paper. We recycle it in special green bins.*

5b Managing the environment

Vocabulary results and figures

1 Work in pairs. Discuss the questions.

1 How often do you read news about the environment? Is it usually good news or bad news?
2 Do you have any good news about the environment in your country?

2 Read a newspaper report about Portugal. Is it good news or bad news?

> Portugal powered the whole country using only solar, wind, and hydroelectric energy for **about a hundred** hours last week. **Exactly a year** ago, the country produced **under a quarter** of its electricity from wind power, and **nearly half** of its total energy came from renewable energy. So it's a huge achievement for the country to live off renewable energy for **over four days**.

3 Look at the phrases in **bold** in the newspaper report above. Match these phrases with the exact information in a–e below.

a 48% _____
b 107 _____
c from May 7 to May 11 _____
d 22% _____
e 12 months _____

4 Work in pairs. Answer these questions about your life using *over, under, almost,* and *about*.

1 How much of your day do you spend looking at a screen (e.g., computer, TV)?
I spend about a third of my day looking at a screen.
2 How many hours a week do you spend shopping?
3 How many people live in your town or city?
4 How much money do you spend on buying clothes each month?
5 How many months a year do you spend at school or at work?

Listening

5 ▶ 37 Work in pairs. Listen to a news report about two environmental projects and answer the questions.

1 What four deserts does the report mention?
2 Where are the two environmental projects?
3 What type of wall are the countries building?

6 ▶ 37 Work in pairs. Listen again and answer the questions.

1 What percentage of the Earth's land is desert?
2 When did the Three-North Shelter Forest Program begin?
3 What is its purpose?
4 How long will the wall be when it's finished in 2050?
5 How many countries are working together on the project in Africa?
6 What are the goals of this project?

Grammar articles

▶ ARTICLES *a/an, the*, or no article

1 *In 1978, **China** started planting **a** wall of trees. Now **the** wall has about 66 billion trees.*
2 *It's **the** largest hot desert in **the** world.*
3 ***The** Gobi Desert is getting bigger.*
4 *Countries in **Africa** plan to build **a** wall.*
5 ***People** know about **the** Great Wall of China.*

For more information and practice, see page 164.

7 Look at the grammar box. Complete these rules (a–c) with *a/an*, *the*, or no article (*x*).

a We normally use _____ when we talk about something that isn't specific or when it's the first time we mention something. When we talk about something specific or talk about it again, we use _____ .
b We also use _____ when something is unique (there is only one), with superlatives, or with the names of some places (e.g., oceans, deserts, mountain ranges).
c We use _____ when we talk about people or things in general, and with the names of most places (e.g., continents, countries, cities, lakes).

8 Read about another way to manage the environment. Circle the correct options. Circle "–" if no article is needed.

Ice towers

In the spring and summer, there is often a water shortage in [1] *the* / – Himalayan mountains. So during the winter, [2] *a* / – people make ice towers. They put one end of [3] *a* / – long pipe into a river high in the mountains, and then they take the other end of [4] *a* / *the* pipe down to a village. The water comes out of the pipe and freezes in a fountain to create [5] – / *an* ice tower in the village. When the ice tower melts in the spring, [6] *a* / – farmers can use it to water their fields.

9 Pronunciation /ðə/ **or** /ðiː/

a ▶ 38 Listen to the difference in the pronunciation of *the* before a consonant sound and before a vowel sound.

/ðə/	/ðiː/
the wall	the Earth

b ▶ 39 Listen and circle /ðə/ or /ðiː/. Then listen again and repeat.

1	the river	/ðə/	/ðiː/
2	the ice	/ðə/	/ðiː/
3	the world	/ðə/	/ðiː/
4	the desert	/ðə/	/ðiː/
5	the oldest	/ðə/	/ðiː/
6	the largest	/ðə/	/ðiː/
7	the Atacama Desert	/ðə/	/ðiː/

10 Work in pairs. Look at these questions from a general knowledge quiz. Complete the questions with *a/an* or *the* where necessary. Then try to answer the questions.

Around the world quiz

1 There is _____ river that flows through parts of _____ Brazil, Colombia, Peru, and Ecuador. What is its name?
2 _____ White House is in _____ USA. Who lives there?
3 There is _____ natural satellite that goes around _____ Earth every day. What is it?
4 In 1998, Larry Page and Sergey Brin set up _____ global search engine. What is its name?
5 _____ Arctic Ocean is _____ smallest ocean in the world. Which is _____ largest?

11 Check the quiz answers on page 155.

Writing and speaking myLife

12 You are going to write five more quiz questions. Work in two pairs in a group of four.

Pair A: Turn to page 153 and follow the instructions.

Pair B: Turn to page 154 and follow the instructions.

13 Work in your group. Take turns asking and answering your five questions. Find out which pair has greater general knowledge.

5c A boat made of bottles

Reading

1 Work in pairs. These words and phrases are from the article on page 63. What do you think the article is about?

plastic bottles	special boat	sail
the Pacific Ocean	San Francisco	Sydney

2 Read the article and complete the fact file with numbers about the *Plastiki*.

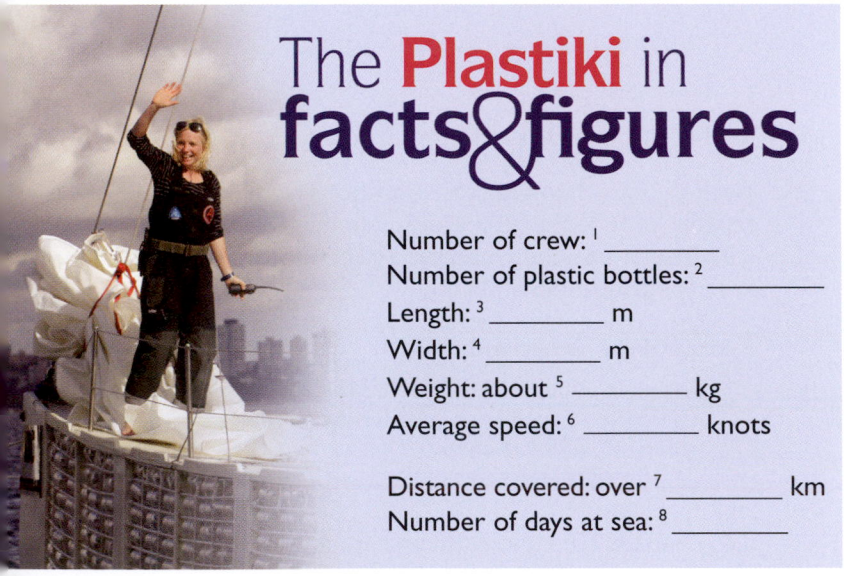

Critical thinking reading closely

3 Read the sentences (1–6). Circle the correct option for each sentence.

T = The sentence is **true**. The information is in the text.
F = The sentence is **false**. The information is in the text.
NG = We don't know if it's true or false. The information is **not given** in the text.

1 The *Plastiki* is made of the same material as other boats.	T	F	NG
2 Humans recycle most of their plastic bottles.	T	F	NG
3 Plastic in the ocean is killing animals.	T	F	NG
4 The *Plastiki* is environmentally friendly.	T	F	NG
5 The size of the "Great Garbage Patch" is growing.	T	F	NG
6 The journey took longer than de Rothschild had planned.	T	F	NG

Word focus *take*

4 Work in pairs. Find and underline five expressions in the article with the word *take*. Then match the expressions with the uses (1–4).

1 transportation: *take a taxi,* _____
2 daily routines: *take a walk,* _____
3 lengths of time: *take a few days,* _____
4 idioms: *take time,* _____

5 Complete the sentences with the correct form of *take* and the words in the box.

~~a break~~	many days	care	a plane

1 The work was tiring, and the crew sometimes needed to ___*take a break*___ and relax.
2 The journey across the Great Garbage Patch was longer than expected—it _____.
3 Most people _____ from San Francisco to Sydney, so they don't know about the pollution in the ocean.
4 _____ of the environment is a global responsibility.

Speaking myLife

6 Work in groups and discuss these questions.

1 Do you think environmental projects like the *Plastiki* can make people change their behavior? Why or why not?
2 In your country, does anyone try to change people's behavior in these areas? How do they do this?

- recycling more trash
- stopping smoking
- driving over the speed limit
- eating too much food
- anything else?

The government tries to stop people from smoking cigarettes by ...

A BOAT *made of* BOTTLES

▶ 40

A boat with a difference

1 The *Plastiki* looks similar to many other boats in Sydney Harbour. It's eighteen meters long, six meters wide, and it weighs about twelve thousand kilograms. It carries a crew of six people and has an average speed of five knots.[1] However, once you get near the *Plastiki*, you realize there's a big difference: It's made of twelve thousand five hundred reused plastic bottles.

How did the *Plastiki* begin?

2 David de Rothschild is an environmentalist who has crossed Antarctica and explored the Ecuadorian Amazon. One day, he was reading some information about all the plastic in the seas and oceans. He couldn't believe what he was reading. For example, humans throw away four out of every five plastic bottles they use, and plastic trash causes about eighty percent of the pollution in the ocean. In addition, scientists think that around one million seabirds die every year from plastic pollution. De Rothschild decided he wanted to get involved in the fight against ocean pollution. To help more people understand the problem, he started building a boat made of plastic bottles.

Designing the *Plastiki*

3 In addition to building the boat with recycled plastic, it was important to make the boat environmentally friendly and user-friendly. The boat uses renewable energy, such as wind power and solar energy. The crew can make meals with vegetables from the small garden at the back of the boat. They can take a break from work and get some exercise by using the special exercise bicycle. The energy from the bike provides power for the boat's computers. And if anyone needs to take a shower, the boat's shower uses saltwater from the ocean.

The journey

4 De Rothschild sailed the *Plastiki* across the Pacific Ocean from San Francisco to Sydney. That's more than fifteen thousand kilometers. On the way, he took the special boat through the "Great Garbage Patch." This is a huge area in the Pacific with 3.5 billion kilograms of trash. You can see every kind of human trash here, but the worst problem is the plastic. It kills birds and ocean life.

How well did the *Plastiki* survive the journey?

5 The journey wasn't always easy, and de Rothschild and his crew had to take care during storms. There were giant ocean waves, and winds of over one hundred kilometers per hour. The whole journey took one hundred and twenty-nine days. Originally, de Rothschild thought the boat could only travel once, but it lasted so well that he is planning to sail it again one day.

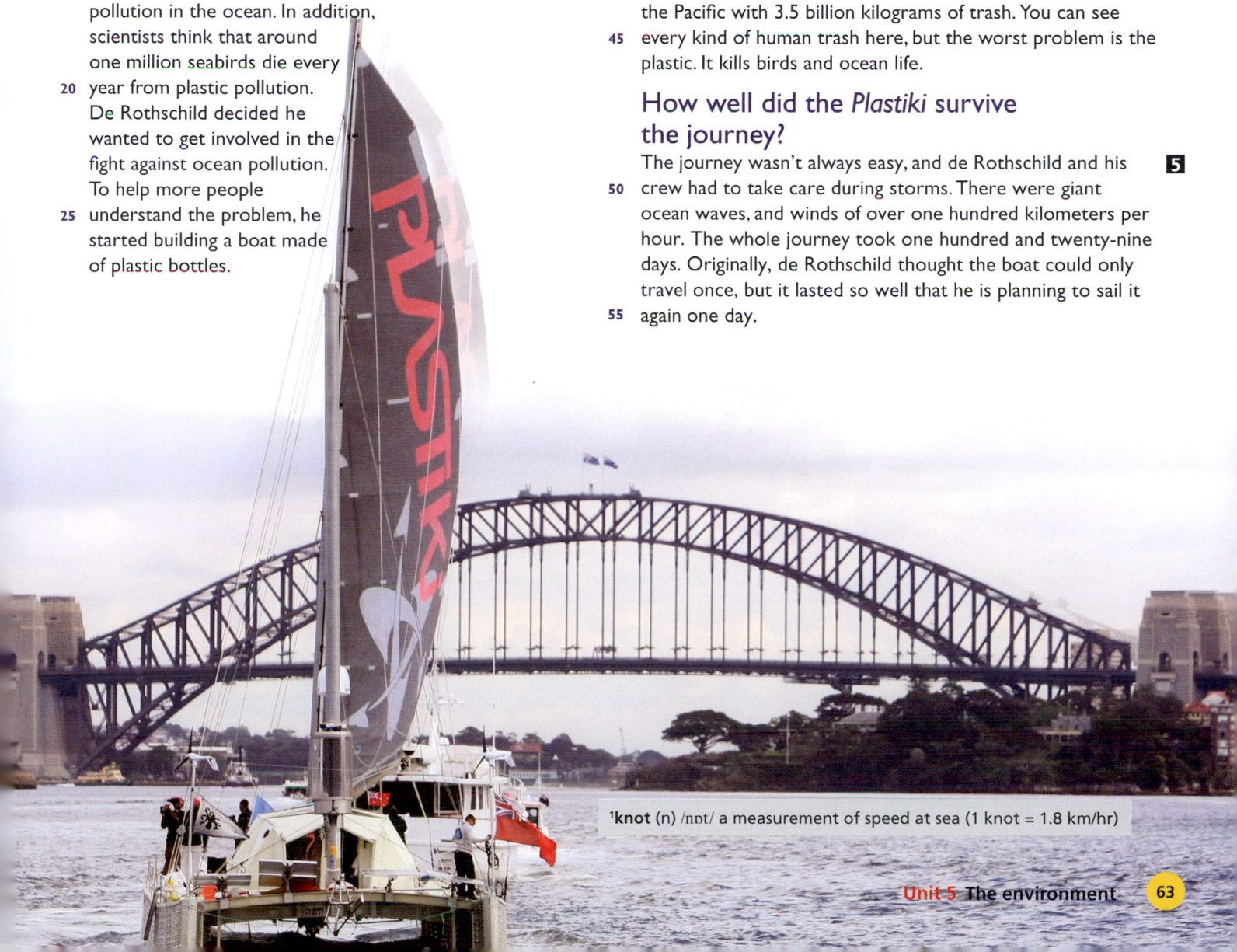

[1]**knot** (n) /nɒt/ a measurement of speed at sea (1 knot = 1.8 km/hr)

5d Online shopping

Reading

1 Work in pairs. Do you normally go to stores or do you prefer shopping online? Why?

2 Look at the website and email order. What did the customer order? What is the problem?

WWW.TECOART.COM

HOME | MY ACCOUNT | SHOPPING CART | CHECKOUT

We have lots of different clocks, and they are all made from recycled computers!

Computer Hard-Drive Clock with Circuit Board. $39.00

Apple iPod® Hard-Drive Clock on a Circuit Board. $35.00

Order number: 80531A
Order date: March 20

Thank you for your order. Unfortunately, the model you ordered is currently not available. We expect more stock to arrive in seven days. We apologize for the delay. For more information about this order, speak to a customer service representative at 555-1754.

Item Number	Description	Quantity	Price
HCV1N	Hard-drive clock	1	$39

Real life calling about an order

3 ▶ 41 The customer is calling customer service about her order. Listen to the conversation. Work in pairs and answer the questions.

1 What information does the customer service representative first ask for and check?
2 Why does the customer want the clock quickly?
3 What does she decide to do?
4 What will the customer service representative email her?

4 ▶ 41 Look at the expressions for calling about an order. Then listen to the conversation again. Circle the sentences the customer service representative uses.

▶ CALLING ABOUT AN ORDER

Telephone expressions
Good morning. How can I help you?
I'm calling about an order for a clock.
Can I put you on hold for a minute?
Is there anything else I can help you with?

Talking about an order
Do you have the order number?
Would you like to order a different product?
Would you like to cancel the order?
Would you like a refund?
Would you like confirmation by email?

Checking and clarifying
Is that A as in America?
Let me check.
So that's F for Freddie?
That's right.

5 Pronunciation sounding friendly

a ▶ 42 Listen to these sentences from a telephone conversation. Does the speaker sound friendly (F) or unfriendly (U)? Circle your answers.

1	Good morning. How can I help you?	F	U
2	Can I put you on hold?	F	U
3	Is that A as in America?	F	U
4	I'm calling about an order.	F	U
5	Is there anything else I can help you with?	F	U
6	Do you have the order number?	F	U

b ▶ 43 Listen to the sentences again. This time, they are all friendly. Work in pairs. Listen and repeat with a similar friendly intonation.

6 Work in pairs. Practice two phone conversations similar to the one in Exercise 3.

Student A: Turn to page 153 and follow the instructions.

Student B: Turn to page 154 and follow the instructions.

A: Good morning. How can I help you?
B: Hello. I'm calling about some clothes I ordered online. I received an email saying ...

5e Emails about an order

Writing emails

1 Read the correspondence between a customer and a customer service representative. Put the emails (A–E) in order (1–5).

A

Dear Mr. Martinez:

I would like to inform you that the e-book reader you ordered is now in stock. I would be delighted to deliver this item immediately. Please reply to confirm you would still like to purchase this item.

Charlotte Lazarro

B

Dear Sir or Madam:

I recently ordered an e-book reader online. However, I received an email that said this was not currently available. Please refund my money back to my credit card.

Yours sincerely,

Carlos Martinez

C

Thanks, but I bought the same product at a store yesterday. Therefore, please cancel the order and, as requested, send me my refund.

Carlos

D

As requested, here is the order number: 80531A

E

Dear Mr. Martinez:

Thank you for your email. I apologize for the difficulties with your order. In order to provide you with the necessary assistance, could you please send me the order number?

Best regards,

Charlotte Lazarro

Customer Service Representative

2 Read the emails in Exercise 1 again. Underline any phrases and expressions that ask for something or give instructions.

3 Writing skill formal words

a The language in the emails in Exercise 1 is quite formal. Match the formal language in the emails to these less formal words (1–9).

1 got *received*
2 happy _____
3 asked for _____
4 give _____
5 give back (money) _____
6 help _____
7 say sorry _____
8 tell _____
9 want _____

b Work in pairs. Make these sentences more formal.

1 I want my money back.
2 I'm writing to tell you that I didn't get the delivery.
3 Do you want any help?
4 Please give us your credit card details.
5 Sorry, but I can't give you your money back.

4 Imagine you ordered a printer online two weeks ago. You paid for delivery within 24 hours, but it hasn't arrived. Write an email to the supplier and request a refund.

5 Work in pairs. Read your partner's email. How formal is the language?

5f Recycling Cairo

Using Egypt's greatest natural resource on the rooftops of Cairo

Before you watch

1 Key vocabulary

Match these words and phrases with the pictures (1–6).

water tank ____	solar panel ____	goat ____
satellite dish ____	rooftop ____	garbage ____

2 Work in pairs. You are going to watch a video about using recycled objects in Cairo. What do you think is the connection between the words and phrases in Exercise 1?

While you watch

3 5.1 Watch the video. Were your predictions in Exercise 2 correct?

4 5.1 Watch the video again. Work in pairs and answer the questions.

1 How does the narrator describe the streets of Cairo?
2 How does he describe the rooftops of Cairo?
3 What is Thomas Culhane helping Egyptians to do?
4 What is Egypt's great natural resource?
5 What is the new solar hot water system made of?
6 The new solar heaters provide hot water, so what do they reduce?

After you watch

5 Vocabulary in context

5.2 Watch the clips from the video. Choose the correct meaning of the words and phrases.

6 Write a short summary of the video (about 100 words). Use these phrases.

People in Cairo use the rooftops for ...
Thomas Culhane is helping some local people to ...
They make the solar water heaters out of ...
The new heaters provide ...
Culhane thinks the solar heaters demonstrate that ...

7 5.3 Work in pairs. You are going to be the narrator of the video. Watch a shorter version of the video with no sound. Your teacher will play this video twice. As it plays, take turns reading your summary from Exercise 6 to your partner.

8 In the video, Thomas Culhane says, "One man's garbage is another's goldmine." What does he mean by this? Circle a, b, or c.

a Everyone thinks the garbage is worth a lot of money.
b Some people think the garbage is useless, but other people think it's very useful.
c You can sell the garbage for a lot of money.

9 Work in pairs. List some things people often use and throw away that other people could recycle or reuse.

UNIT 5 REVIEW AND MEMORY BOOSTER

Grammar

1 Circle the correct options to complete the article about recycling.

Recycling around the World

A new report looks at recycling in different countries and what they can learn from each other.

Japan

[1] *A / The* Japanese have different types of recycling bins, so local people only throw away [2] *a little / a few* household items. For example, they recycle about 100% of their drink cans, which is a lot higher than some countries in [3] *– / the* Europe.

USA

Overall, [4] *– / the* USA doesn't recycle as [5] *many / much* trash as Japan, but it has introduced [6] *a lot of / any* new projects in recent years. This year, it recycled 48% of its paper, 40% of its plastic bottles, and 65% of its cans.

Senegal

Senegal recycles [7] *a few / a little* of its waste industrially, but people generally don't throw away [8] *any / much* items that they can use for something else. For example, you can buy shoes made from old plastic bags, and drinking cups made from cans.

2 >> MB Work in pairs. Look at the photos. Answer these questions for each photo.

1 What project does the photo show?
2 What is the purpose of this project?

I CAN	
use quantifiers and articles	☐

Vocabulary

3 Work in pairs. What materials are these objects made of?

book	bookshelf	bottle	can
jar	magazine	cell phone	radio

4 >> MB Work in pairs. Think of two more objects for each material in Exercise 3.

5 Look at the percentages in the article in Exercise 1. Match the percentages to these phrases (1–4).

1 a full amount ____
2 just over a third ____
3 about two-thirds ____
4 almost half ____

6 >> MB Write the percentage of time you spend doing these things each day. Then work in pairs. Explain how you spend your time to your partner.

- at work or at school ____
- sleeping ____
- texting friends ____
- watching TV ____
- eating ____

I spend over a third of my day at school.

I CAN	
talk about materials	☐
talk about results and figures	☐

Real life

7 Work in pairs. Practice making a telephone call about an order. Take the roles of someone who works for the company (A) and a customer (B). Use these ideas.

A: Hello. How can / help /?
B: calling / an order / a clock. It hasn't arrived.
A: Do you / order number?
B: It / AG-100234L.
A: Sorry, can / repeat /?
B: Yes, it's /.
A: Let / check. Is / A / America?
B: That's correct.
A: Sorry, this product / currently not in stock. Would / change / order?
B: No. I'd like / refund.
A: That's fine. Would / like confirmation / email?
B: Yes, please.
A: Is / anything else / can help you with?
B: No /. Goodbye.

8 Practice the conversation again, but this time Student B closes their book. Then change roles.

I CAN	
call about an order	☐

Unit 6 Stages of life

Women chat on a station platform in Winterthur, Switzerland.

FEATURES

70 Changing your life
How one couple quit their jobs for a life of adventure

72 World party
Join in some of the world's biggest and most colorful parties

74 Coming of age
A look at how different societies celebrate becoming an adult

78 Steel drums
A video about the steel drums of Trinidad and Tobago

1 The photo shows three generations of people. Check (✓) the three options that describe their stages of life.

- ☐ toddler
- ☐ child
- ☐ teenager
- ☐ young adult
- ☐ middle-aged person
- ☐ elderly person

2 ▶ 44 Work in pairs. Listen to someone talking about the photo. Why does the speaker like the photo?

3 Look at these different life events. Work in pairs and answer the questions.

get your driver's license	buy your first house
get married	go to college or university
leave home	raise a family
start your career	retire from work

1 At what age do people in your country usually do these things?
2 Do you think there is a correct time in your life to do each one?

6a Changing your life

Vocabulary describing age

1 In some countries, it is rude to ask the question "How old are you?" Is it rude to ask this question in your country? When is it appropriate to ask this question? Discuss with a partner.

2 We use the phrases in B to talk about general age (e.g., *He's in his mid-twenties*). Work in pairs. Match the ages in A with the phrases in B.

A	25	14	83	39	53

B	early teens	mid-twenties	fifties
	late thirties	early eighties	

3 Work in pairs. Think of five famous people you both know. How old do you think they are?

Reading

4 Work in pairs. Read the article on page 71 about Rich and Amanda. How old do you think they were when they quit their jobs? Give reasons for your answer.

5 Work in pairs. Read the article again and answer these questions.

1 What did Rich and Amanda realize they wanted to do?
2 Why did they buy an RV?
3 Where did they plan to travel to by ship?
4 What did their friends think they were crazy to do?
5 What did Rich and Amanda start to do after they left home?

Grammar infinitive forms

▶ INFINITIVE FORMS

1 *We **intend to leave** our jobs.*
2 *Let's **buy an RV to travel** in.*
3 *It's **difficult to understand** your decision.*

For more information and practice, see page 166.

6 Look at the grammar box. Match the sentences (1–3) with the different forms (a–c).

a a verb + an infinitive ____
b an adjective + an infinitive ____
c the infinitive explains the purpose of an action ____

7 Read about three people's future plans. Circle the correct options. How old do you think each person is?

"One day I plan [1] *go / to go* to college, but this year I'm working in a supermarket [2] *earn / to earn* some money. Then I'd [3] *like / to like* to travel around the world for six months."

"I'm so happy [4] *retire / to retire*! Some people tell me I should [5] *relax / to relax* at this stage in my life, but I don't want [6] *sit / to sit* at home doing nothing. I hope [7] *do / to do* some volunteer work."

"These days, it's really difficult [8] *buy / to buy* a house. My husband and I can't [9] *afford / to afford* one, so we're living with his parents and saving money [10] *buy / to buy* a place of our own."

CHANGING your life

▶ 45

Rich and Amanda Ligato were professional people with successful careers. Every week, they worked hard. They always intended to do something fun and exciting on the weekends, but in the end, there was never enough time. One day they asked themselves, "Is this all there is?"

They realized that they wanted to stop working and, instead, to go traveling. Or, as Rich said, "to buy our freedom." But first, they needed to save some money. Every month, they lived on Rich's salary and saved Amanda's. Then they bought an RV to travel from the bottom of South America to Brazil, and from there they hoped to get to Africa on a container ship.

Colleagues at work found it difficult to understand Rich and Amanda's decision. Even their closest friends thought they were crazy to go on this kind of journey. But finally, the day came. Rich and Amanda left their home and started to live their dream.

8 Work in pairs. Look at the correct options in Exercise 7. Which options use the infinitive? Match them to the uses (a–c) in Exercise 6.

9 Match the beginnings of the sentences (1–4) with their endings (a–d).

1 One day, I
2 I'd
3 I want to be good at
4 I want to take a year off

a be happy to live in another country. ____
b intend to buy my own house. ____
c playing the piano. ____
d to travel overseas. ____

10 **Pronunciation** /tə/

▶ 46 Work in pairs. Listen to the sentences from Exercise 9. Is ***to*** pronounced /tuː/ or /tə/? Listen again and repeat.

11 Write your own sentences using the sentence beginnings (1–4) in Exercise 9. Then work in pairs. Read your sentences aloud and compare your ideas.

One day, I plan to start my own business.

Speaking myLife

12 Work in pairs. You plan to take six months off and take the trip of a lifetime! Discuss the following questions and make notes about your plans.

- Where do you plan to visit?
- Why do you want to visit these places?
- What type of transportation do you intend to use?
- What do you hope to do in each place?
- What do you think will be easy to do on the trip? What do you think will be difficult to do?

13 Present your trip of a lifetime to the rest of the class.

*We **plan to visit** parts of Asia. First of all, **we want to visit** Vietnam **to see** its beautiful natural attractions, such as ...*

6b World party

WORLD PARTY ▶ 47

People in different countries celebrate Mardi Gras with live music, costumes, fireworks, parades, and lots of good food. The most famous celebrations are in New Orleans, Venice, Rio de Janeiro, and Port-of-Spain.

a **Venice, Italy**
Mardi Gras is called *Carnevale* in this beautiful city. The first celebrations were in the 11th century, and it is still a big celebration today. Visitors to the city can enjoy the costumes, candles, and fireworks from a gondola in Venice's canals.

b **New Orleans, USA**
Small parties for Mardi Gras began in the 18th century. By the 19th century they were huge events with masks, costumes, and jazz bands. Visitors should also try "king cake" with its gold, purple, and green decorations.

c **Rio de Janeiro, Brazil**
The world-famous parades started in the mid-19th century, with decorated floats and thousands of people dancing the samba. People eat a famous meat and bean stew called *feijoada*.

d **Port-of-Spain, Trinidad and Tobago**
The French arrived here in the 18th century and brought Mardi Gras with them. These days, everyone enjoys the parties and concerts with the famous steel drums playing from morning to midnight.

Reading and vocabulary celebrations

1 Work in pairs. Which events do you celebrate in your family or country? When do you have parties?

2 Work in pairs. Look at the first paragraph of the article. Why is the article called *World Party*?

3 Read the article. Match the sentences (1–5) with the four cities mentioned in the article (a–d).

1 There were no Mardi Gras celebrations here before the mid-19th century. ____
2 It has the oldest celebration. ____
3 One type of food is decorated with different colors. ____
4 One type of musical instrument is especially important. ____
5 People can travel to the party on a type of boat. ____

4 Find words in the article for these pictures.

1 _____ 2 *floats* 3 _____

4 _____ 5 _____ 6 _____

5 Work in groups. Describe your favorite festival or celebration in your country. Answer these questions.

- When and why did it begin?
- Is there any special food?
- Do people wear special costumes or masks?
- Do people walk around the streets or ride on floats?
- Do you have fireworks at night?
- Is music important? What kind of music is there?

Listening

6 ▶ 48 Listen to a news report about one of the celebrations in the article. Which celebration is it about?

7 ▶ 48 Work in pairs. Listen again. Answer these questions with *Yes*, *No*, or *Don't know* (if the news report doesn't say).

1 Are a lot of people going to come to the celebration?
2 Is Lorette going to dance in the parade?
3 Is Lorette wearing her mask when the interview starts?

Grammar future forms

▶ FUTURE FORMS

1 ***Are*** *you* ***going to be*** *in the parade this afternoon?*
2 *Everyone* ***is meeting*** *at the float at six-fifteen.*
3 Reporter: *Do you have a mask?*
Lorette: *Sure. Here it is.* ***I'll put*** *it* ***on****.*

For more information and practice, see page 166.

8 Work in pairs. Look at the grammar box. Answer these questions.

a Which sentence is about an arrangement with other people at a fixed time, made before the conversation?
b Which sentence is about a decision made at the time of speaking?
c Which sentence is about a general plan or future intention? (It was decided before the conversation.)

9 Circle the correct options to complete the sentences.

1 One day when I'm older, I'm *visiting / going to visit* Venice.
2 A: Did Jeff email the times of the parade?
B: I don't know. *I'll check / I'm checking* my inbox right away.
3 A: Have you bought Mark a present for his birthday?
B: Yes, *I'm going to / I'll* give him a tie.
4 A: Hey, this costume would look great on you.
B: Really? I don't think so, but *I'm trying / I'll try* it on.
5 A: What time *will we meet / are we meeting* everyone for the parade?
B: Julie said to be at the main square at two.

10 Pronunciation contractions

▶ 49 Listen to sentences 1–4 in Exercise 9. Notice how the contractions are pronounced. Listen again and repeat.

11 Complete the sentences with a future form of the verbs in parentheses.

1 At the end of this year, I _____ (quit) my job and write a book.
2 What time _____ we _____ (meet) everyone today?
3 A: My car won't start, and I have a meeting at nine!
B: Don't worry. I _____ (take) you in my car.
4 I think we also need more decorations for the party, so I _____ (buy) those.

Speaking myLife

12 Work in groups. Imagine your town is going to be five hundred years old. Have a town meeting to plan and prepare the celebration. Discuss this list. Decide what you would like to do, and who is in charge of organizing each item.

- type of celebration
- type of food
- type of music
- type of place
- date and time
- anything else

A: We're ***going to have*** *a party with fireworks! I'll* ***buy*** *the fireworks. What about the food?*
B: I'll ***buy*** *the food!*

6c Coming of age

Reading

1 Work in pairs. Discuss these questions.

1 At what age can people legally do these things in your country?

drive a car	get married
buy cigarettes	work full-time
vote	open a bank account

2 At what age do you think people become adults?

3 Do you have special celebrations in your country for young people as they become adults?

2 Look at the photos and the title of the article on page 75. What do you think the expression "coming of age" means? Discuss with your partner.

3 Read about the three different coming-of-age ceremonies. Are these sentences true (T) or false (F)?

1 *Quinceañera* is celebrated in many different countries.	T	F
2 The writer thinks the Spanish introduced coming-of-age celebrations to South America.	T	F
3 The Hamar groom-to-be must pay money to the bride's family.	T	F
4 In Hamar culture, a husband is usually younger than his wife.	T	F
5 In Japan, you have more legal rights when you turn twenty years old.	T	F
6 The attitudes of some young people toward *Seijin-no-Hi* are changing.	T	F

4 These pairs of words (1–4) are in the article. Match the words with their definitions (a or b).

1 country *b* culture *a*
   a the ideas and customs of a group of people
   b an area of land with its own government

2 celebration ___ ceremony ___
   a an enjoyable event such as a party
   b a traditional and formal event on a special day

3 bride ___ groom ___
   a a man on his wedding day
   b a woman on her wedding day

4 legal rights ___ social traditions ___
   a what the law allows you to do
   b activities or behavior based on the past

Critical thinking analyzing the writer's view

5 The three sections in the article look at the topic in different ways. Match the paragraphs (1–3) with these three ways of looking at the topic (a–c). Underline the words or phrases that help you decide.

a **Historical view:** The writer includes information about the past. ___
b **Social view:** The writer includes information about society and how it is changing. ___
c **Economic view:** The writer includes information about costs. ___

6 Work in pairs and compare your answers.

Word focus *get*

7 Work in pairs. Look at the highlighted word *get* in the article. What word could replace *get* in this expression?

8 Read the description of a wedding. Match the uses of *get* (1–6) with their meanings (a–f).

> Once a couple [1] **gets** engaged, people start to [2] **get ready** for the big day! On the morning of the wedding, everyone [3] **gets up** early. Family and friends sometimes have to travel long distances, but it's a great chance for everyone to [4] **get together**. At the wedding, the bride and groom [5] **get** a lot of presents. When they [6] **get back** from their honeymoon, they move into their new home with all their presents.

a becomes	___	d receive	___
b meet	___	e return	___
c prepare	___	f starts the day	___

Speaking myLife

9 Work in pairs. Choose one of these events and describe what happens in your family or country on this day. Try to use the word *get* three times in your description.

a birthday	a religious holiday
New Year's Day	your country's national day
Valentine's Day	another special occasion

COMING of AGE

For some people, the age when you become an adult is the age you learn to drive or leave your parents' home. It can also be when you get married, buy a house, or have children. Or perhaps it's when you finish school and get a job. Different cultures have their own ideas and their own celebrations to symbolize coming of age.

Quinceañera

1 In Latin American countries, *Quinceañera* is a well-known celebration for girls around their fifteenth birthday. Attended by family and friends, the festivities include music, food, and dance. Many people believe the celebration started when the Spanish first came to parts of the Caribbean, Central America, and South America. Of course, ancient tribes[1] like the Inca, Maya, and the Aztecs probably already had their own coming-of-age ceremonies, but the Spanish changed these to include European features,[2] such as the *Quinceañera* waltz.[3] This waltz between the teenage girl and her father symbolizes[4] her coming of age.

Bull jumping

2 The Hamar tribe in southern Ethiopia is known for its unique custom of "bull jumping"—part of the coming-of-age ceremony for boys in Hamar culture. A row of fifteen bulls are lined up, and the boy has to jump over them. He must run back and forth twice across the backs of the bulls. The bulls are covered in dung to make them slippery. If the boy falls off, he must wait a year to try again. Hamar men have to do this before they can marry. After choosing a wife, the groom-to-be will have to pay the bride's family a "bride price" of about thirty goats and twenty cows. Because of the costs involved, Hamar men are usually in their mid-thirties and the women aged about seventeen when they marry. As a result, the husband often dies many years before his wife, so many Hamar households are headed by women who have survived their husbands.

Seijin-no-Hi

3 The second Monday of January is a public holiday in Japan. It's a day when all twenty-year-olds are supposed to celebrate their coming of age. Called *Seijin-no-Hi*, the young men and women wear formal clothes and attend ceremonies. Twenty is an important age in Japanese society because you get several adult legal rights, such as the right to vote in elections. However, in recent years, the number of young people celebrating *Seijin-no-Hi* has decreased. This is partly due to Japan's low birth rate, but it could also be because modern twenty-year-olds are less interested in these kinds of social traditions.

[1]**tribe** (n) /traɪb/ a group of people who share the same language and culture
[2]**feature** (n) /ˈfiːtʃər/ a quality or an important part of something
[3]**waltz** (n) /wɔːls/ a traditional and formal dance
[4]**symbolize** (v) /ˈsɪmbəlaɪz/ represent

6d An invitation

Speaking

1 Work in pairs. Which of these events are very formal? Which are less formal? Which could be either?

a graduation party
a barbecue with family and friends
a retirement party for a work colleague
your grandfather's ninetieth birthday party
a dinner with a work client

Real life inviting, accepting, and declining

2 ▶ 51 Listen to two conversations. Work in pairs and answer the questions.

Conversation 1

1 What event does Ian invite Abdullah to?
2 Why does Abdullah decline the invitation at first?
3 How does Ian convince Abdullah to come?
4 Does Abdullah need to bring anything?

Conversation 2

5 When is Sally leaving?
6 Where does Joanna invite Sally to?
7 Does Sally accept the invitation?
8 Do you think this conversation is more or less formal than conversation 1? Why?

3 ▶ 51 Look at the expressions below. Listen to the conversations again. Circle the expressions the speakers use.

INVITING, ACCEPTING, and DECLINING	
Less formal	**More formal**
Inviting	
Do you want to ...? How about *-ing*? Why don't you ...?	Would you like to come ...? I'd like to invite you to / take you to ...
Accepting	
It sounds great/nice. OK, thanks. That would be great.	That would be wonderful. I'd like that very much. I'd love to.
Declining	
Thanks, but ... Sorry, I can't.	I'd like/love to, but I'm afraid I ... It's very nice of you to ask, but I ...

4 **Pronunciation emphasizing words**

▶ 52 Listen to these sentences. Circle the word with the main stress in each sentence. Then listen again and repeat.

1 I'd love to.
2 That would be wonderful.
3 It's very nice of you to ask.
4 I'd like to, but I'm afraid I'm busy.

5 Work in pairs. Take turns inviting each other to different formal and informal events from Exercise 1. Think about how formal you need to be. Practice accepting and declining.

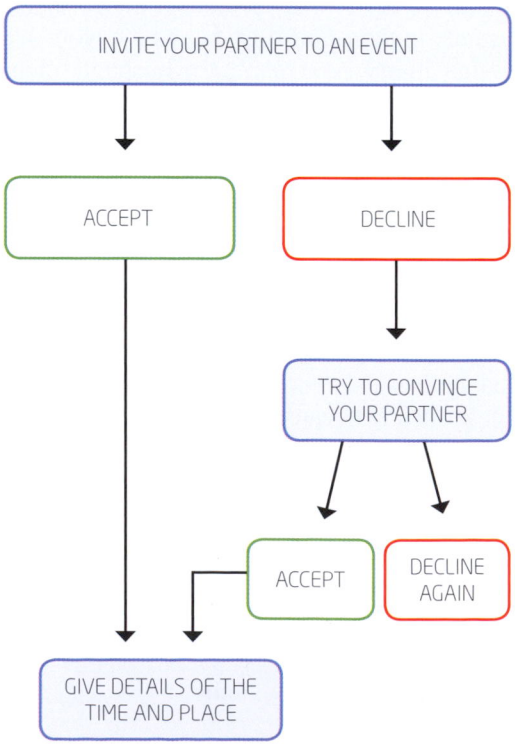

6e A wedding in Madagascar

Writing a description

1 Read this post from a travel blog. Circle the topics in the box that the writer describes.

food and meals	clothes
people	cities and buildings
music	transportation

I was staying in Madagascar with a family, and they invited me to their daughter's wedding. On the big day, I arrived outside an enormous tent. There was a zebu (a type of cow) at the entrance brought by the groom. He offered the zebu to the bride's parents to thank them for raising such a wonderful daughter. Inside the tent, there were beautiful decorations, and over 300 excited relatives and guests. The women wore colorful dresses. The older men wore formal suits, but the younger men were less formally dressed. Finally, the ceremony began with some speeches. The crowd listened politely, and sometimes they laughed and clapped. Then the oldest and most respected family members gave the couple their blessing. Finally, it was dinner, and we were served massive plates of meat. It was delicious! The meal for the bride and groom was served on a special plate, and they ate it using only one spoon to show that they were now joined as one. After the ceremony, the couple went back to their new home to begin their life together.

2 **Writing skill** descriptive adjectives

a When you write about places or special events, it's important to use interesting and very descriptive adjectives. Match the highlighted adjectives in the travel blog with these less descriptive adjectives (1–3).

1 big *enormous* , _____
2 nice *wonderful* , _____ , _____
3 happy _____

▶ WORDBUILDING synonyms

Some words have the same meaning, or a similar meaning. These are called synonyms.
old = ancient, big = huge, boring = dull
Using synonyms can improve a description and make it more interesting to read.

For more practice, see Workbook page 51.

b Work in pairs. Improve these sentences with more descriptive adjectives. You can use the words above or your own ideas.

beautiful *ancient*

1 Istanbul is a ~~nice~~ city with lots of ~~old~~ buildings.
2 The USA is a big country. It will take days to drive across it.
3 The parade was kind of boring after a while.
4 The crowd was happy because the fireworks had started.
5 All the costumes were nice.
6 I tried sushi for the first time, and it was really good.

c Work in pairs. Look at the topics in the box in Exercise 1. Think of two or three interesting adjectives for each one. Use a dictionary to help you. Then work with another pair and compare your adjectives.

food and meals: delicious, tasty, disgusting

3 Choose one of the topics below and write a short description (one paragraph) for a travel blog.

- a day you remember from a holiday
- your favorite place in the world
- a hotel you stayed at recently
- a festival or celebration

4 Work in pairs. Read your partner's description. Does it include interesting adjectives?

6f Steel drums

A steel drumming competition in Port-of-Spain during Trinidad and Tobago's Carnival celebrations

Before you watch

1 Work in pairs. Look at the photo on page 78 and discuss these questions.

1 What kind of musical instrument is the woman playing?
2 How important is music in your country?
3 Does your country have a traditional type of music and musical instrument?

2 Key vocabulary

Read the sentences (1–5). The words and phrases in **bold** are used in the video. Write these words and phrases next to their definitions (a–e).

1 Before you can play a guitar, you have to **tune** it.
2 Young children are **influenced** by their parents.
3 Oil companies store and transport the oil in **drums**.
4 In most countries, smoking is **banned** in public places.
5 The didgeridoo is a long wooden musical instrument. It's **native to** the aboriginal people of Australia.

a comes from _____
b affected or changed _____
c round metal containers _____
d not allowed (by law) _____
e change the sound of an instrument so it sounds nice _____

While you watch

3 6.1 Watch the video. Number these actions in the order you see them (1–4).

____ Beverly and Dove learn to play the drums.
____ Children and adults play together in a steel band.
____ Tony Poyer says that the steel drum, or pan, was invented in Trinidad and Tobago.
____ Honey Boy tunes a drum.

4 6.1 Watch the video again. Work in pairs and answer the questions.

1 What are the islands of the Caribbean region famous for?
2 According to Tony Poyer, when was the steel pan invented?
3 Why did Trinidad have many oil drums?
4 Do most steel drum musicians play by reading music?
5 Who do you find in a "panyard"?

After you watch

5 Vocabulary in context

a 6.2 Watch the clips from the video. Choose the correct meaning of the words and phrases.

b Complete the information about the Australian didgeridoo with these words and phrases.

play by ear	performers	backgrounds
goes back	escape	

The didgeridoo is a musical instrument that [1] _____ about 1,500 years. It is made from a long piece of wood with a hole down the middle. Aborigines of different tribes and [2] _____ play the didgeridoo. They don't read from music but [3] _____ . As you travel around Australia, you can't [4] _____ its famous sound. You'll often see [5] _____ playing the instrument at special Aboriginal celebrations because it's an important symbol of their culture.

6 Work in pairs and discuss these questions.

1 Musical instruments can be important national and cultural symbols. What are some other important symbols of your country or culture?
2 Plan a two-minute video about your country's symbols. Which ones will you show in the video? What will you say about them?
3 Present your idea for the video to the class.

UNIT 6 REVIEW AND MEMORY BOOSTER

Grammar

1 >> MB Work in pairs. Look at these sentences about the future. Can you explain the difference in meaning between the different verb forms?

1 I'm going to major in English in college.
2 I think I'll study for my English test next.
3 I'm meeting my friend at two o'clock to study English together.
4 I plan to study English in college.

2 Circle the correct options to complete the sentences.

1 We *hope / 're going to* visit my family this weekend.
2 A: I need someone to carry these books for me.
B: I *'m helping / 'll help* you!
3 It isn't easy *win / to win* the lottery.
4 A: When *are you going to start / starting* your homework?
B: In a few minutes.
5 Rachel *will have / is having* a party tonight. She planned it months ago.

3 >> MB Work in pairs. Tell each other about:

- your plans for this weekend.
- your future career intentions.

I CAN	
use infinitive forms	☐
use different future forms	☐

Vocabulary

4 Work in pairs. Match the verbs in A with the words in B to make phrases.

A	go	learn	buy	raise
B	a house	to school	to drive	a family

5 >> MB Work in pairs. Look at the phrases in Exercise 4 and answer these questions.

1 In what order do these things typically happen in life?
2 Which things have you done?
3 How old were you when you did them?
4 How did you feel at the time?
5 When do you plan to do the other things?

6 Complete the text about the Asakusa Samba Carnival with these words.

costumes decorations drums floats parade

Every year on the last Saturday of August, over 500,000 people gather in Tokyo for the Asakusa Samba Carnival. The [1] _____ starts on Umamichi Street and lasts for about five hours. A music group beats out a rhythm on a variety of [2] _____ . Samba teams from all over the country wear bright, glittering [3] _____ . The performers dance in the streets and ride on large [4] _____ that are covered in colorful [5] _____ .

I CAN	
talk about age and the stages of life	☐
talk about parties and celebrations	☐

Real life

7 Look at the sentences (1–3). Replace the phrases in **bold** with these phrases in the box.

I'd like to that sounds would you like to

1 **Why don't you** come with me to the movies?
2 **It's nice of you to ask**, but I won't be home this evening.
3 Thanks. **That'd be** great.

8 Work in pairs. Take turns inviting each other to do something this week. Accept or decline the invitation.

I CAN	
invite people and accept or decline invitations	☐

Unit 7 Work

A woman working in a steel mill in Pennsylvania, USA

FEATURES

82 Changes in Pennsylvania

How the discovery of natural gas changed people's lives

84 X-ray photographer

Looking inside a place of work

86 Twenty-first century cowboys

How similar is the Hollywood cowboy to the real thing?

90 My working life

A video of people talking about their jobs

1 Work in pairs. Look at the photo above. Describe the woman's job using some of these words.

interesting	dangerous	physical	hard
boring	skilled	challenging	tiring

2 ▶ 53 Listen to the woman above talking about her job. Circle the correct options.

1 When she graduated from high school, she had a *full-time / part-time* job in a restaurant.
2 She did some *office / manual* work for a construction company.
3 She works *as part of a team / on her own* at the steel mill.
4 It's *easy / hard* work with *normal / long* hours.

3 We often put two words together to make names for jobs, e.g., *steel + worker = steel worker*. Match the words in A with the words in B to make five jobs.

A	hotel	sales	police	fashion	computer
B	clerk	designer	programmer	officer	receptionist

4 Work in pairs. Describe each job in Exercise 3 using words from Exercise 1. Which of the jobs would you enjoy doing? Which wouldn't you enjoy? Give reasons.

7a Changes in Pennsylvania

Vocabulary jobs

1 In the US, some jobs are difficult to fill because there aren't enough people qualified to do them. Work in pairs. Look at these jobs. Which five jobs do you think are most difficult to fill? Check your answers on page 155.

accountant	chef	financial advisor
home health aide	journalist	nurse
software engineer	teacher	truck driver

▶ WORDBUILDING suffixes in job words

We often make words for jobs by adding suffixes to verbs and nouns.
verb + suffix: *teach—teacher*
noun + suffix: *journal—journalist*
Some job titles do not use a suffix: *chef, nurse,* etc.

For more practice, see Workbook page 59.

2 Look at the wordbuilding box. Underline the suffixes in the jobs in Exercise 1.

3 Work in pairs. Make jobs from these words using the suffixes from Exercise 1.

farm	economics	science
act	build	train

Reading

4 Read the article about people living and working in Pennsylvania, USA. Match these jobs (1–3) with the people in the article (A–C).

1 businessman ____
2 trainee driver ____
3 farmer ____

5 Work in pairs. Read the article again and answer the questions.

1 When did the energy company first discover natural gas in Pennsylvania?
2 What does Donald get from the energy company?
3 What training is Lee doing?
4 Why is Paul's business "looking good"?

▶ 54

WHEN JOBS CAME TO PENNSYLVANIA

In 2004, an energy company discovered gas under the ground in the State of Pennsylvania in the USA. Now there are lots of energy companies in Pennsylvania, and many people's lives have changed.

A ***Donald Roessler*** lives on a farm. He has lived there for most of his life, but he hasn't made much money from it. Two years ago, however, an energy company wanted the gas under his farm. Now they pay Donald a regular monthly income for the energy.

B ***Lee Zavislak*** hasn't had a job since she lost her old job at a bottle factory. But recently, a lot of the energy companies have employed new drivers, so now she's learning to drive trucks.

C ***Paul Battista*** has run his company selling construction equipment for about thirty-five years. He has had some bad times, but since natural gas was discovered in the area, Paul's profits have increased and business is looking good.

Grammar present perfect and simple past

▶ PRESENT PERFECT and SIMPLE PAST

1 *In 2004, an energy company **discovered** gas under the ground.*
2 *Many people's lives **have changed**.*
3 *Donald Roessler **has lived** on his farm for most of his life, but he **hasn't made** much money from it.*

For more information and practice, see page 168.

6 Look at the sentences in the grammar box. Underline the verb(s) in the simple past and circle the verb(s) in the present perfect. Then circle the correct options in these sentences (a–c).

a If we say when something happened, we use the *simple past / present perfect*.
b If we don't know or don't say when something happened, we use the *simple past / present perfect*.
c For something that started in the past and continues in the present, we use the *simple past / present perfect*.

7 Look at the article on page 82 again. Underline the verbs in the present perfect (*have / has* + past participle). Then write the past participles in the correct category below.

- Regular past participles: *changed,* _____
- Irregular past participles: *made,* _____

8 Read about an engineer working for an energy company in Pennsylvania. Circle the correct options.

[1] *I've started / I started* college when I was nineteen, and [2] *I've graduated / I graduated* with a degree in engineering about four years later. Now I live here in Pennsylvania with my wife and children, but we [3] *haven't lived / didn't live* here very long. [4] *I've worked / I worked* in six other places, and last year [5] *I've spent / I spent* three months working overseas. But now I think we'll stay in Pennsylvania. [6] *It's been / It was* good for us living here. At first, some of the local people [7] *haven't been / weren't* very friendly because they were worried about the company's impact on the environment. But the natural gas industry [8] *has improved / improved* the local economy, so things are better now.

9 You are going to listen to an interview with a scientist for a natural gas company. Write questions to ask about his life. Use the present perfect or the simple past.

1 how long / work / for your company?
How long have you worked for your company?
2 where / you / go / to college?
_____
3 you / always / want / to be a scientist?
_____
4 what / make / you / change your mind?
_____
5 you / ever / work / overseas?
_____
6 it / be / easy living here?
_____

10 ▶ 55 Work in pairs. Listen to the interview. Check your questions from Exercise 9 and discuss the scientist's answers.

Grammar present perfect with *for* and *since*

▶ PRESENT PERFECT with *FOR* and *SINCE*

Interviewer: *How long have you worked for your company?*
Scientist: ***For** five years. **Since** I graduated from college.*

For more information and practice, see page 168.

11 Look at the grammar box above. Read the scientist's answer to the question and complete this sentence with *for* and *since*.

We use [1] _____ with a point in time (e.g., 2015, yesterday); and we use [2] _____ with a period of time (e.g., ten minutes, six months).

12 Complete these phrases with *for* or *since*.

1	_____ 2008	4	_____ one o'clock
2	_____ two weeks	5	_____ I started work
3	_____ six days	6	_____ January 1st

Speaking myLife

13 Work in pairs. Practice asking and answering questions about these topics using the present perfect and simple past.

current job/studies	where you live	travel
interests/hobbies	people you know	languages

*A: **Have** you ever **studied** Chinese?*
*B: No, I **haven't**, but I **studied** Arabic when I **was** younger.*
*A: Really? How long **did** you **study** it for?*

7b X-ray photographer

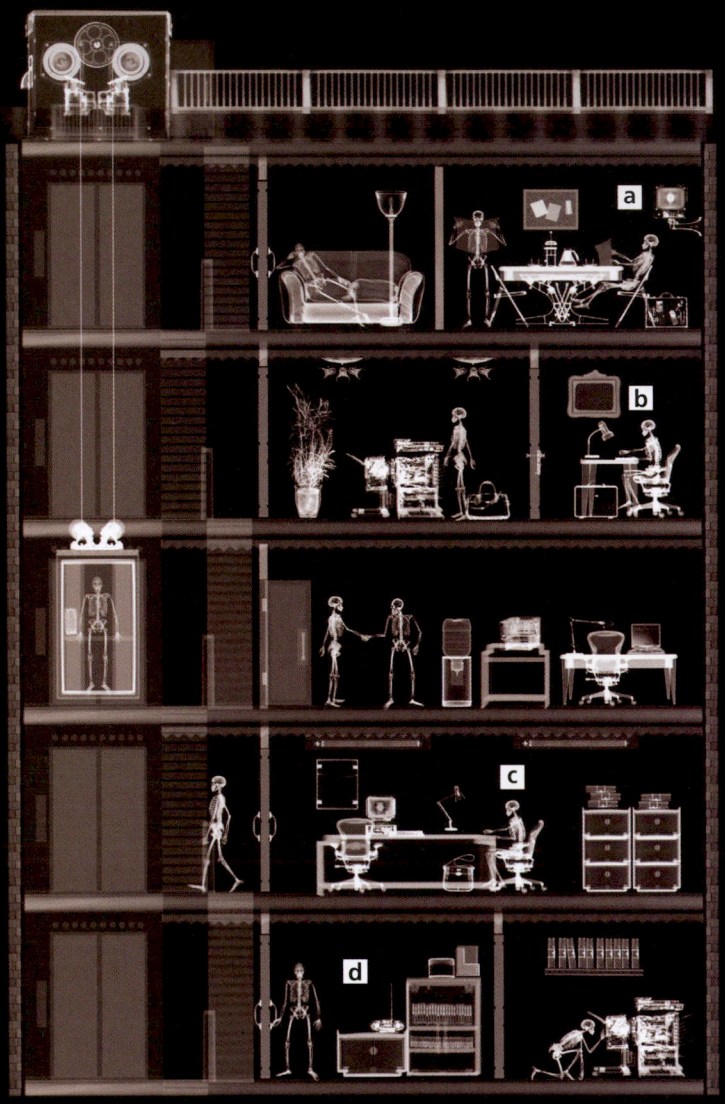

Nick Veasey is a photographer who works with X-rays. Nick likes taking photos showing the inside of people, buildings, flowers, and everyday objects. This photo of an office building was made by taking a series of X-ray photographs and putting them together in one picture.

Vocabulary parts of a building

1 Work in pairs. Look at the photo and read about the photographer. Answer these questions.

1 What type of photography is it?
2 How did Nick make this photo?
3 Do you like this kind of photography?

2 Complete the sentences (1–5) with these parts of an office building. Two options are extra.

cafeteria	hallway	emergency exit
entrance	first floor	elevator
~~office~~	reception	stairs

1 I work in an ___*office*___ on the second floor.
2 Speak to the person at _____ when you arrive.
3 When the _____ isn't working, we have to walk up the _____ .
4 I normally eat my lunch in the _____ , but sometimes I go to the diner down the road.
5 I work on the _____ . Walk down the _____ and my office is on the left.

3 Work in pairs. Think about the building you are in now. Which options from Exercise 2 are parts of your building?

4 Work in pairs. Look at the photo of the office building again. With your partner, describe different parts of the building and say what the people are doing there.

On the ground floor, someone is fixing the copy machine.

Listening

5 ▶ 56 Work in pairs. Listen to two telephone conversations with people who work in the building in the photo. Answer the questions.

Conversation 1
1 Where is Jeff calling from?
2 Where is Kristina's desk in the photo: a, b, c, or d?

Conversation 2
3 Why is the man visiting the building?
4 Where is Richard's office in the photo: a, b, c, or d?

6 ▶ 56 Listen again and write the missing prepositions you hear.

1 Is it _____ your desk?
2 I think it's _____ my computer.
3 Maybe it's _____ the filing cabinet _____ your desk.
4 Try the top drawer _____ the left.
5 I'm standing _____ the entrance to the building.
6 Go _____ the third floor.
7 Go _____ the door and you'll see the photocopy room.
8 My office is _____ it.

Grammar prepositions of place and movement

▶ PREPOSITIONS OF PLACE AND MOVEMENT

Prepositions of place
*It's **opposite** the door.*
*It's **on** the third floor.*
*It's **at** the top of the building.*

Prepositions of movement
*Go **down to** the basement.*
*Come **up** the stairs.*
*Walk **out of** the building.*
Note: Prepositions of movement follow verbs of movement (e.g., *go*, *come*, *walk*).

For more information and practice, see page 168.

7 Work in pairs. Look at the grammar box. Then look at the sentences in Exercise 6. Which sentences have prepositions of place? Which have prepositions of movement?

8 Circle the correct options.

1 There's coffee *on / in* the table. Help yourself.
2 You need to go *up / down* these stairs to get to the basement.
3 I need some fresh air. Let's go *inside / outside* for a walk.
4 Once you get here, see the person *at / on* reception.
5 When you go *past / through* a mailbox, can you mail this letter for me?
6 The cafeteria is *opposite / between* the main building.
7 Go *down / on* the hallway and my office is *at / on* the right.

9 Complete the messages with these prepositions.

at	down	in	into
next to	on	through	up

Let's meet [1] _____ the coffee area at 11. It's the room [2] _____ the top of the building. See you there.

Can you fix my printer for me? My office is [3] _____ the third floor. The printer is [4] _____ my desk.

The elevator is out of order today, so please go [5] _____ the reception area to the fire exit and walk [6] _____ the emergency stairs.

We got [7] _____ the elevator on the fifth floor, and now it won't go [8] _____ to the ground floor. Please help!

10 Pronunciation intrusive /w/

▶ 57 Sometimes when a verb ends in a vowel and the next word starts with a vowel, we add the /w/ sound. Listen and repeat these examples with *go* + preposition.

1 go /w/ in
2 go /w/ on
3 go /w/ out
4 go /w/ into
5 go /w/ up
6 go /w/ across

Speaking myLife

11 Work in pairs. Take turns giving directions from where you are now to these other parts of the building. Listen to your partner and name the part of the building.

the elevator or stairs	the cafeteria
the restroom	the reception area
another classroom/office	

7c Twenty-first century cowboys

Reading

1 Work in pairs. Look at the photo. What is a cowboy? Which country is most famous for cowboys?

2 Read the article on page 87. What is the article mainly about? Circle a, b, or c.

a how modern cowboys really live and work
b the truth about Hollywood cowboys
c why people don't want to be cowboys anymore

3 Read the article again. Circle the correct option (a–c) to complete these sentences.

1 The writer explains that real life as a cowboy is ____ .
   a like a Hollywood movie
   b adventurous and romantic
   c hard work and not well-paid
2 Modern cowboys spend a lot of time ____ .
   a meeting people
   b outdoors on their own
   c on the phone
3 Blaine and Tyrel Tucker grew up ____ .
   a on a ranch
   b in the city
   c in different places
4 People like Pat Crisswell become cowboys for ____ .
   a the long vacations
   b the salary
   c job satisfaction

Critical thinking analyzing comparisons in a text

4 Work in pairs. The writer uses comparisons to help us understand the life of a modern cowboy. Look at the pairs of ideas (1–4). Find words and phrases from the article that describe each idea, and decide if the two ideas are similar or different.

1 a the cowboy in Hollywood movies *freedom, adventure*
   b the real life of a cowboy *hard, dangerous, physical, long hours, low pay*
   The two ideas are very different.
2 a the life of a cowboy in the past
   b the life of a modern cowboy
3 a cowboys like Blaine and Tyrel
   b cowboys like Pat Crisswell
4 a the advantages of an office job in the city
   b the advantages of working as a cowboy

Word focus *make* or *do*

5 Find phrases in paragraphs 2 and 4 with *make* or *do* and complete these phrases.

1 _____ breakfast
2 _____ good money
3 _____ something different

6 Complete these phrases with *make* or *do*. Use a dictionary to help you, if necessary.

1 _____ your homework
2 _____ a mistake
3 _____ a decision
4 _____ someone a favor
5 _____ well at school
6 _____ your bed
7 _____ a noise
8 _____ a job

7 Work in pairs. Ask your partner three questions using phrases with *make* or *do*. Take turns asking and answering.

*What kind of job do you want to **do** in the future?*
*Do you think it is important to **make** a lot of money?*

Speaking myLife

8 Work in pairs. Read the last paragraph of the article again. Do you think Pat Crisswell was crazy to give up his job in the city? Do you think job satisfaction is more important than money?

9 Work in pairs. When you look for a job, which things on this list are most important? Number the items in order of importance (1 = most important, 9 = least important). Give reasons for your order.

- learning new skills ____
- earning a good salary ____
- working with a team of people ____
- making your own decisions ____
- getting regular promotions ____
- working outdoors ____
- having travel opportunities ____
- being given a lot of vacation time ____
- working close to your house ____

I think working with a team is important because it's more interesting than working on your own.

TWENTY-FIRST *century* COWBOYS

▶ 58

1 Cowboys have lived and worked in the American West and Southwest for over three centuries. They are a famous symbol of the USA. When you watch old Hollywood cowboy films from the fifties and sixties, you don't see a job; you see a life of freedom and adventure. However, the real job of an American cowboy has always been hard and sometimes dangerous. It's physical, with long hours and low pay.

2 Life hasn't changed much for cowboys since the early days. The cattle still walk across huge plains[1] to eat grass, and the cowboys ride on their horses to bring the cattle home. Like the cowboys of the past, a twenty-first century cowboy still gets up early on freezing cold mornings and makes breakfast over a fire. He can't take days or weekends off, and there are no paid holidays. And when you are in the middle of nowhere,[2] your cell phone doesn't work, so you can't call your family or friends if you feel lonely.

3 So why does a man—because it is usually a man—become a cowboy? For some, it isn't a choice—they are born into the life. Men like Blaine and Tyrel Tucker, both brothers, have worked with cows since they were children. Their mother had a ranch,[3] and they rode horses before they could walk. Both Blaine and Tyrel have large moustaches and wear traditional cowboy clothes, with the famous hat and boots. They prefer the traditional cowboy culture: "It's a real life about you, your horse, and the open country." Last winter, they looked after 2,300 cows. Every day, from December to April, they rode across nearly 100,000 acres[4] of land with only the cattle and horses for company.

4 But some people choose the job later in life. Pat Crisswell had an office job with the US government. He made good money,[5] but he didn't like city life and spending all day indoors. He wanted to do something different. So one day, he gave up his job and moved to a ranch in Texas, earning much less money as a cowboy. Pat's colleagues in the city all thought he was crazy, but he wanted more job satisfaction. And for a cowboy, job satisfaction doesn't come from the money or a comfortable office; it comes from being free to wake up under the sky and being your own boss.

[1]**plain** (n) /pleɪn/ a large area of flat land with very few trees
[2]**middle of nowhere** /ˈmɪd(ə)l əv ˈnəʊweər/ a place far away from a town, city, or other people
[3]**ranch** (n) /raːntʃ/ a large farm for cattle, horses, or sheep
[4]**acre** (n) /ˈeɪkər/ a measure of land area
[5]**good money** /gʊdˈmʌni/ a lot of money

7d A job interview

Vocabulary job ads

1 Work in pairs. Look at the job ad below. Answer the questions.

1 When does the restaurant need people?
2 Would you apply for this kind of job? Why or why not?

2 Work in pairs. Find words in the ad with these meanings.

1 people who work for a business or company
2 formal word for "jobs" with a company
3 necessary or needed
4 formal word for "give"
5 ask for something (e.g., a job) by writing or filling out a form
6 a document with information about you, your qualifications, and work experience
7 information including name, phone number, and address

Real life a job interview

3 ▶ 59 Natalia applied for the job in the ad in Exercise 1. Listen to parts of her interview with the manager. Are these sentences true (T) or false (F)?

1	The manager has read Natalia's résumé.	T	F
2	Natalia wants a full-time job at the restaurant.	T	F
3	Natalia liked dealing with customers in her last job.	T	F
4	Natalia asks the manager what her working hours will be like.	T	F

4 Do you think Natalia is a good person for the job? Why or why not? Discuss with a partner.

5 ▶ 59 Work in pairs. Listen again and complete these questions from the interview. Then match questions 1–3 with the categories in **bold** in the box below.

1 _____ do you want this job?
2 _____ did you like about your last job?
3 _____ did you deal with any difficult situations?
4 _____ you have any questions for me?

▶ A JOB INTERVIEW

Your current life and job
What are you doing at the moment?
Tell me about your current job.

Reasons for applying
Can you tell me your reasons for applying for this job?
Why did you apply for this job?

Past experience and qualifications
Have you worked in a restaurant before?
What qualifications do you have?

Questions for the interviewer
What are the typical hours?
Can you tell me the salary?

6 Work in pairs. Look at the job ad below. You are going to practice an interview for this job.

Student A: You are the manager of the store.

Student B: You have applied for the job of sales clerk.

When you are both ready, begin the interview. Then change roles and repeat the interview.

7e Applying for a job

Writing a résumé

1 Complete the résumé with these headings.

Address	Date of birth	Education	Home telephone
Interests	References	Skills	Work experience

Résumé

Juan Luiz Santos

Nationality	Brazilian
1 _____	September 17, 1992
2 _____	Rua Martin Luther King 1286 Araçatuba, São Paulo, 16020-190
Email	juan.luiz.santos@ingcenter.com
3 _____	+55 (11) 2992-3083
Mobile	+55 (11) 98550-2794
4 _____	
2013–2014	MA in Design Studies, Parsons School of Design
2010–2013	BA in Graphic Design, Universidade de São Paulo
5 _____	
Current position:	Web Designer: create websites for clients; design webpage layout; organize and update content; manage small team of 3
2014–2016	Graphic Designer: created brand logos; worked in a team; designed advertisements, brochures, magazines, and reports
Summer 2013	Photographer at a summer camp in the USA: took photos of activities and produced camp video
6 _____	

Languages: Portuguese (native), English and Spanish (fluent)
Computing: Word, Excel, Photoshop, Illustrator, web design

7 _____

Photography: portrait and street photography
Captain of local soccer team
Jiu-jitsu

8 _____

Dr. Alex Striani, Professor of Art and Design, 261 Morningview Lane, New York
Marcia Pinto, Rua Olegário Ferreira 1081, Rio de Janeiro

2 Work in pairs. How similar is a résumé in your country? Would you use these headings? Would you add any other information?

3 **Writing skill** **leaving out words in résumés**

a Work in pairs. Compare these full sentences with the sentences in **bold** from a résumé. Which words are missing in the résumé sentences? Which verb forms do the résumé sentences use?

1 I am working part-time in a restaurant.
Working part-time in restaurant.
2 I've worked in a four-star hotel in Dubai.
Have worked in four-star hotel in Dubai.
3 I had to meet guests in the reception area.
Met guests in reception area.

b Work in pairs. Underline the sentences in Juan Luiz Santos's résumé starting with verb forms. How would you normally write each sentence?

c Rewrite these sentences for a résumé.

1 ~~I am~~ studying mathematics at Boston University.
Studying mathematics at Boston University.
2 I made pizza in the student cafeteria.
_____
3 I've competed in athletic competitions for my school.
_____
_____
4 I had to train new employees.
_____
5 I am learning to play the drums.
_____
6 I've given presentations to large groups of people.
_____
_____

4 Think about what you are currently doing and your past work and studies. Write six sentences for your résumé.

5 Now write your complete résumé.

6 Work in pairs. Exchange résumés. Use these questions to check your partner's résumé.

- Does it have clear headings?
- Does it use present and past participles correctly?

7f My working life

These Italian actors are working in Istanbul, Turkey. They are performing *Romeo and Juliet*.

Before you watch

1 Key vocabulary

Read the sentences (1–5). The words and phrases in **bold** are used in the video. Write these words and phrases next to their definitions (a–e).

1 Eating right and exercising are essential for a healthy **lifestyle**.
2 My job is challenging, but the **pay** is good.
3 The positive parts of my job **outweigh** the negatives.
4 I like the **variety** in my job. Every day is different.
5 When you have a party, you can **bring together** all your friends in one place.

a are more important than _____
b have everyone in the same place _____
c a particular way of living _____
d money received in exchange for work _____
e the quality or state of being different or diverse _____

2 You are going to watch two people talking about their jobs. Look at the photos and descriptions (1–2). Then predict which person says each sentence (a–f). Circle V (Virginia) or M (Marcus).

1 Virginia is a language teacher.
2 Marcus is an actor.

a	"At the moment, I'm in a play called *Romeo and Juliet*."	V	M
b	"I like sharing my culture with other people."	V	M
c	"Sometimes the work involves a lot of paperwork or marking."	V	M
d	"I really like the sense of achievement that I get from creating something."	V	M
e	"There's a lot of travel involved."	V	M
f	"It's a fun job, and I enjoy it very much."	V	M

While you watch

3 7.1 Watch the video. Were your predictions in Exercise 2 correct?

4 7.1 Watch the two people in the video again. Complete this chart to answer the three questions.

	What's your typical working day like?	What do you like about the job?	Is there anything you don't like about the job?
1	• 4:00 p.m. teach at pupil's houses • 6:30–8:30 p.m. [1] _____ _____	• sharing my culture • bringing [2] _____ together through languages	• paperwork and marking can be [3] _____ • traveling from home to home can be [4] _____
2	• sometimes start first thing in the morning and finish at midnight • sometimes travel up and down the country	• the [5] _____ – no two days are the same • working as a [6] _____ • sense of achievement	• [7] _____ hours • travel • [8] _____ isn't great

5 7.1 Work in pairs and compare your notes. Then watch the video again to check your answers.

After you watch

6 Vocabulary in context

a 7.2 Watch the clips from the video. Choose the correct meaning of the words and phrases.

b Work in pairs. Ask and answer these questions.

1 What is your dream job? What does it involve?
2 When was the last time you felt lucky?
3 When was the last time you felt a sense of achievement?

7 Which of the two jobs in the video would you prefer? Tell the class your reasons.

UNIT 7 REVIEW AND MEMORY BOOSTER

Grammar

1 Complete the conversation with the present perfect or simple past form of the verbs in parentheses.

A: How long [1] _____ you _____ (work) here?
B: About three years. I [2] _____ (join) the newspaper when I graduated from college.
A: So, [3] _____ you always _____ (want) to be a reporter?
B: Not particularly. But when I [4] _____ (be) young, I wrote stories.
A: What [5] _____ you _____ (study) in college?
B: Spanish.
A: [6] _____ you ever _____ (live) in Spain?
B: No, but I [7] _____ (spend) a summer in Argentina during my college years.
A: Really? That sounds like fun!

2 >> MB Write three questions starting with *How long have you …?* Then ask and answer your questions with a partner. Use *since* or *for* in your answers.

3 Complete the sentences with these prepositions.

across at in on opposite through

1 Walk _____ to the other side of the parking lot and you'll see the factory.
2 Can you pass me that book _____ the shelf?
3 I think Paulo is _____ the basement.
4 Go _____ those doors at the end and you'll see the copy machine.
5 The cafeteria is _____ the top of the building on the fifth floor.
6 We sit _____ each other in the office.

I CAN	
use the present perfect and the simple past	☐
use prepositions of place and movement	☐

Vocabulary

4 >> MB Can you remember the missing part of these compound nouns from Unit 7?

1 financial a*dvisor*
2 fashion d_____
3 sales c_____
4 c_____ programmer
5 e_____ exit
6 contact i_____

5 Complete the text about the balloon seller with the correct form of ***make*** or ***do***.

Nguyen [1] _____ two jobs. During the day he sells balloons, and in the evening he [2] _____ money by working in a restaurant. He helps to [3] _____ food in the kitchen. He works long days, but he is saving so he can complete his studies. If he [4] _____ well at school, he can go to university.

6 Work in pairs. Which of Nguyen's two jobs do you think he enjoys more? Why?

I CAN	
talk about jobs and places of work	☐

Real life

7 Match these questions at a job interview (1–5) with the responses (a–e).

1 Why did you apply for this job? ___
2 What are you doing at the moment? ___
3 Have you worked in a hotel before? ___
4 What do you like about your current job? ___
5 Do you have any questions for me? ___

a Meeting different people.
b No, but I have experience dealing with customers.
c So I can use my language skills.
d Yes, can you tell me ...?
e I'm working at a café downtown.

8 >> MB Work in pairs. Take turns asking the questions in Exercise 7 and responding with your own answers.

I CAN	
ask and answer questions about a job	☐

Unit 8 Technology

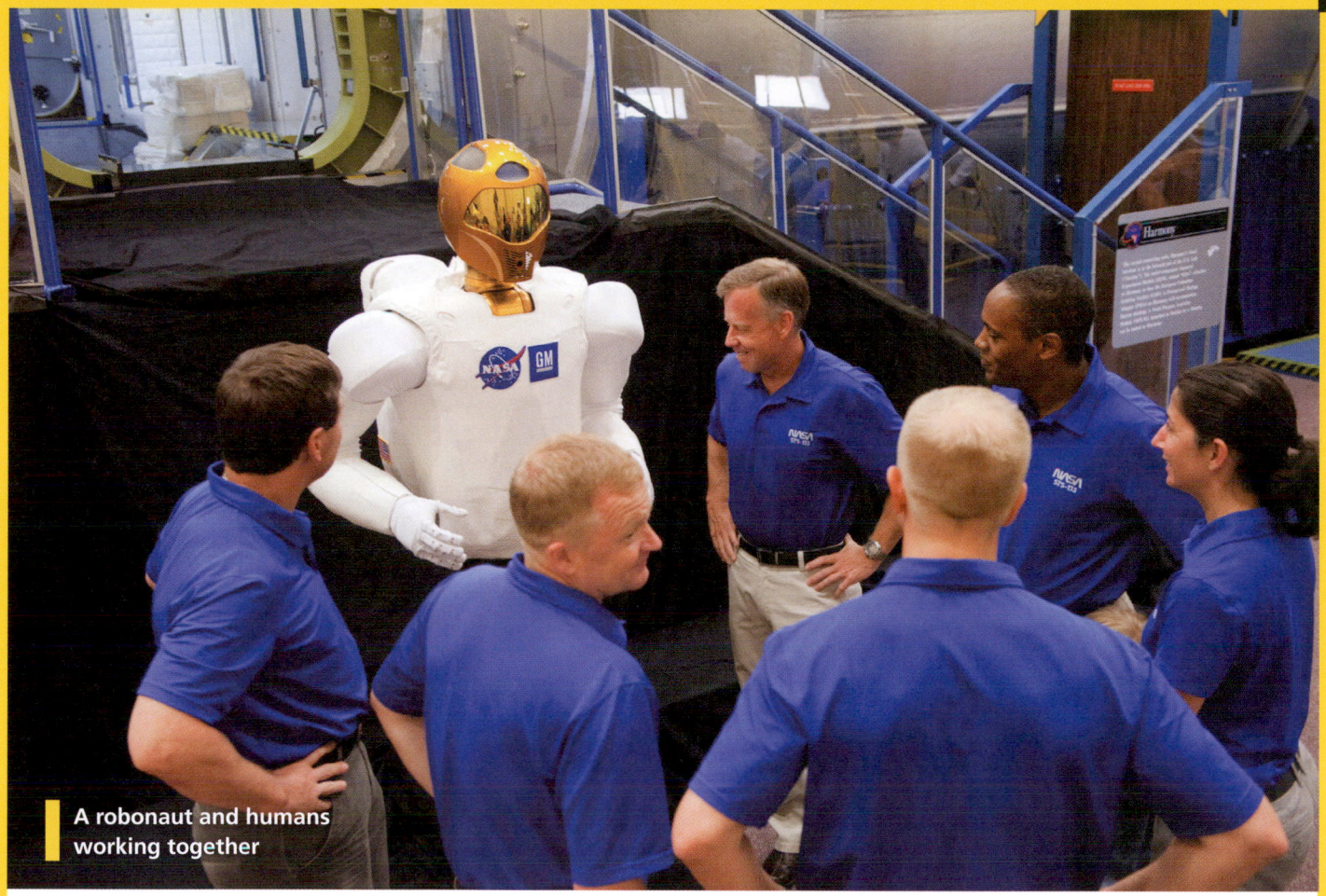

A robonaut and humans working together

FEATURES

94 Mobile technology
How technology is changing the world

96 Invention for the eyes
An inventor finds a solution to make the whole world see

98 Designs from nature
What we can learn from plants and animals

102 Ancient languages, modern technology
A video about how technology can save ancient languages

1 Work in pairs. Look at the photo and the caption. How do you think the robonaut and the humans are "working together"? In what other ways do robots work with humans?

2 ▶ 60 Work in pairs. Listen to someone talking about the importance of technology in our lives. Answer the questions.

1 How does technology help us in our everyday lives?
2 Why does technology sometimes make mistakes?
3 Where does the robot in the photo work? What does it do?

3 Work in pairs. Look at this list of things humans can do. Which can robots do?

fall in love	get bored	have new ideas
make decisions	make mistakes	sleep
solve problems	speak a language	understand instructions

4 What simple or repetitive jobs do you do at work, at school, or at home? Which of these jobs could you give to a robot in the future? Discuss with a partner.

8a Mobile technology

Vocabulary internet verbs

1 Think about the different ways you have used the internet in the last 24 hours and make a list. Then work in pairs and compare your lists.

to find out information on train times, to check my email, to get directions

2 Complete the sentences with these verbs.

connect	download	log in	search
~~set up~~	subscribe	upload	write

1 To ___*set up*___ a new online account, type in your personal details and click "enter."
2 I don't buy CDs anymore. It's much easier to _____ music.
3 When I need to find information, I _____ the internet.
4 My friends and family _____ their photos to social networking sites like Facebook.
5 There's no Wi-Fi here, so I can't _____ to the internet.
6 I use online banking because it's so convenient. You just _____ with a password and your account details.
7 I _____ a weekly blog to tell readers about my family's news.
8 I _____ to a daily podcast that gives me all the latest news.

3 Work in pairs. Which of the sentences in Exercise 2 are true for you?

I write a blog, but I don't write about my family. I write about what my friends and I like doing.

Reading

4 Work in pairs. Read the blog about the Kamchatka Project. Who do you think wrote it? Why did the person write it?

5 Read the blog again. Circle the correct options to complete these sentences.

1 The team had a *short / long* journey to the Karimskaya River.
2 The weather was *good / terrible* when they arrived.
3 The writer thinks social media is *a waste of time / useful* for modern explorers.
4 *The writer / Someone else* touched a strange plant.

www.kamchatkaproject.org/blog

kamchatka project

▶ 61

Posted July 15, 2:55 PM

After traveling through three international airports and nineteen time zones, we are here at last! We are at the start of the Karimskaya River in the region of Kamchatka. It's the middle of nowhere, but I have a signal on my phone. It's a sunny afternoon, and if the weather stays the same for the next few days, everything will go well.

Posted July 16, 8:05 AM

We had a good night's sleep and are about to cook breakfast. I've already connected to the internet and checked my email. It's funny to think that in the past, explorers couldn't share their news until months after the trip. Nowadays, if anything interesting happens, explorers blog about it before breakfast!

Posted July 18, 7:20 PM

Twitter and Facebook are great if you have a problem. We were working in a forest today, and someone in our group touched a strange plant. Suddenly his skin became red, hot, and painful. I posted a photo of the plant on Twitter and asked for advice. Minutes later, I got a reply from someone who knows this region well. "It's a pushki plant. It won't kill you if you touch one, but it will hurt!"

Grammar zero and first conditionals

▶ ZERO and FIRST CONDITIONALS

Zero conditional
*Twitter and Facebook **are** great **if** you **have** a problem.*
***If** anything interesting **happens**, explorers **blog** about it before breakfast!*

First conditional
***If** the weather **stays** the same, everything **will go** well.*
*It **won't kill** you **if** you **touch** one.*

For more information and practice, see page 170.

6 Look at the grammar box. Circle the correct options to complete these sentences.

1 We use a *zero / first* conditional sentence to talk about things that are generally true.
2 We use a *zero / first* conditional sentence to talk about a possible future situation.
3 In a *zero / first* conditional sentence, we use *if* + simple present + simple present (or simple present + *if* + simple present).
4 In a *zero / first* conditional sentence, we use *if* + simple present + *will* (or *will* + *if* + simple present).
5 *If* can come at the beginning of the sentence or in the middle. If it is at the beginning, we *use / don't use* a comma after the *if*-clause.

7 Match the beginnings of the sentences (1–6) with the endings (a–f).

1 If I get lost on the way to your house,
2 If there's a red sign or an error message on the computer screen,
3 You can't read the articles on the website
4 If you click on this link,
5 I'll call you from the top of the mountain
6 I only write my blog

a you have a virus. ____
b it downloads the video for free. ____
c if you don't subscribe. ____
d I'll use the GPS in my car. ____
e if I have something interesting to write about. ____
f if I get a phone signal. ____

8 ▶ 62 Complete the sentences with the correct form of the verbs in parentheses. Then listen and check your answers.

1 When I _____ (go) on vacation, I take lots of sunscreen.
2 We _____ (need) a flashlight if we go out late tonight.
3 We always get lost if my brother _____ (drive).
4 I can't buy food if the supermarket _____ (not / be) open.
5 If you have any questions, _____ (call) this number.
6 If you don't try harder, you _____ (not pass) your exam.

Speaking myLife

9 Work in groups. You are going to the mountains for two days. The weather forecast is for sun on the first day and rain on the second. You have tents, backpacks, and food. Look at the photos below. Discuss these items and choose the five most useful. Give reasons for taking them.

*A: **If** we **take** …, we **won't need** …*
*B: We'**ll need** … **if** it **rains** …*

8b Invention for the eyes

Speaking

1 Work in groups. Discuss the importance of these inventions. Rank them from 1 (the most important) to 7 (the least important).

____ the airplane
____ the bicycle
____ the camera
____ the steam engine
____ the internet
____ the cell phone
____ the washing machine

2 Present your ranking to the class and compare it with other groups. What other important inventions would you add to the list? Why?

Listening

3 ▶ 63 Work in pairs. Listen to a science program. Answer the questions.

1 What is a problem for more than one billion people in the world?
2 What has Joshua Silver invented?

4 ▶ 64 Listen to the first half of the program again. Number the steps below in the correct order (1–4).

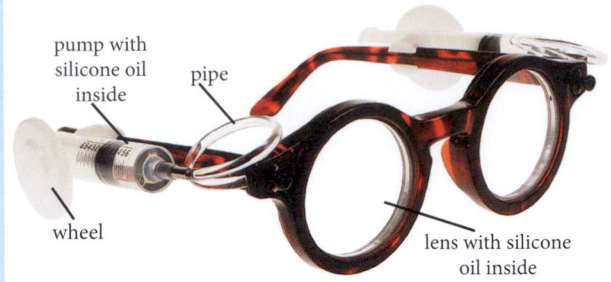

____ The lens changes shape.
1 You turn the wheels on each side.
____ The silicone oil moves into the lens.
____ The pump pushes the silicone oil through the pipe.

5 ▶ 65 Listen to the second half of the program again. Are these sentences true (T) or false (F)?

1	Silver had to do many experiments with the glasses before they worked properly.	T	F
2	A man in Ghana used the glasses first.	T	F
3	Silver started a center that works with students in developing countries.	T	F
4	The glasses are expensive to produce.	T	F

Grammar defining relative clauses

▶ DEFINING RELATIVE CLAUSES

The underlined part of each sentence below is a defining relative clause. This clause gives essential information about the noun.

*There is a scientist **who** has solved the problem.*
*Joshua Silver has invented glasses **that** don't need an optician.*
*They live in places **where** there aren't any opticians.*

For more information and practice, see page 170.

A Tibetan man wearing Joshua Silver's invention

6 Look at the sentences in the grammar box on page 96. Which word (*who, that,* or *where*) do we use:

a for people? _____
b for things? _____
c for places? _____

7 Look at these sentences from the listening. Underline the relative clauses.

1 There is a pump on each side that contains silicone oil.
2 You turn a wheel that controls the pump.
3 A man in Ghana was the first person who used the new glasses.
4 The center works with schools in countries where students can't get glasses easily.

8 Complete these sentences with *who* or *where*.

1 Tim Berners-Lee is the person _____ invented the World Wide Web.
2 I live in a village _____ there is no public transportation.
3 Joshua Silver is the physicist _____ founded the Center for Vision in the Developing World.
4 Silicon Valley is a place _____ many successful technology companies are based.
5 I want to live in a country _____ everyone has access to the internet.
6 Maria Beasley was the inventor _____ made the first life raft.

9 Look at the photo on the right and read the information about another invention called the LifeStraw. Complete the text with *who, that,* or *where* and these phrases.

~~cleans water~~	like hiking and camping
there is a lake	can break
there is no safe	

10 Think of a famous person, an invention, and a place or city. Write a sentence to define or explain each one, but don't name the person, invention, or place. Then exchange sentences with a partner. Can your partner guess what they are?

*He was **the astronaut who** became the first person to walk on the moon. (Neil Armstrong)*

*It's **a thing that** you use to find information and to contact people. (a cell phone)*

*It's **the city where** you can see the Space Needle. (Seattle)*

LIFESTRAW

LifeStraw is an invention
1 _____*that cleans water*_____ while you drink, so it's useful in areas
2 _____ water supply. It's also small, so you can carry it to places
3 _____ or a river. It's popular with people
4 _____.
LifeStraw can clean up to 1,000 liters of water, and it doesn't have any moving parts
5 _____. Today, *LifeStraw* is used in more than 64 countries around the world.

Speaking myLife

11 Work in groups. Invent something that will help you, your family, or your friends in their everyday lives. Discuss these questions and draw a simple design of the invention with any important information on a large sheet of paper.

- What is the invention for?
- Who will use it?
- Where can you use it?

12 As a group, prepare a short presentation about your invention. Give your presentation to the class.

*Our invention is a machine **that** …*
*It's for people **who** …*
*You can use it in places **where** …*

8c Designs from nature

Reading

1 Work in pairs. Photos 1–5 on page 99 show inventions. Which animals or plants (photos a–e) do you think inspired these inventions? Before you read, write a–e next to each invention.

2 Read the article and check your answers from Exercise 1.

3 Read the article again. Choose the correct option (a or b) to complete these sentences.

1 Geckos are amazing because they can ____ .
   a walk upside down
   b walk on glass and plastic
2 The wind turbine engineers and the car manufacturer studied ____ .
   a birds
   b sea animals
3 George de Mestral got the idea for Velcro ____ .
   a after doing many experiments
   b by chance
4 Wilhelm Barthlott got his idea from ____ .
   a the inside of a lotus leaf
   b the outside of a lotus leaf
5 The writer thinks designers ____ .
   a will learn a lot from nature in the future
   b have already looked at most of the possibilities in biomimetics

Wordbuilding dependent prepositions

4 These eight words often have prepositions after them. Find these words in the article and write the prepositions.

1 problem _____
2 good _____
3 interested _____
4 depend _____
5 work _____
6 think _____
7 similar _____
8 idea _____

▶ WORDBUILDING dependent prepositions

Many verbs, adjectives, and nouns often have a preposition after them. These are called "dependent prepositions."
verb + preposition: *I* ***agree with*** *you.*
adjective + preposition: *I'm* ***bad at*** *soccer.*
noun + preposition: *I have* ***a question about*** *this.*

For more practice, see Workbook page 67.

5 Work in pairs. Look at the wordbuilding box. Match the words in Exercise 4 with the categories (verb, adjective, noun).

6 Choose three of the words from Exercise 4 and write a sentence with each word and its dependent preposition. Then work in pairs. Take turns reading your sentences, but do not say the preposition. Your partner must say the preposition.

Critical thinking the writer's sources

7 Work in pairs. To write an article, a writer often uses different sources to find information. Which of these sources (1–6) do you think were used for writing *Designs from nature*? Say which parts of the article used information from the sources.

1 photographs
2 biographies
3 questionnaires
4 interviews with people
5 books about the topic
6 articles in magazines

8 Work in pairs. If you had to write about these topics (1–3), which sources would you use? Consider the sources listed in Exercise 7 or use your own ideas.

1 people's favorite type of everyday technology
2 famous inventors throughout history
3 technologies that will shape the future

Speaking myLife

9 Work in pairs. You are going to do some research for a short article about different people's favorite technology. Prepare interview questions to find out these things from other people.

- what their favorite technology is
- how often they use it
- what it's used for
- its design (color, shape, size)
- its manufacturer
- anything else that's important

10 Work with other pairs and interview them using your questions from Exercise 9.

A: What's your favorite piece of technology?
B: Definitely my phone. I love it! I take it everywhere!

DESIGNS *from* NATURE

When we have a problem, nature often has the answer.

▶ 66

1 In a room at Stanford University, scientists have a problem with their robot. It can walk up and down walls made of glass and plastic, but it can't walk upside down. So today, they have a gecko in the room. The gecko is an amazing animal. Like the robot, it's very good at moving up and down trees, but the gecko can also walk upside down. In particular, the scientists are interested in the gecko's feet. They want to learn from its feet and use the same design on their robot.

2 Animals and plants can teach humans a lot about design and engineering. As a result, many engineers, scientists, and designers spend time studying the natural world. When they have a question, nature often has the answer. This science is called biomimetics. *Bio-* means "living things," and *mimetics* means "copying." In other words, these scientists—or *biomimeticists*—depend on animals and plants to help them solve design problems.

3 Two types of sea animals helped engineers in Canada and Germany. When engineers in Canada were working on improving wind turbines, they studied a whale's flippers[1]—because whales move so easily through water. And when the car company Mercedes-Benz wanted to think of a new design for a car, it looked at a boxfish. The result was a car that was similar to the shape of a boxfish and that used less fuel than other cars.

4 The world of plants helped with the invention of Velcro and a new type of paint. In 1948, the Swiss engineer George de Mestral was walking in the countryside when he pulled a plant's bur[2] from his pants. He noticed how the bur stuck really well to his clothes, and this gave him the idea for Velcro. And in 1982, Wilhelm Barthlott—an inventor who was studying the leaves of a lotus plant—noticed that water always ran off the leaf. Barthlott copied the lotus leaf's design and produced a type of paint that stays cleaner than regular paint because water and dirt run off it.

5 Biomimetics has helped to solve modern human problems, and there are many more possibilities. It might take a long time to discover all of them, because, after all, it has taken nature millions of years to design its animals and plants.

[1]**flipper** (n) /ˈflɪpər/ the flat arm or leg of a sea animal, used for swimming
[2]**bur** (n) /bɜː/ a rough, prickly case or covering around the seeds of certain plants

a boxfish

b lotus leaf

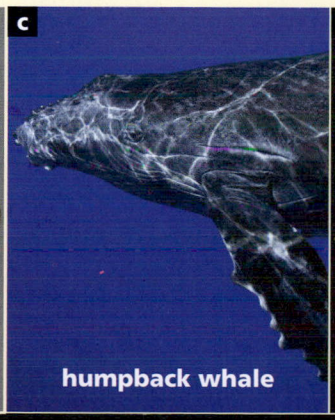
c humpback whale

d bur

e gecko

8d Gadgets

Vocabulary instructions

1 Work in pairs. When you buy new technology for the first time, do you usually:

- read the instruction manual?
- watch a "How to" video online?
- ask a friend for help?
- call a customer helpline?
- just turn it on and see what happens?

2 Match the verbs (1–5) with the phrases on the right to make instructions. Then match the instructions with the pictures (A–E). Write 1–5 next to each picture.

1	turn it on with	○	○ the battery
2	pull	○	○ the button
3	charge	○	○ the remote control
4	press	○	○ the lever forwards
5	push	○	○ the lever backwards

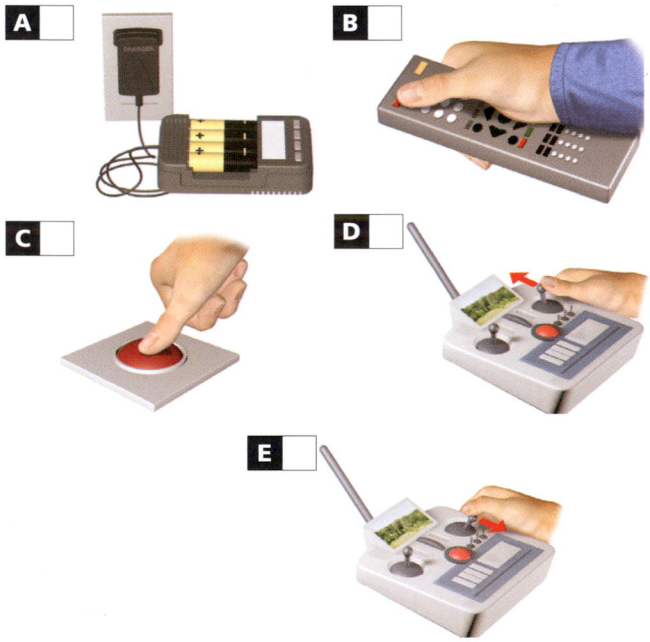

3 **Pronunciation linking**

a ▶ 67 A word ending with a consonant sound links to the next word if it starts with a vowel sound. Listen and practice saying these instructions.

1 Turn‿it‿on.
2 Charge it‿overnight.
3 Press‿it down.
4 Push‿it forwards.
5 Pull‿it back.

b Work in pairs. Think of items you often use and make sentences about them using the verbs in Exercises 2 and 3a. Be careful with linking where necessary.

Real life finding out how something works

4 ▶ 68 Listen to two people talking about a drone. In what order do they talk about the pictures (A–E) in Exercise 2? Complete the sequence below.

A → ___ → ___ → ___ → ___

5 ▶ 68 Read the list of expressions for finding out how something works. Then listen to the conversation again and circle the questions you hear.

▶ FINDING OUT HOW SOMETHING WORKS

Can you show me how it works?
Can you explain the instructions to me?
Have you charged the battery?
How do I turn it on?
How did you do that?
What is this (other lever) for?
What does this (lever) do?
What happens if I press this (big) button?
How do you make it (record / go up)?

6 Work in pairs. Choose objects from the box below or gadgets in your bag or in the school. Take turns asking and explaining how they work.

a video game	your favorite app
a cell phone	a copy machine
a printer	a tablet
a USB stick	a vending machine

A: Can you show me how this works?
B: Yes. First of all, you need to turn it on, here.

8e An argument for technology

Writing a paragraph

1 Read this paragraph. Where do you think it comes from? Choose the correct option (a, b, or c).

a an instruction manual
b a report on LED lights
c a message to a colleague at work about the lighting

LED lighting is a very efficient form of modern lighting technology. Firstly, LED lighting lasts longer than regular lighting. For example, a regular light bulb lasts for around 5,000 hours. LED light bulbs last 100,000 hours. In addition, LED light bulbs change 80% of electricity into light. Regular bulbs only change 20% into light—the rest is heat. In other words, LED lights need less electricity to produce more light. On the other hand, LED lights are more expensive than regular lights. However, you don't have to change them every year, and they use less energy. As a result, LED lights are cheaper over a long period of time.

2 Writing skill connecting words

a Look back at the highlighted connecting words in the paragraph in Exercise 1. Match the highlighted words with their uses (1–6).

1 to put ideas and sentences in order *Firstly*
2 to introduce contrasting information _____, _____
3 to say the same thing in a different way _____
4 to introduce an example _____
5 to introduce a result _____
6 to add extra information to support your main idea _____

b Complete this paragraph with connecting words from Exercise 2a.

Since the late twentieth century, the internet has completely changed our lives. [1] *Firstly*, it has delivered information to every house with a computer. [2] _____, if you want to find out more information about drones, you can type in the word "drone" and find thousands of pages on the subject. [3] _____, with faster download speeds, you can watch movies and videos online. [4] *On the other hand*, some people think the internet can be dangerous, especially for young children. [5] _____, if we teach people how to use it responsibly, then it's like having a library in your home. For me, the benefits clearly outweigh the disadvantages.

3 Read these notes for a paragraph about GPS technology. The notes give the main idea of the paragraph, and the arguments for and against. Write a paragraph using these notes and the connecting words from Exercise 2.

GPS is a good idea for anyone who travels a lot

- GPS maps are always up-to-date and correct
- safer to use when driving
- devices more expensive than a paper map
- saves time (and money on gas)

4 Choose one of these types of technology or use your own idea. Plan a paragraph about why it is useful. Make notes like the ones in Exercise 3.

email	cell phones
music downloads	wireless technology

5 Now write your paragraph. Use connecting words.

6 Exchange paragraphs with a partner. Does your partner's paragraph:

- introduce the main idea?
- give reasons why the technology is useful?
- use connecting words?

8f Ancient languages, modern technology

Using modern technology to record ancient languages in Arunachal Pradesh, India

Before you watch

1 Work in pairs. Look at the photo and the caption. What kind of technology can you see? How do you think these people are using it?

2 Key vocabulary

Read the sentences (1–5). The words and phrases in **bold** are used in the video. Write these words and phrases next to their definitions (a–e).

1 How much **awareness** is there of the problem?
2 Many languages could **die out** in the next few years because no one speaks them.
3 Humans can't **survive** without water.
4 In recent years, there has been a **shift** in the way we communicate because of technology.
5 Don't **neglect** your schoolwork during your vacation.

a a change in something _____
b knowledge or understanding of a situation _____
c become less common and finally disappear _____
d not pay attention to _____
e continue to live or exist in a difficult situation _____

While you watch

3 8.1 Watch the video. Number these actions in the order they happen (1–4).

____ The team goes to a region in northeast India where there are many different languages.
____ The three men leave, but they hope that the local communities will use the technology kits.
____ The team visits Australia to interview the last speaker of a language.
____ The team visits a large village where the older people speak a language called Apatani.

4 8.1 Watch the video again. Are these sentences true (T) or false (F)?

1 David, Greg, and Chris are trying to help save ancient languages that are disappearing and dying out.	T	F
2 The Australian man speaks a language that most people thought had already disappeared.	T	F
3 There used to be seven thousand known languages in the world, but now there is only half that amount.	T	F
4 One language disappears every two weeks around the planet.	T	F
5 In India, the team has problems with the recording equipment.	T	F
6 No one in the village speaks both English and Apatani.	T	F
7 The team teaches the local people how to use the recording equipment themselves.	T	F

After you watch

5 Vocabulary in context

8.2 Watch the clips from the video. Choose the correct meaning of the words and phrases.

6 Complete this paragraph about a language using the correct form of the words and phrases from Exercises 2 and 5. The first letter is provided.

National Geographic's Enduring Voices Project
In North America, there are between 150 and 170 [1] k*nown*_____ languages. Many of these are Native American languages that are [2] d_____ . The Enduring Voices Project is trying to help native speakers save their languages so we don't lose them [3] f_____ . Researchers use special recording [4] e_____ to interview older people speaking the language, and try to translate some of the [5] b_____ words. As a result of this work, the language of Salish has [6] s_____ . A few years ago, only about 50 people over age 75 spoke the language of Salish; but now the tribe offers courses in Salish, and the children are [7] s_____ in the language.

7 Work in groups. Discuss these questions.

- Is your country's native language a global or important language? Why or why not?
- How much is your native language changing? For example, does it use any English words?
- How important is a global language like English in your country?
- How do you use technology for learning English?

UNIT 8 REVIEW AND MEMORY BOOSTER

Grammar

1 Complete the sentences with the simple present or *will* form of the verbs in the box.

not call	not go	pass	press	work

1 When you _____ this button, the TV comes on.
2 If you put new batteries in, it _____ again.
3 If he _____ , we won't know what time to meet him.
4 I _____ hiking if the weather is bad tomorrow.
5 If you work hard, you _____ the exam.

2 Complete the defining relative clauses with *who, that,* or *where.*

1 The internet is an invention _____ has changed the modern world.
2 Sam is the one _____ showed me around when I first moved here.
3 They live in a place _____ there is no internet access.
4 A GPS is something _____ tells you your location.

3 >> MB Complete these sentences so they are true for you. Then work in pairs. Read your sentences to your partner and give reasons.

1 _____ is someone who is important in my life.
2 _____ is an invention that improves my life.

I CAN	
use zero and first conditionals	☐
use defining relative clauses	☐

Vocabulary

4 Complete these sentences with one word. The first letter is provided.

1 To s*et* _____ up an account, create a password.
2 P_____ the button here.
3 Plug it in here to c_____ the battery.
4 I'm interested i_____ robots.
5 Use your email to l_____ in.
6 I have a question a_____ this grammar point.
7 I'm working o_____ a big project.

5 >> MB Choose three more words from the unit. Write a sentence with each word, but leave out the key word. Then work in pairs. Take turns reading your sentences and guessing the missing word.

I CAN	
talk about technology	☐
use dependent prepositions	☐

Real life

6 Work in pairs. Put these words in the correct order to make questions.

1 turn / it / how / do / I / on?
2 can / me / you / how / this / works? / show
3 you / did / that? / do / how
4 charged / battery? / the / you / have
5 this / button / do? / what / does

7 Match these responses (a–d) with the questions in Exercise 6 (1–5). One response matches two questions.

a Sure. First, turn it on. ___
b Yes, I have. It should work now. ___
c By pressing this. ___
d It restarts the device. ___

8 >> MB Work in pairs. Look at these two inventions from Unit 8. Describe what they do and how they work.

It's something that ...

If you turn this, ...

I CAN	
find out how something works	☐
give instructions	☐

Unit 9 Vacations

Zoltan Takacs travels around the world studying venomous snakes.

FEATURES

106 Vacation stories

Do you have an interesting vacation story?

108 A different kind of vacation

Interview with an adventure travel tour guide

110 Two sides of Paris

Two different views of the famous European city

114 Living in Venice

A video about daily life in this famous city

1 Work in pairs. Look at the photo of Zoltan Takacs. How do you think his vacations are similar to his working life?

2 ▶ 69 Work in pairs. Listen to Zoltan and two other people talking. What is similar about their working life and their vacations?

3 ▶ 69 Listen again. Which accommodation and activities does each person talk about? Write the number of the speaker (1–3) next to the words they use. One type of accommodation is mentioned by two speakers.

bed and breakfast ___ hotel ___ , ___ tent ___

camping ___ diving ___ sightseeing ___ hiking ___

4 Work in pairs. Discuss these questions about your vacations.

1 When was your last vacation?
2 Where did you go?
3 What type of accommodation did you stay in?
4 What activities did you do?
5 What do you think makes a good vacation?

9a Vacation stories

Reading

1 Work in groups. Have you ever had these problems or other problems on vacation? What did you do?

- It rained all the time.
- You missed your plane / train / bus / ferry.
- You couldn't find your bag at the airport.
- You got lost when you went sightseeing.

2 Work in pairs. Read a story about a vacation. Why wasn't the tourist happy with her hotel room? What did she do?

▶ 70

Vacation Story

I was in a foreign country for the first time in my life. It had sounded amazing in the brochure: "Enjoy seven days in one of the most beautiful cities in the world while staying at a luxury hotel."

I had been excited about the trip, but now I wasn't so sure. I had waited at reception for fifteen minutes before someone checked me in. And my room was small and dark, with a window looking over a parking lot. I tried to be positive as I unpacked my bags. I decided to take a shower before going sightseeing. However, the shower wasn't working, so I called hotel reception.

An hour later, a maintenance man arrived. He hit the pipes a few times. "Sorry, but I can't fix it today. Maybe tomorrow," he said. Then he held out his hand. He wanted a tip for doing nothing! I was furious. But suddenly, I had a thought. He hadn't fixed my shower, but I tipped him anyway. Two minutes later, I was at the reception desk. I explained the problem to the hotel manager and gave him a very large tip.

Fifteen minutes later, I moved into room 405. It was twice the size of my original room, it had a wonderful view of the city, and—most importantly—the shower worked fine.

3 Read the story again. Number the events below in the order they happened (1–9).

____ gave the manager a tip
____ arrived at the hotel
____ the maintenance man looked at the shower
____ gave the maintenance man a tip
____ booked the vacation
____ tried to turn on the shower
____ called reception
____ moved to a larger room
____ waited at reception

4 Work in pairs. Do people tip in your country? If so, when and how much do they give?

Vocabulary vacation collocations

5 Complete the sentences with these verbs.

book call check in tip go stay unpack

1 I plan to _____ **overseas** next year for the first time in my life.
2 When did you _____ **your vacation**?
3 We hope to _____ **at a hotel** in the center of the city.
4 We need to _____ **at reception**.
5 Let's _____ **our bags** and then go sightseeing!
6 Can you _____ **reception** and ask someone to come and clean the room?
7 Do you always _____ **waiters** in this country?

6 Match these verbs to the groups of words below to make collocations.

book go rent stay

1 _____ : on a tour, diving, online
2 _____ : at home, at a campsite, out all night
3 _____ : a table (in a restaurant), a flight, a hotel room
4 _____ : a car, an apartment, skis

Grammar past perfect

▶ PAST PERFECT

1 *I **had been** excited about the trip, but now I **wasn't** so sure.*
2 *He **hadn't fixed** my shower, but I **tipped** him anyway.*
Note: In informal English, we often use *'d.*
(*I'd been = I had been*)

For more information and practice, see page 172.

7 Work in pairs. Look at the grammar box. How do we form the past perfect?

8 Work in pairs. Answer the questions below for each sentence (1–2) in the grammar box.

a Which is the main action? Which action happened earlier?
b Which verb is in the simple past and which is in the past perfect?

9 ▶ 71 Read this conversation between two friends about a vacation. Circle the correct options. Then listen and check your answers.

A: Hey, you're back! How was your vacation?
B: Umm…to be honest, I'm happy to be home.
A: Why? What [1] *happened / had happened*?
B: Well, on the first day, someone stole my bag. I was waiting at reception to check in, and someone just grabbed it.
A: No way! Did you catch the person?
B: No. He'd [2] *ran / run* off before anyone could stop him. The hotel [3] *reported / had reported* it to the police, but I never got my bag back.
A: That's horrible.
B: Yeah. Luckily, I [4] *put / 'd put* my passport and money in my pocket before reaching the hotel. So as soon as I checked in, I [5] *bought / 'd bought* some new clothes and went sightseeing.
A: That's good. How was the rest of the trip?
B: It was OK, but one night, the lights in the hotel suddenly went out and there was no electricity. I looked for the manager, but she [6] *left / 'd left* for the night.
A: Oh, no! What did you do?
B: Some of the hotel guests [7] *had / had had* flashlights, so we sat in the lobby and sang songs. That was fun, actually. In fact, that [8] *was / had been* probably the best night of the trip!

10 Complete the sentences with the simple past or the past perfect form of the verbs in parentheses.

1 We landed late in London, so our connecting flight to Dubai _____ (leave).
2 The hotel hadn't expected them until the evening, so they _____ (go) for lunch while the hotel staff prepared the rooms.
3 We _____ (not eat) for hours, but we finally arrived downtown and found a restaurant that was open.
4 I realized I _____ (lose) my passport as soon as I put my hand in my pocket.
5 We'd had a wonderful meal, so we _____ (give) the waiter a big tip.

11 Pronunciation *'d*

▶ 72 Listen to sentences 4 and 5 in Exercise 10. Notice the pronunciation of *'d*. Then listen again and repeat.

Speaking myLife

12 You are going to tell a story about a vacation. You can invent the story, or it can be about something that happened to you or someone you know. Prepare five sentences about it using these ideas.

A few weeks before the trip, we had …

When we got to the hotel / airport, we realized / remembered that we had …

One day, we'd just visited …

On the last day, …

After we got home, we found out that …

13 Work in pairs. Take turns telling your story to your partner. Do you think your partner's story is true?

9b A different kind of vacation

Listening

1 Work in groups. Do you prefer traveling in a group or on your own?

2 ▶ 73 Work in pairs. Listen to an interview about a different kind of vacation. Answer the questions.

1 What new job does Madelaine have?
2 What is she responsible for?

3 ▶ 73 Listen to the interview again. Are these sentences true (T) or false (F)?

1 Madelaine has led her first tour.	T	F
2 Madelaine is going to the Galápagos Archipelago for the first time.	T	F
3 Some people on the tour come on their own.	T	F
4 You have to do the same activities as other people in the group.	T	F

4 Work in pairs. Would you like to go on one of Madelaine's vacations? Which parts of the world would you like to visit or work in? Give reasons for your answers.

Wordbuilding *-ed / -ing* adjectives

▶ WORDBUILDING *-ed / -ing* adjectives

*I know that you're very **excited** about your new job.*
*My first tour is very **exciting**.*

For more practice, see Workbook page 75.

5 Work in pairs. Look at the wordbuilding box. Answer these questions. Then find other *-ed* and *-ing* adjectives in track 73 of the audioscript on page 187.

1 Which adjective describes how a person feels?
2 Which adjective describes a place or a thing?

6 Circle the correct adjectives to complete the conversation.

A: So, how was your vacation?
B: I had an [1] *amazed / amazing* time. I'm so [2] *bored / boring* back at work.
A: I'm sure. Where did you go exactly?
B: We went hiking in Patagonia! It's a [3] *fascinated / fascinating* place.
A: Yes, I watched an [4] *interested / interesting* TV program about it once. The mountains there are enormous. It looked like a [5] *frightened / frightening* place to climb.
B: Well, we had a fantastic guide, so I wasn't [6] *worried / worrying*. Though there was one man who was [7] *annoyed / annoying* about all the climbing. He kept complaining and saying he was [8] *tired / tiring* all the time.
A: Sounds like he booked the wrong vacation!

7 Pronunciation number of syllables

▶ 74 Listen to the sixteen adjectives from Exercise 6. Write the number of syllables you hear in each word. Then listen again and repeat.

1 amazed (2), amazing (3)

8 Work in pairs. Use *-ing* and *-ed* adjectives formed from these verbs to talk about the topics below (1–4).

amaze	bore	excite	fascinate
interest	tire	worry	annoy

1 a place you visited recently
2 a project you are working on
3 the last book you read
4 a TV show you saw last week

*I recently visited Cape Town. I had been **excited** about the trip because it was my first time there, but I actually found it kind of **boring**.*

The Galápagos Archipelago

Grammar subject questions

▶ SUBJECT QUESTIONS

Subject questions
Who books these types of vacations?
How many people go on the tour?
Who has been here before?
What happened next?

Other questions
How much does it cost?
When did you go on vacation?
Where do they live?
Why did you choose this vacation?

For more information and practice, see page 172.

9 Look at the grammar box. Circle the correct options to complete the rules (1–2).

1 In *subject questions / other questions*, the question word replaces the subject.
2 In subject questions, we *use / do not use* the auxiliary verb *do* or *did*.

10 Circle the correct options to complete these questions.

1 How many students *study / do study* English in your class?
2 How many days *you stayed / did you stay* in the hotel?
3 Which artist *painted / did paint* the Mona Lisa?
4 Where *you lived / did you live* when you were young?
5 What *happened / did happen*? I thought you were on vacation!
6 Which places *I should visit / should I visit* in Brazil?
7 Who *can you help / can help* me with my homework?
8 How much money *you take / did you take* with you?

11 ▶ 75 A group of four friends are planning their next vacation together. Complete their questions with the words in parentheses. Then listen and check your answers.

Ryan: OK, so what's our budget? How much money [1] _____ (we / want) to spend?
Maggie: Not too much! How about going to the beach?
Ryan: Good idea. Who [2] _____ (want) to go to the beach?
Adriana: I heard that Prainha Beach in Brazil is beautiful.
Maggie: We'll have to fly there, though, and flights are expensive.
Peter: Who [3] _____ (have) a car? Maybe we can drive somewhere. That's cheaper than flying.
Ryan: Good idea. I can borrow my brother's car. We drove to California last summer, and it was beautiful.
Adriana: [4] _____ (you / go) to any beaches there?
Ryan: Yes, we went to the beach in Santa Barbara, but I don't mind going again. It was really fun!
Maggie: Great. How many people [5] _____ (agree) to go? We can leave on Friday.

Speaking myLife

12 Work in groups. Imagine you have won $10,000 from a travel magazine to spend on a one-week group vacation. Ask your group members questions about:

- the type of trip they want to take.
- the accommodations and places they want to visit.
- the types of activities (daytime and evening) they want to do.

Agree on and plan a vacation that everyone in the group will enjoy.

9c Two sides of Paris

Reading

1 Work in pairs. What tourist attractions is Paris famous for?

2 Read the article. What two parts of Paris is it about?

3 Read the first two paragraphs again and complete these notes about what a tourist can do in Paris. Use words from the article.

1 see famous art and *architecture*
2 go up the _____
3 visit _____
4 eat some of the best _____
5 go _____
6 choose from lots of _____
7 visit tunnels called _____
8 walk down steps to see _____

4 Read the article again. Choose the correct option (a–c) to answer these questions.

1 Are tourists allowed to see the catacombs?
   a Yes, nowadays they can see the catacombs.
   b It depends on where they want to go.
   c No, the catacombs are closed off.
2 Why are the tunnels dangerous?
   a They might collapse.
   b There are criminals down there.
   c The writer doesn't say.
3 How have people used other parts of the tunnels?
   a for somewhere to live
   b for studying the architecture
   c for fun and entertainment
4 Why is it difficult to find Dominique and Yopie's room?
   a It isn't on a map.
   b It's far away from other rooms.
   c They never take anyone there.

Critical thinking the author's purpose

5 Work in pairs. Check (✓) the two options that describe the author's purpose. Give reasons for your answers.

☐ to compare and contrast two sides of Paris
☐ to support the police in their work to stop people from entering the tunnels
☐ to tell readers something they don't know
☐ to criticize people who use the unofficial tunnels

Word focus *place*

6 Read these sentences (1–3) from the article. Write the phrases in **bold** next to their uses and meanings (a–c).

1 After a busy morning, it's time to find **a good place to** eat.
2 Theater performances sometimes **take place** in the tunnels.
3 It's **no place for** anyone who is afraid of the dark or small places.

a to advise people not to go somewhere _____
b to say something happens _____
c to recommend somewhere _____

7 Work in pairs. Ask and answer these questions about your town or city.

1 Are there a lot of things for tourists to do? Why or why not?
2 Where are the best places for tourists to go sightseeing and shopping?
3 What special events take place there every year?

Speaking myLife

8 Work in pairs. Plan a two-minute presentation for a group of tourists about the place you live in or a place you know well. List what tourists can see and do there, using some of these ideas.

- art galleries
- cafés and restaurants
- good places for sightseeing
- museums
- nightclubs
- places with a good view (e.g., a tower)
- shopping
- special events
- theaters

9 Work with another pair. Take turns giving your presentations. Try to convince the other pair to visit your place.

There are a lot of things for tourists to do. For example, lots of different festivals take place here …

TWO SIDES OF PARIS

▶ 76

1 When tourists visit Europe, Paris is often at the top of their lists. It's a city where you can see some of the most famous art and architecture in the world. Most tour groups start by going to the top of the Eiffel Tower for a view of the city, or they visit a museum or an art gallery. After a busy morning, it's time to find a good place to eat. There's nothing better than sitting outside at a café or restaurant in Paris, watching people walking by, and eating some of the best food in the world. The city is also famous for its fashion, so after lunch it's time for some shopping. In the evening, there's a huge number of theaters and nightclubs to choose from.

2 That's the city that most tourists see when they visit Paris. But there is another amazing part of Paris most tourists don't know about—and it's underground. Paris has hundreds of kilometers of tunnels. Tourists are allowed to visit part of these tunnels, called catacombs, where over six million people were buried in the nineteenth century. Tourists have to walk down two hundred steps and through long, dark corridors to see the bones and skeletons.[1]

3 However, this public part of the tunnels is quite small. There are another 250 kilometers of the tunnels that are closed to the public. They are dangerous, and the police don't want people to go down there. Nevertheless, a lot of people find their way into these tunnels through secret entrances. The police often search the area; once, they found a movie theater down there. It's well-known that art shows and theater performances sometimes take place in the tunnels, and that they are popular with university students for parties.

4 There are unofficial tours of the tunnels with tour guides like Dominique and Yopie (not their real names). If you pay, they will take you deep underground. It's no place for anyone who is afraid of the dark or small places. The stone tunnels are small, and it's easy to hit your head on the ceiling. After two hours, you arrive in a room that isn't on any official map. Yopie and his friends built it. It's comfortable and clean, with a table, chairs, and a bed. Yopie says there are many other rooms like this under Paris. "Many people come down here to party, some people to paint. We do what we want here."

[1] **skeleton** (n) /ˈskelɪt(ə)n/ the bones of a human or an animal

9d Tourist information

Tarxien Temples, Malta

Real life requesting and suggesting

1 Work in pairs. Look at the information brochure for the Tarxien Temples on the right. Would you visit this kind of place on vacation? Why or why not?

2 Work in pairs. There is information missing in the brochure. What questions can you ask to get the information (1–5)?

3 ▶ 77 Listen to a conversation at a tourist information office. Complete the information about the Tarxien Temples in the brochure.

4 ▶ 77 Look at the expressions for requesting and suggesting. Listen to the conversation again and circle the expressions you hear.

▶ REQUESTING AND SUGGESTING

Requesting information
I'm interested in visiting ...
Do you know the opening hours?
What time does it open / close?
Could you tell me the price?
How much does a ticket cost?
Is there any public transportation to the site?
Are there any ...?

Suggesting options
How about ...-ing ...?
Another option is to ...
You can also ...
Or you could take ...

5 **Pronunciation** /dʒə/

▶ 78 Work in pairs. Listen to these two questions. How does the speaker pronounce the first two words? Then listen again and repeat.

Do you know the opening hours?
Could you tell me the price?

The **Tarxien Temples** *in Malta*

Information for visitors

This is a UNESCO World Heritage Site. The four temple structures are around 5,000 years old.

Address: Neolithic Temple Street, Tarxien

Hours: Open [1] _____ days a week, from 10 a.m. to [2] _____ p.m. (Last admission at 4:30 p.m.)

Tickets: Book in advance or buy at the entrance

Adults: €6.00
12- to 17-year-olds, seniors (over 65), and students: € [3] _____
Children (ages 6–11): €3.00
Ages 5 and under: Free

Official guided tour: €20.00 with tour guide and lasts [4] _____ hours

Transportation to the site: Buses every hour from outside the [5] _____

6 Work in pairs. Practice a conversation similar to the one in Exercise 3.

Student A: You are the tourist. Turn to page 155.

Student B: You work at a tourist information booth. Turn to page 154.

A: Hi. I'm interested in visiting the Caves of Lascaux. What time does it open?
B: It opens at ...

9e Requesting information

Writing an email requesting information

1 Work in pairs. When you want to take a vacation, how do you find out information? (e.g., online, from a travel agent, by email, by phone)

2 Read the email and answer the questions.

1 What is the writer's reason for writing?
2 What two things does he want to know?

Dear Sir or Madam,

I am writing to request more information about the "Explorer's Vacations" on your website. In particular, could you provide me with more details of your next tour to Alaska?

Currently, the website says that you will confirm the exact dates of tours in the near future. I would be grateful if you could inform me as soon as these dates become available.

My second question is about accommodations. The tour seems to include camping and staying in hotels, but the information on the site is not very clear. I would like to receive more details about this.

Thank you in advance for providing this information.

I look forward to hearing from you.

Best regards,

William Fong

3 **Writing skill formal expressions**

Work in pairs. Find formal expressions in the email that have a similar meaning to these informal expressions.

Starting
1 Hi
2 I'm writing to ask about ...

Requesting more information
3 Can you send me …?
4 Please tell me …
5 when you have them
6 I'd like to get …

Ending
7 Thanks for the information.
8 Hope to hear from you soon.

4 Work in pairs. Circle any contractions (e.g., *I'm, it's, you're*) in the email and in Exercise 3. Do we use contractions more in formal or in informal writing?

5 Circle the more formal option in each sentence.

1 *I'm writing to ask for / I am writing to request* more information about your product.
2 *I would also like / I also want* a copy of the vacation brochure.
3 *Thanks / Thank you* for your *help / assistance*.
4 *I'll tell / I will inform* you when they are *ready / available*.
5 Please let me know when *I will receive / I'll get* the payment.
6 *Hope to hear / I look forward to hearing* from you soon.

6 You have looked at a vacation website for cruises around the Caribbean. Write an email to the tour company and request information about:

1 how long the cruise lasts (in weeks).
2 when and where the cruise starts and ends.
3 the cost of a cabin.

7 Work in pairs. Exchange emails with your partner. Has your partner used formal expressions?

9f Living in Venice

For tourists in Venice, Italy, a gondola is the best way to travel.

Before you watch

1 Work in pairs. Look at the photo of Venice and answer these questions.

1 Why do you think Venice is popular with tourists?
2 What do you think it's like to live and work in Venice?

2 Key vocabulary

Read the sentences (1–7). The words and phrases in **bold** are used in the video. Write these words and phrases next to their definitions (a–g).

1 The **traders** at the market sell lots of different foods and local products.
2 Young people have to **face the challenge** of finding their first job.
3 My father is a **gondolier**. He takes tourists around Venice.
4 Most people can't buy a place to live in the city because **property** costs a lot of money.
5 Many young people **move away** to more modern cities.
6 Did you ever **get to** meet anyone famous?
7 Good health is a **gift** in life—especially as you get older!

a a person who steers a traditional canal boat in Venice _____
b leave one place to live in another _____
c buildings that people own (e.g., houses, apartments) _____
d people who buy and sell things _____
e deal with the difficulties _____
f a present or something you are lucky to have _____
g have the opportunity to _____

While you watch

3 9.1 Watch the video. Number these actions in the order you see them (1–5).

____ Traders sell their food in an outdoor market.
____ The early morning sun lights up the Piazza San Marco.
____ The sun sets over Venice.
____ A group of musicians play for tourists.
____ Giovanni dal Missier gives an interview in a gondola.

4 9.1 Work in pairs. Watch the video again and answer these questions about living in Venice.

1 When is the best time of day for shopping in the outdoor markets?
2 How does Fabrizio Copano describe Venice?
3 What does Gino Penzo say about his son?
4 What is happening to the population of Venice?
5 What is particularly expensive in Venice?
6 What does Giovanni dal Missier say about the tourists?
7 What kind of jobs do most people do in Venice?
8 How does Gino Penzo describe the cities of Florence and Rome?
9 How does Giovanni dal Missier describe the experience of living in Venice?

After you watch

5 Vocabulary in context

9.2 Watch the clips from the video. Choose the correct meaning of the words and phrases.

6 Work in pairs. Ask and answer these questions about a town or city you know well.

1 Is it clean and easy to live in, with a high quality of life?
2 How expensive is property and housing?
3 Is it difficult to earn a living there?
4 Do you think young people are moving away? If so, why?

7 Work in pairs. You are going to practice a conversation between a tourist and a tour guide.

Student A: You are a tour guide showing a visitor your town or city. Make notes about these things.

- the best places to see
- good places to eat
- good places for shopping and entertainment

Student B: You are a tourist visiting your partner's town or city. Find out what it's like to live there. Look at these ideas and prepare questions to ask your tour guide.

- the best places to see
- the advantages of living in the town or city
- the disadvantages of living in the town or city

8 Practice the conversation using your notes. Then change roles and have another conversation. Try to choose a different town or city.

A: Welcome to _____ !
B: Thank you. Which places should I visit here?
A: Well, there's …

UNIT 9 REVIEW AND MEMORY BOOSTER

Grammar

1 Complete the conversation with the simple past or the past perfect form of the verbs in parentheses.

A: How was your vacation?
B: It was fine, in the end.
A: Why? What [1] _____ (happen)?
B: Well, when we [2] _____ (arrive) at the hotel, they were full and so we [3] _____ (not / have) a room.
A: Oh, no! Why [4] _____ you _____ (not / book) the hotel?
B: I had! But someone [5] _____ (make) a mistake with the reservation. Anyway, they [6] _____ (get) us a room in another hotel, but it was in another part of town.
A: So what [7] _____ you _____ (do)?
B: Well, I was really angry after everything that [8] _____ (happen), but the manager [9] _____ (pay) for a taxi to the other hotel.
A: That was nice of him.

2 >> MB Work in pairs. The phrases in the box are from the Vacation Story on page 106. Can you remember and tell the story using these phrases?

one of the most beautiful cities in the world	
had waited at reception for 15 minutes	
was small and dark	decided to take a shower
wasn't working	a maintenance man arrived
"I can't fix it today"	a tip for doing nothing
explained the problem to the hotel manager	
moved into room 405	

3 Work in pairs. Circle the correct options to complete the questions. Which are subject questions?

1 How many tourists *visit / do visit* your town or city every year?
2 What places *enjoy they / do they enjoy*?
3 Where *they usually stay / do they usually stay*?
4 Who *shows / does show* the tourists around?
5 How much *costs a tour / does a tour cost*?

I CAN	
use the past perfect	☐
use subject questions and other questions	☐

Vocabulary

4 Complete each sentence with a pair of verbs.

check in + get	call + book	unpack + go

1 Can you _____ the restaurant and _____ a table?
2 Let's _____ our bags and _____ sightseeing.
3 First, _____ at the airport and then _____ on the plane.

5 Complete the adjectives with *-ing* or *-ed*.

1 What's the matter? Do you feel bor____ ?
2 This book is very interest____ .
3 We had an amaz____ time in Peru.
4 I'm so excit____ about our trip!

I CAN	
talk about vacations	☐

Real life

6 >> MB Work in pairs. Look at the photos. What can you remember about these places? Discuss the questions.

1 What are these places called? Where are they?
2 What do you think you can see there?

7 Work in pairs. Put these words in the correct order to make sentences.

1 interested / caves / the / in / visiting / I'm
2 know / do / you / the / hours? / opening
3 another / is / to / a / option / take / taxi
4 about / tour? / a / taking / how / sightseeing
5 tours? / any / there / are / guided

8 >> MB Work in pairs. Practice a conversation.

Student A: You are the tourist. Ask questions about a museum.

Student B: You work at tourist information. Answer the tourist's questions and suggest options.

I CAN	
request information	☐
suggest options	☐

Unit 10 Products

Carrying baskets in Hung Yen, Vietnam

FEATURES

118 A lesson in logos

Why Apple turned its logo around

120 Product design

The story of a classic design

122 Is stuff winning?

An article about how we have too much "stuff" in our lives

126 Wind turbines

A video about a product that can earn money and help the environment

1 Work in pairs. Look at the photo and the caption. What products is the man selling? What do you think they are used for?

2 ▶ 79 Work in pairs. Listen to part of a radio program about the man in the photo. Answer the questions.

1 Who makes these baskets?
2 Who are his customers? Why do they buy the baskets?
3 Where does he sell the baskets?

3 Work in pairs. Do you usually buy things from small local producers or from international companies?

4 What was the last thing you bought (e.g., clothing, an electronic device)? Tell your partner. Answer these questions about the product.

- What was it?
- Where did you buy it?
- Why did you buy it?
- Do you know what brand it is?
- Do you know where it was made?

10a A lesson in logos

Reading

1 Work in pairs. Look at the photo below. Do you recognize the logo on the laptop? What is wrong with it? Read the article and check your ideas.

▶ 80

A LESSON IN LOGOS

A logo is what people recognize about your company. When you see a "Swoosh" logo on an advertisement, for example, you know it's Nike sportswear; the golden arches says McDonald's; and everyone knows who made the technology you are using when it has an apple on it.

The Apple logo is one of the simplest and most successful logos in the world. Apple products are used in millions of homes and offices. Over five hundred iPhones are sold every minute, and the company makes more than two hundred billion dollars a year. An Apple product is recognized by people all over the world because of its design and the famous logo.

However, when the first Apple laptops were produced in 1999, Apple discovered a problem with its logo. When the laptop was closed, the customer saw the Apple logo on the lid. But when the laptop was open, the logo was upside down. This wasn't a problem for the person using the laptop, but it didn't look good to other people. In the end, the logo was turned around so that it was seen correctly by other people.

Why was this so important to Apple? Because when you see other people using a product, you are more likely to buy it.

Steve Wozniak, co-founder of Apple

2 Read the article again. Are these sentences true (T) or false (F)?

1 The writer thinks everyone knows about Apple products. T F
2 On the first Apple laptops, the company didn't use the Apple logo. T F
3 When you are using a modern Apple laptop, other people can see the logo correctly. T F

3 Discuss these questions as a class.

1 Do you agree with the last sentence in the article? Is it true for you? Why or why not?
2 How important do you think logos are? Do they make you buy products?

Wordbuilding word forms

4 Work in pairs. Match these word forms with their definitions (1–5).

ad	advertise	advertisement
advertiser	advertising	

1 (verb) to tell the public about a product, job, or service
2 (noun) short for the word *advertisement*
3 (noun) a person or company that advertises
4 (noun) a notice, picture, or video telling people about a product, job, or service
5 (noun) the activity of telling the public about a product, job, or service

▶ WORDBUILDING word forms

When you learn a new word, try to learn its other forms. Use a dictionary to help you.
produce (v), *product* (n), *productive* (adj), *production* (n), *producer* (person / company)

For more practice, see Workbook page 83.

5 Look at the wordbuilding box. Complete these sentences with the correct form of *produce*.

1 I work for Mercedes. We _____ cars and other vehicles.
2 The iPad is one of the most popular _____ in the world.
3 Wine _____ in France are worried about low sales this year.
4 My brother works in video _____ . He makes videos for online advertising.
5 I've had a very _____ day, and I've finished all my work.

6 Pronunciation stress in different word forms

▶ 81 Listen and underline the stressed syllable in each of these words. Then listen again and repeat the words.

ad	advertising	product	productive
advertise	advertisement	produce	production
advertiser		producer	

Grammar the passive

▶ THE PASSIVE

Simple present passive

1 *An Apple product **is recognized** by people all over the world.*
2 *Apple products **are used** in millions of homes and offices.*

Simple past passive

3 *The first Apple laptops **were produced** in 1999.*
4 *The logo **was turned** around.*

For more information and practice, see page 174.

7 Work in pairs. Look at the sentences in the grammar box. Answer these questions.

a In a passive sentence, we use the past participle of the main verb. What other verb do we use?
b Compare sentence 1 with this active sentence: *People all over the world recognize an Apple product.*
In which sentence is *people* the subject, and in which sentence is *an Apple product* the subject?
c Sentences 2, 3, and 4 don't say who does the action. Why is this?
d Sentence 1 says who does the action. Which word introduces this?

8 Complete the information about YouTube with the simple present passive and the simple past passive form of the verbs in parentheses.

YouTube in numbers

- Six billion hours of YouTube video [1] _____ (watch) every month.
- Four hundred hours of video [2] _____ (upload) every minute.
- The first YouTube video [3] _____ (call) "Me at the zoo." It [4] _____ (make) by Jawed Karim in 2005.
- Ten years ago, the site [5] _____ (visit) by 20 million people per month. Today, the YouTube website [6] _____ (use) by 1.5 billion people per month.

9 Read about another logo. Circle the correct options.

In the world of business, logos [1] *design / are designed* very carefully, and millions of dollars [2] *spend / are spent* on them. Customers often [3] *prefer / are preferred* products with a famous logo.

So when companies [4] *try / are tried* to change their logo, they have to be very careful. Gap is a good example of how companies sometimes [5] *make / are made* mistakes with logos. Gap clothes [6] *buy / are bought* all over the world, and the simple blue logo [7] *recognize / is recognized* in every shopping mall. However, in 2010, the company [8] *decided / was decided* to change its logo.

Many customers [9] *complained / were complained*, and a week later, Gap [10] *changed / was changed* the logo back. The company hadn't realized how much its logo [11] *loved / was loved* by its customers.

10 Complete these sentences so they are true for you. Use the passive form of the verbs in parentheses.

1 My bag _____ (make) in _____. (which country?)
2 My favorite movie _____ (direct) by _____. (who?)
3 My home _____ (build) in _____. (when?)
4 My favorite book _____ (write) by _____. (which author?)

Speaking myLife

11 Work in pairs. Take turns choosing a type of product from the box below. Think of a famous brand. Your partner has to ask a maximum of ten questions and guess the company. Use the ideas below or your own ideas.

a drink | a car | clothes | furniture | technology

Was it invented in this country?
Where is it made?
How is it normally sold?
Can you describe the logo?

*A: **Was it invented** in this country?*
*B: No, it **was invented** in the USA.*

10b Product design

Vocabulary describing design

1 Read the sentences (1–7). Write the adjectives in **bold** next to their definitions (a–g).

1 You don't need to read the instructions for this device because it's so **user-friendly**.
2 I know my clothes are **old-fashioned**, but I can't afford anything new.
3 I still use the same phone I had five years ago. It looks very **basic**, but it works.
4 I can sell you this device now, but a more **up-to-date** model comes out in three weeks.
5 That style of dress is very **fashionable** this summer. Everyone's wearing it.
6 I like her taste in clothes. She always wears **classic** designs.
7 My mother gave me this bag. It's very **useful** because it can hold everything I need.

a easy to learn how to use _____
b practical or effective _____
c simple, not complicated _____
d simple and traditional, but always in fashion _____
e out-of-date, not modern _____
f the latest or newest _____
g popular at the moment _____

2 Work in pairs. Use the adjectives in **bold** from Exercise 1 to describe the designs of objects in the photo above, in your classroom, or in your bag.

Listening

3 Work in pairs. How do you listen to music? Do you use:

1 vinyl records?
2 cassettes?
3 CDs?
4 downloads?
5 streaming?

4 ▶ 82 Work in pairs. Listen to a radio program about a famous product called the Sony Walkman. Which thing(s) from Exercise 3 did it play?

5 ▶ 82 Listen again. Read the questions and choose the correct option (a or b).

1 What does the speaker say about listening to music in the seventies?
   a People didn't listen to as much music then as they do now.
   b You couldn't listen to music on your way to school or work.
2 What showed that the Sony Walkman was successful?
   a It won awards for its design.
   b Other companies copied the idea.
3 Why did some people think the Sony Walkman was a crazy idea?
   a It was too basic.
   b It was too expensive.

Grammar *used to*

▶ USED TO

*People **used to buy** music on vinyl records.*
*My mother **used to have** a Sony Walkman.*
*We **didn't use to download** music.*
***Did** you **use to buy** CDs?*

For more information and practice, see page 174.

6 Work in pairs. Compare this sentence with the sentences in the grammar box. Answer the questions (1–2).

He bought his first record in 1973.

1 Which form do we use to describe a single action at a specific time in the past?
2 Which form do we use to describe a habit in the past that is not true now?

7 Circle the correct options to complete these sentences.

1 I *used / use* to buy CDs, but now I download all my music.
2 We *used to go / went* to our first music concert when we were fourteen.
3 Musicians *used to play / played* live all the time, but nowadays they spend more time in recording studios.
4 My brother *didn't use to / didn't use* have long hair, but he grew it when it became fashionable.
5 I *didn't use to learn / didn't learn* the guitar until I was twelve years old.
6 Did you *use / used* to like this song?
7 When did you *move / use to move* to the United States?

8 Pronunciation /s/ **or** /z/

▶ 83 Work in pairs. Listen to these sentences. Which **bold** words have the sound /s/ and which have the sound /z/? Listen again and repeat the sentences.

I **used** to buy CDs, but I didn't **use** to buy records. Nowadays, I **use** my cell phone to download music.

9 Complete the sentences with *used to, didn't use to,* or *did you use to* and the verb given in parentheses.

1 My family ___*used to spend*___ (spend) every summer on a boat. It was great.
2 I _____ (eat) vegetables when I was a kid, but I love them now.
3 Before you got that cell phone, _____ (have) a camera?
4 My sister _____ (play) the guitar in a rock band when she was younger. They sounded terrible, but she loved it!
5 He _____ (earn) much money compared to what he earns nowadays.
6 _____ (write) letters before email was invented?

Speaking myLife

10 Write five true sentences about your past with *used to* or *didn't use to*. Then write the question form.

*I **used to play** the guitar. **Did** you **use to play** the guitar?*
*I **didn't use to like** vegetables. **Did** you **use to like** vegetables?*

11 Work in pairs. Take turns asking and answering your questions from Exercise 10. Find similarities and differences between you and your partner.

A: Did you use to play the guitar?
B: No, but I used to take piano lessons.
A: Did you use to like vegetables?

10c Is stuff winning?

Reading

1 Work in pairs. Read this conversation between two people. Answer the questions.

1 Where do you think this conversation is taking place?
2 Who do you think the conversation is between?

A: This room is so messy. There's so much **stuff** everywhere.
B: I know. I'll clean it, but I don't have anywhere to put some of these **things**.
A: Well, let's throw some away. For example, what's this **thing**?
B: No, don't throw that away. I like to keep **stuff** like that, just in case.

2 Work in pairs. Look at the words *stuff* and *thing* in the conversation above. Which is countable? Which is uncountable?

3 Work in pairs. Look at the photo on page 123. Is your home full of stuff like this? Or is it very neat?

4 Read the article quickly. What is it mainly about? Choose the best option (a, b, or c).

a Some people are buying too much stuff and need to spend less.
b Some people are bored because they have nothing to do.
c Some people are trying to have less stuff in their lives.

5 These sentences (a–e) are missing from the ends of the paragraphs in the article. Read the article again and match these sentences with the paragraphs (1–5).

a All these people are interested in leading a "minimalist" life. ____
b They buy more stuff in order to avoid getting bored. ____
c Maybe one way to begin is by going offline for fifteen minutes a day and seeing if you feel better! ____
d By the end of the month, you'll have thrown away lots of your stuff. ____
e I also need to reply to a few text messages from work. ____

Critical thinking fact or opinion?

6 The sentences below (1–6) are from the article. Which sentences:

a give facts?
b give the author's opinion?
c report other people's opinion?

1 My email inbox contains 243 unread emails. __a__
2 The good news is that now there is an excellent website to help people like me. ____
3 When Ryan Nicodemus and Joshua Fields Millburn set up this website, they had 52 visitors in the first month. ____
4 Some people think that there is a problem with having lots of stuff in our heads. ____
5 Some people said they were bored with their screens and online life. ____
6 Spending more time away from our devices could be the first step toward this. ____

7 Work in pairs. Underline the words in Exercise 6 that helped you to answer. Which types of words or phrases did you underline:

1 for factual information?
2 for opinions and reporting opinions?

8 Work in pairs. Look at the article again. Which statement (a–c) do you agree with? Give reasons for your answer.

a On the whole, the article is based on facts and results.
b On the whole, the article is based on the writer's opinion and the opinions of others.
c On the whole, the article is a good balance of fact and opinion.

Speaking myLife

9 Work in pairs. Prepare a short presentation to convince other people to have less stuff in their homes or to spend less time online. Use ideas from the article and add your own opinions. Make sure to present the **problem**, the **reasons**, and the **solutions**.

10 Work with another pair. Take turns giving your presentations and convincing the other pair of your opinions.

Today, we'd like to talk to you about the stuff in your home. Do you spend time every day shopping at malls or buying things online?

IS STUFF WINNING?

▶ 84

1 I bought another book today and have put it with a pile of unread books on my new coffee table. There's no more space on the table, which also has on it digital devices, coffee cups, and some clothes I need to put away in my bedroom. But my bedroom is also full of stuff. I pick up my phone. My email inbox contains 243 unread emails. I've already missed three calls this morning.

2 I know that I want less stuff in my life, but at the moment, the stuff is winning. I seem to spend all my time buying things and then putting them away, when really I'd like more time for family, friends, and hobbies. The good news is that now there is an excellent website to help people like me, called The Minimalists. When Ryan Nicodemus and Joshua Fields Millburn set up this website, they had 52 visitors in the first month. Two years later, the website has over two million visitors a month.

3 Nicodemus explains how it began. He was working between sixty and eighty hours a week and spending his free time buying more products to make himself feel better. One day, he decided to start working fewer hours and to get rid of all his stuff. After a while, he realized he was much happier, and he wanted to share his ideas with other people. So he set up the website with Millburn to give advice to others about how to become "minimalists."[1] On the website, there are blog posts and lots of practical ideas. One of these ideas is to play the thirty-day minimalism game. On day 1, you throw out, sell, recycle, or give away one object in your life. Then on day 2, two objects. On day 3, three objects.

4 In the same way that stuff can fill the space in our homes, some people think that there is a problem with having lots of stuff in our heads. Often people go online because they don't want to be doing nothing, so they keep their brains busy with unnecessary activities. According to a recent survey, most people born between 1980 and 2000 use their phones when they have nothing else to do: 46% check social media, 43% play games, and a fifth do some online shopping.

5 In the same survey, some people said they were bored with their screens and online life. For example, 27% said they were bored of watching TV, and 14% were bored of social media. So perhaps we need to simplify our heads in the same way Nicodemus and Millburn have simplified their homes. Spending more time away from our devices could be the first step toward this.

[1]**minimalist** (n) /ˈmɪnɪməlɪst/ a person who uses a small number of things in their work and life

10d Website design

Vocabulary websites

1 Complete these sentences with the words and phrases in the box.

"About Us"	ads	contact	content
home	links	search	

1 The _____ page is the first page you see on a website.
2 Most websites have _____ to other websites.
3 You can send a message to the owner of a website using the _____ page.
4 The _____ page has background information about the company or the person who owns the website.
5 Some websites have _____ that appear on the top or the side of the screen. They can be really annoying!
6 Visitors want to read and watch up-to-date _____ on a website.
7 The _____ box helps you find specific information more quickly.

2 Work in groups. Discuss the questions.

1 Which websites do you visit when you want to do these things?

- listen to music
- find the translation of a word into English
- buy clothes, books, or music
- find out the latest news

2 Why do you prefer these websites?
3 What do you think makes one website better than another?

Real life discussing opinions

3 ▶ 85 Sergio and Rachel own a store called Retake Records, which sells second-hand records and CDs. They are planning a new website for online customers. Listen and check (✓) the topics they discuss.

- ☐ the website name
- ☐ the home page
- ☐ ads
- ☐ a search box
- ☐ the "About Us" page
- ☐ links to other sites
- ☐ the contact page
- ☐ payment methods

4 ▶ 85 Listen again and complete the sentences with the words you hear.

1 Great. I think we _____ buy it today.
2 Let me show you. What do you _____ ?
3 I see what you _____ , but we can have a photo of the store at the top.
4 In my _____ , it's more important that people see the records for sale as soon as they arrive on the home page.
5 R: Also, we need a search box so customers can find the record they want.
S: Yes, you're _____ .
6 R: Lots of other websites have an "About Us" page. _____ you could put this text there?
S: Good _____ .
7 I'm not _____ about that. Regular customers will want to call or email us directly.

5 Look at the expressions for discussing opinions and check your answers in Exercise 4.

▶ DISCUSSING OPINIONS

Asking for an opinion
What do you think?
What's your opinion?

Giving your opinion
I think we should ...
In my opinion, ...
I'm not sure about ...

Agreeing and disagreeing
I agree. / You're right. / Good idea.
I see what you mean, but ...
I disagree. / I don't agree.

Making suggestions
Maybe you could ...
I suggest you ...

6 Work in groups. You are going to plan a new website. Discuss these questions. Use the expressions for discussing opinions.

1 What are you going to sell from your website?
2 What is the name of your business?
3 What pages do you need?
4 How will you show your product on the page?
5 What else will you have on the website (e.g., videos)?

7 As a group, present your plans to the rest of the class.

10e A review

Writing a review

1 Work in pairs. Read the review of a website and answer these questions.

1 What is the purpose of the website?
2 Why does the writer like the website?
3 What is one problem with the site?
4 What is the writer's conclusion about the site?

> One of my favorite websites is a free photo-sharing site called flickr.com. It's a great place for photographers to share their photos with other people.
>
> The site has quite a few good features. Firstly, it's easy to find photographs that you are interested in. The photos are organized into different categories like "travel," "food," or "people," so you can search for things you want to look at. Another good thing is that you can comment on each other's photos. There are a lot of professional photographers in the community. In my opinion, you can learn a lot from their comments.
>
> The only problem is that the site has too many ads. I think that's how it makes money, but when you are looking at beautiful photos, it's annoying when an ad appears on the screen.
>
> On the whole, it's a useful website for anyone who loves taking photos and communicating with other people about them.

2 Writing skill giving your opinion

a Work in pairs. What are some useful phrases in the review that:

a give positive opinions?
One of my favorite … is …
b give negative opinions?
c sum up the writer's main opinion?

b Match these phrases (1–4) to the uses (a–c) in Exercise 2a.

1 One thing I really like is that … ___
2 In general, … ___
3 Another bad point is that … ___
4 One big advantage is that … ___

3 Think of a website you often use. Make notes to answer these questions and plan a review of the website.

Paragraph 1:
What is the website? What is it used for?
Paragraph 2:
In your opinion, what are its good points?
Paragraph 3:
Are there any bad points or problems with the site?
Paragraph 4:
On the whole, what do you think about the site?

4 Write your review. Use the useful phrases in Exercise 2.

5 Exchange reviews with a partner. Use these questions to check your partner's review.

- Does it explain the purpose of the website?
- Does the review give positive opinions?
- Does it give negative opinions?
- Does it sum up the writer's main opinion?

10f Wind turbines

Wind turbines can help save money and the environment.

Before you watch

1 Work in pairs. Look at the photo and answer these questions.

1 Do you have wind turbines in your local area?
2 How do you think wind turbines work? What do they produce?

2 Key vocabulary

Read the sentences (1–7). The words and phrases in **bold** are used in the video. Write these words and phrases next to their definitions (a–g).

1 The land is very **flat** in this area.
2 I **paid off** the loan on the car.
3 This tower can **withstand** very strong winds.
4 Our electricity comes from the national **grid**.
5 The price can be **anywhere between** one hundred and two hundred dollars.
6 This truck weighs **a ton**.
7 The farmer grows **crops** like corn and wheat on his land.

a gave back all the money owed _____
b a network of electrical wires and equipment that supplies electricity to a large area _____
c not be damaged by something _____
d a very large amount _____
e with no hills or mountains _____
f plants that are grown in large quantities for food _____
g a phrase used when you don't have the exact figure _____

While you watch

3 10.1 Watch the video. Match the numbers and years in the box to the information (1–8).

6,000	2	81,530	180
130	257	1993	140,000

1 The number of wind turbines at the schools in Spirit Lake: _____
2 The amount of money the smaller turbine has saved the district: $ _____
3 The year the first wind turbine was built: _____
4 The total amount that the two turbines save the schools each year: $ _____
5 The height of a wind turbine: _____ feet
6 The speed of wind that the turbine can withstand: _____ miles per hour
7 The amount of money Charles Goodman thinks he will make in a year from his wind turbines: $ _____
8 The number of wind turbines in this part of the countryside: _____

4 10.1 Work in pairs. Watch the video again and answer the questions.

1 Why was the second turbine built?
2 How are the turbines fixed in the ground so they don't fall over?
3 Where is the power from the two turbines sent?
4 Apart from their crops, what else do the farmers in the countryside sell?
5 Why does Charles Goodman smile when the wind is blowing?
6 Why are the wind turbines useful in class?
7 To sum up, what are the two uses of wind power in Spirit Lake?

After you watch

5 Vocabulary in context

10.2 Watch the clips from the video. Choose the correct option to complete each sentence.

6 Work in pairs. List the reasons why wind turbines are good for the area of Spirit Lake.

7 With your partner, prepare a short, two-minute presentation about building wind turbines near your town or city. Do extra research if necessary. Explain:

- how a wind turbine works.
- the different reasons why wind turbines are good.
- why the town or city needs to build wind turbines.

When the wind blows, …
One good thing about wind turbines is that …
Our town/city needs to build wind turbines because …

8 Work with another pair and take turns giving your presentations. How similar were your reasons for building wind turbines?

UNIT 10 REVIEW AND MEMORY BOOSTER

Grammar

1 Circle the correct options to complete the text about IKEA.

IKEA furniture [1] *sold / is sold* in nearly 400 different stores around the world and online. However, IKEA [2] *didn't used / didn't use* to make furniture. The company [3] *started / was started* in Sweden in 1943 by Ingvar Kamprad. Kamprad [4] *use / used* to sell small objects like watches and pens by mail. As the company grew, it [5] *produced / was produced* larger household furniture. Today, it [6] *sells / is sold* around 12,000 different products, including chairs, beds, and cupboards.

IKEA is famous for changing the way we buy products. In the past, furniture [7] *assembled / was assembled* in the factory, and customers [8] *were bought / used to buy* it ready-made. But modern IKEA furniture [9] *assembles / is assembled* by the customer after they buy it. Also, furniture stores [10] *used / use* to be in the center of cities, but IKEA [11] *built / was built* its stores outside the downtown area. Nowadays, you often see large stores in the suburbs.

I CAN	
use the passive form of the simple present and simple past	☐
use *used to*	☐

Vocabulary

2 Complete this chart of words.

verb	adjective	company	other nouns
advertise	–		_____, advertising
produce			product, _____

3 Rearrange the letters to make adjectives that describe products.

1 suer-rifelndy _____
2 casib _____
3 hasionfable _____
4 slacsic _____
5 lufuse _____
6 lod-asfihoned _____
7 pu-ot-tade _____

4 Work in pairs. Write three products or brands and match them with the adjectives in Exercise 3.

Gap clothes – *classic, fashionable*

1 _____ – _____
2 _____ – _____
3 _____ – _____

5 >> MB Which part of a website (a–d) do you click on to do these things (1–4)?

a "About Us" page
b contact page
c home page
d search box

1 to send a message to the site owners ____
2 to look for specific information on the site ____
3 to return to the main page ____
4 to learn more about the site owners ____

I CAN	
talk about products and advertising	☐
talk about websites	☐

Real life

6 Read a discussion between three people about the color of a new logo for a store. Write the missing words. The first letter is provided.

A: The designers have sent the new logo in three different colors. Which [1] d_____ y_____ t_____ is the best color?
B: [2] I_____ m_____ o_____, the black and white logo is the best. It's easy to see.
C: I [3] d_____. Black and white is boring.
A: OK, let's look at the other two. [4] M_____ we c_____ use the yellow logo.
C: No, I [5] d_____ a_____. This shade of yellow is difficult to see from the street.
A: Yes, [6] y_____ r_____. Then I [7] s_____ we use the blue logo.
B: [8] G_____ i_____. Let's do that.

7 >> MB Work in pairs. Identify the phrases in Exercise 6 for:

- asking for an opinion.
- giving an opinion.
- agreeing and disagreeing.
- making suggestions.

I CAN	
ask for and give opinions	☐
agree, disagree, and make suggestions	☐

Unit 11 History

Captain Robert Falcon Scott's hut was left with all its contents in 1917, and was only found again in 1956.

FEATURES

130 The history of video gaming

How video gaming became popular

132 Messages from the past

A local fisherman finds a message in a bottle and sets a record

134 Stealing history

How Egypt is trying to save its history

138 The Golden Record

A video about the messages on Voyager 1

1 Work in pairs. The hut in the photo is about one hundred years old. Where do you think it is? What do you think Captain Scott did?

2 ▶ 86 Work in pairs. Listen to a historian talking about the hut in the photo and check your ideas from Exercise 1. Then answer these questions.

1 What objects can you see inside the hut?
2 Why is it important to preserve the hut?
3 The historian says, "The hut has become a time capsule." What do you think he means by a *time capsule*?

3 Work in groups. Plan your own time capsule, which you will bury under the ground. Discuss which five objects will be most useful for future historians. Use these examples or your own ideas.

a copy of today's newspaper	drawings and diaries
a memory stick with music and movies	a clock
a menu from a restaurant	money (coins and bills)
a popular novel	a can of food

4 As a group, present your final list of objects for the time capsule to the class. Explain the reasons for your choices.

11a The history of video gaming

Reading

1 Work in pairs. Look at the photo below and discuss these questions.

1 When do you think the photo was taken?
2 How many differences can you think of between the game in the photo and modern video games?

The game in the photo is black and white …

2 Work in pairs. Read the timeline of video gaming. Answer the questions.

1 Which video games does the timeline mention?
2 What do you know about these games?
3 Does anyone still play these games today?

3 Read the timeline again. Are these sentences true (T) or false (F)?

1 Pong was a competitive game.	T	F
2 Space Invaders became popular in the 1990s.	T	F
3 A Game Boy was easy to carry around.	T	F
4 The Wii attracted new players to video games.	T	F

Wordbuilding verb + preposition

WORDBUILDING verb + preposition

Many verbs are often used with a preposition. When you learn a new verb, try to also learn the different prepositions you can use with it.
play with (someone), play against (someone), play for (a team), play on (teams)

For more practice, see Workbook page 91.

4 Complete the questions with these prepositions.

about for on with (x3)

1 Do you often play video games _____ friends?
2 Which video games are most people talking _____ these days?
3 How much do you normally pay _____ a mobile video game?
4 How much do you spend _____ video games every month?
5 When you leave the house, what do you always take _____ you?
6 Some people think video games are bad for you. Do you agree _____ them?

5 Work in pairs. Take turns asking and answering the questions in Exercise 4.

87

A timeline of VIDEO GAMING

1970

The first video games appeared in the 50s and 60s, but the first really successful game was Pong, which came out in 1972. People said that they had never seen anything like it before. It was one of the first home video games that you played against another person for points.

1980

When people remember playing video games in the late 70s and early 80s, they often think of Space Invaders. That's because everyone was talking about it at the time. People of all ages said they loved it!

1990

Much smaller video game devices became available in the 90s. For example, you could take the Game Boy with you anywhere. It had lots of different games, including Tetris, which was the most popular. Many gamers said they played Tetris for hours and weren't able to stop!

Grammar reported speech

▶ REPORTED SPEECH

We use reported speech to report what someone said in the past.

1 *People said that they **had** never **seen** anything like it.*
2 *People of all ages said they **loved** it!*
3 *Nintendo said they **were working** on a new type of gaming device.*
4 *Nintendo said that they **would** produce games for the whole family to play.*

Note: After the reporting verb *said*, you can use *that* but you don't have to.

For more information and practice, see page 176.

6 Look at the grammar box. Match the sentences with reported speech (1–4) to these sentences with direct speech (a–d).

a People of all ages said, "We love it!" ___
b Nintendo said, "We are working on a new type of gaming device." ___
c Nintendo said, "We will produce games for the whole family to play." ___
d People said, "We've never seen anything like it." ___

7 Look at the verbs in the direct speech in Exercise 6 and in the reported speech in the grammar box. Then complete this chart.

Direct speech	Reported speech
Simple present	1 _____
2 _____	Past continuous
Present perfect or simple past	3 _____
4 _____	*Would*

At the beginning of the 21st century, Nintendo said they were working on a new type of gaming device and that they would produce games for the whole family to play. The device was called a Wii, and—unlike other video games—the games were active and involved exercise. The Wii became popular with a new group of people—people over fifty.

2000

8 Read the first sentence in each item, and complete the second sentence with the correct verb form.

1 The boy said, "I love playing Super Mario."
The boy said that he _____ playing Super Mario.
2 She said that she wanted a new Xbox.
She said, "I _____ a new Xbox."
3 The company said, "We are planning a new version of the game."
The company said they _____ a new version of the game.
4 Their message said they had gone to the movies.
Their message said, "We _____ to the movies."
5 My father said, "I bought my first Game Boy in 1990."
My father said he _____ his first Game Boy in 1990.
6 Julian said he would play against us later.
Julian said, "I _____ against you later."

9 ▶ 88 Listen to a short conversation between Jack and Sonia. Write down what they say.

1 Jack: *I need the TV for my game.*
2 Sonia: _____
3 Jack: _____
4 Sonia: *You're always using the TV. I haven't watched it for ages.*
5 Jack: _____

10 Rewrite the conversation from Exercise 9 as reported speech.

1 Jack said that he *needed the TV for his game.*
2 Sonia said that she _____
3 Jack said that he _____
4 Sonia said that Jack _____ and that she _____
5 Jack said that he _____

Speaking myLife

11 Work in pairs. Take turns asking and answering these questions. Write your partner's answers.

1 What kind of games (e.g., board games, video games) are popular in your country?
2 Do you often play any of these games?
3 What type of games do you prefer?

12 Work with a new partner. Report what your previous partner said.

Aniko said that chess was very popular in her country.

11b Messages from the past

Vocabulary communication

1 Work in pairs. Put these types of communication into the correct category in the chart. Can any of them go in both categories?

an email	a letter or card
a newspaper	a phone conversation
a presentation	a sticky note on the fridge
a radio program	a text message
a Whatsapp message	a Facebook page

Personal (with family and friends)	Public (with lots of people)

2 Work in pairs. Which types of communication in Exercise 1 are normally used for these messages (1–6)? Give reasons for your answers.

1 to tell someone you are getting married
2 to say there is a new president
3 to thank someone who lives in another country for a present
4 to ask or remind your brother to feed the cat while you are on vacation
5 to share some family vacation photos
6 to wish someone happy birthday

Listening

3 Work in pairs. Look at the newspaper headline below and the photos. Who do you think wrote the message? What do you think the message says? Tell the class your ideas.

4 ▶ 89 Listen to the news story about the message in the bottle. Number the three parts of the story (a–c) in the order you hear them (1–3).

a the history of messages in bottles ____
b how someone found this message in a bottle ____
c why someone sent this message in a bottle ____

5 ▶ 89 Listen to the news story again. Choose the correct option (a–c) to answer each question.

1 How did the captain feel when he saw a message inside the bottle?
   a surprised
   b worried
   c curious
2 Why had someone written the message?
   a as a love letter
   b because they were lost at sea
   c as part of a scientific experiment
3 Why is this a world record?
   a It's the longest message in a bottle ever found in the ocean.
   b It's the oldest message in a bottle ever found in the ocean.
   c It's the oldest message in a bottle ever written.
4 Why did the ancient Greeks put bottles in the ocean over two thousand years ago?
   a to find out if the Mediterranean Sea and the Atlantic Ocean were connected
   b to send messages to ships in the Mediterranean Sea and the Atlantic Ocean
   c to help sailors who were lost in the Mediterranean Sea and the Atlantic Ocean
5 In 1915, why did the sailor send a message in a bottle to his wife?
   a to say he was coming home
   b to say that he loved her
   c to say where he was

Fishing captain finds one-hundred-year-old message in a bottle at sea

Grammar reporting verbs (*say* and *tell*)

▶ REPORTING VERBS (*SAY* and *TELL*)

1 *He **told news reporters** that he had been very curious when he'd seen a message inside.*
2 *The message **said** that his boat was sinking and that he loved her.*

For more information and practice, see page 176.

6 Work in pairs. Read the sentences in the grammar box and answer these questions.

1 Which verbs report the words of someone?
2 Which reporting verb is followed by an object (e.g., *you, her, them, reporters*)?
3 Which reporting verb is not followed by an object?

7 Circle the correct options to complete the conversation.

A: Did I [1] *say / tell* you there was a great show on TV last night?
B: No. What was it about?
A: Space travel in the next one hundred years. They [2] *said / told* that humans would soon land on Mars.
B: Really? When did they [3] *say / tell* that would happen?
A: The presenter didn't [4] *say / tell* exactly, but probably in the next thirty years.
B: I read an article that [5] *said / told* there would be a hotel on the moon soon.
A: Yes, but someone [6] *said / told* me a few years ago that there were going to be space hotels orbiting the Earth soon, and nothing's happened yet.

8 Report these messages using *said* or *told*.

1 "Your lunch is in the fridge."
She ___*told*___ him that his ___*lunch was in the fridge*___ .
2 "I'm lost in the middle of the city."
He _____ that he _____ .
3 "We're waiting at the café."
They _____ that they _____ .
4 "I'll call you back later."
Dave _____ me that he _____ .
5 "You need to call this number."
The message _____ that I _____ .

Writing and speaking myLife

9 Write a message to put in a bottle in the ocean. Include information about who you are and why you are writing. Use one of these suggestions or your own idea.

- You are lost at sea.
- You are stuck on a desert island.

10 Exchange your message with a partner. Imagine someone has found the message one hundred years in the future. Write a short news report about your partner's message. What did it say?

Today, someone found a message in a bottle at sea. The message was written 100 years ago. The writer said …

11 Read your news report to your partner.

A fishing boat near the Shetland Islands, Scotland

11c Stealing history

Vocabulary ancient history

1 You are going to read an article that includes these words. Match the people (1–4) with the definitions (a–d), and the objects (5–8) with the photos below (e–h).

People	Objects
1 archeologist	5 tomb
2 soldier	6 pot
3 robber	7 painting
4 collector	8 statue

a someone who buys a certain type of object (e.g., coins, paintings) ____
b someone who is in the army ____
c someone who steals from others (and breaks the law) ____
d someone who studies the buildings and objects of people who lived in the past ____

Reading

2 Work in pairs. Look at the title of the article. What do you think the article is about? Why will it mention the four types of people in Exercise 1?

3 Work in pairs. Read the article and check your answers from Exercise 2. Then answer these questions.

1 What was Abu Sir al Malaq called in the past? Why was it famous?
2 What types of people work at Abu Sir al Malaq? Why do robbers go there?
3 What is Amal Farag trying to do?
4 The robbers steal some historical objects to sell. What do they often do with the objects they don't sell?
5 In the past, who else stole or took valuable objects from Egypt?
6 Why does the problem continue?

Critical thinking emotion words

4 Work in pairs. Look at these sentences (1–3) and compare them with the sentences in the article. What extra words does the author use in the article?

1 These people are here to discover more about Egypt's history. (paragraph 2)
2 Her team is trying to save the ancient objects. (paragraph 3)
3 It continues to be big business. (paragraph 4)

5 Work in pairs. Why does the writer use these words? What do they tell us about the writer's opinion?

Word focus *one*

6 Read these sentences (1–4) from the article. Match the uses of *one* in the sentences to the explanations (a–d).

1 There is only sand and stone, with **one or two** small villages nearby.
2 They are moving the objects **one by one** to museums and other safe places.
3 **One day** in 2012, she was working at ...
4 Maybe **one day** the problem will be solved.

a to talk about a particular day in the past ____
b to talk about a careful process ____
c to talk about a small number of people or things ____
d to talk about some point in the future ____

Speaking myLife

7 Work in groups. You want to open a new museum about your local town or city. Make notes about:

- what your town was famous for in the past.
- what historical objects you can show in the museum.
- what you can tell visitors about.

8 Work with another group. Take turns presenting your ideas. Try to use emotion words in your presentation.

*This town **desperately** needs a new museum for a number of reasons. Firstly, ...*

STEALING HISTORY

▶ 90

1 Abu Sir al Malaq is a place about one hundred kilometers south of Cairo in Egypt. In ancient times, it was called Busiris. Busiris was one of Ancient Egypt's largest cities, famous for its architecture and buildings. Nowadays, there is only sand and stone, with one or two small villages nearby. But the area of Abu Sir al Malaq is still famous because of its history.

2 When you arrive at Abu Sir al Malaq, you meet a lot of archeologists. These hardworking people are here to discover more about Egypt's history. Inside the old tombs, they can find pots and paintings that tell us more about Ancient Egypt. Surprisingly, there are also soldiers with guns who protect the archeologists and the ancient tombs. That's because robbers often come to Abu Sir al Malaq and try to steal things. They can sell these historical items for large amounts of money to collectors around the world.

3 Amal Farag is one person who wants to protect the area from robbers. She works for the government, and her team is desperately trying to save the ancient objects. They are moving the objects one by one to museums and other safe places. However, it's almost impossible to save everything. One day in 2012, she was working at a tomb on a hillside when she suddenly met three men. They were stealing some historical objects from a tomb. When they saw Amal and her colleague, they quickly ran away. Typically, robbers take the good pieces and throw away the rest. "For every nice piece," says Amal, "they destroy hundreds."

4 It's wrong to think that stealing historical objects is a modern problem in Egypt. History books describe how people stole from tombs over three thousand years ago. When Roman armies arrived in Egypt, they took gold and valuable objects back to Rome on their ships. And from the 16th to the mid-20th century, different countries controlled Egypt and took away statues and beautiful art. Nowadays, there are laws controlling the movement of historical objects to and from Egypt. Maybe one day the problem will be solved, but in the meantime, it continues—sadly—to be big business.

11d A journey to Machu Picchu

Real life giving a short presentation

1 Work in pairs. Do you ever give talks or presentations in your own language (or in English)? What are they about? Why would people give talks or presentations in these situations?

- at work
- at school
- at the meeting of a local club or town council
- at a special occasion (e.g., a wedding)

2 ▶ 91 Listen to parts of a presentation about Peru and Machu Picchu. Check (✓) the topics the presenter talks about.

- ☐ the people of Peru and their customs
- ☐ the history of Machu Picchu
- ☐ the history of the Incas
- ☐ the capital city of Peru
- ☐ his own journey through Peru
- ☐ the food in Peru

3 ▶ 91 Listen again and complete the expressions for giving a short presentation with the words you hear.

▶ GIVING A SHORT PRESENTATION

Good morning and [1] _____ all for coming.
Today, I'd like to [2] _____ about ...
Let me [3] _____ by telling you about ...
So, that's everything I wanted to [4] _____ about ...
Now, let's [5] _____ at ...
The [6] _____ part of my presentation is about ...
I'd like to [7] _____ you some of my photos.
To sum [8] _____ , ...
Are there any [9] _____ ?

4 Pronunciation pausing

a ▶ 92 Presenters often pause at the end of a sentence, at the end of a phrase, or before and after important words they want to emphasize. Listen to and read the first part of the presentation. Notice the first four pauses (/) and write in the other pauses.

Good morning / and thank you all for coming. / Today, / I'd like to talk about my vacation in Peru, / and in particular, about my journey to Machu Picchu. Machu Picchu is sometimes called "The Lost City of the Incas." Let me begin by telling you about the history of the city.

b Work in pairs. Take turns reading the same part of the presentation with similar pauses.

5 Prepare a short presentation for your partner. Think about a historical place you have visited and make notes for these questions. Then give your presentation.

- Where is it?
- Why is it important?
- Who lived there in the past?

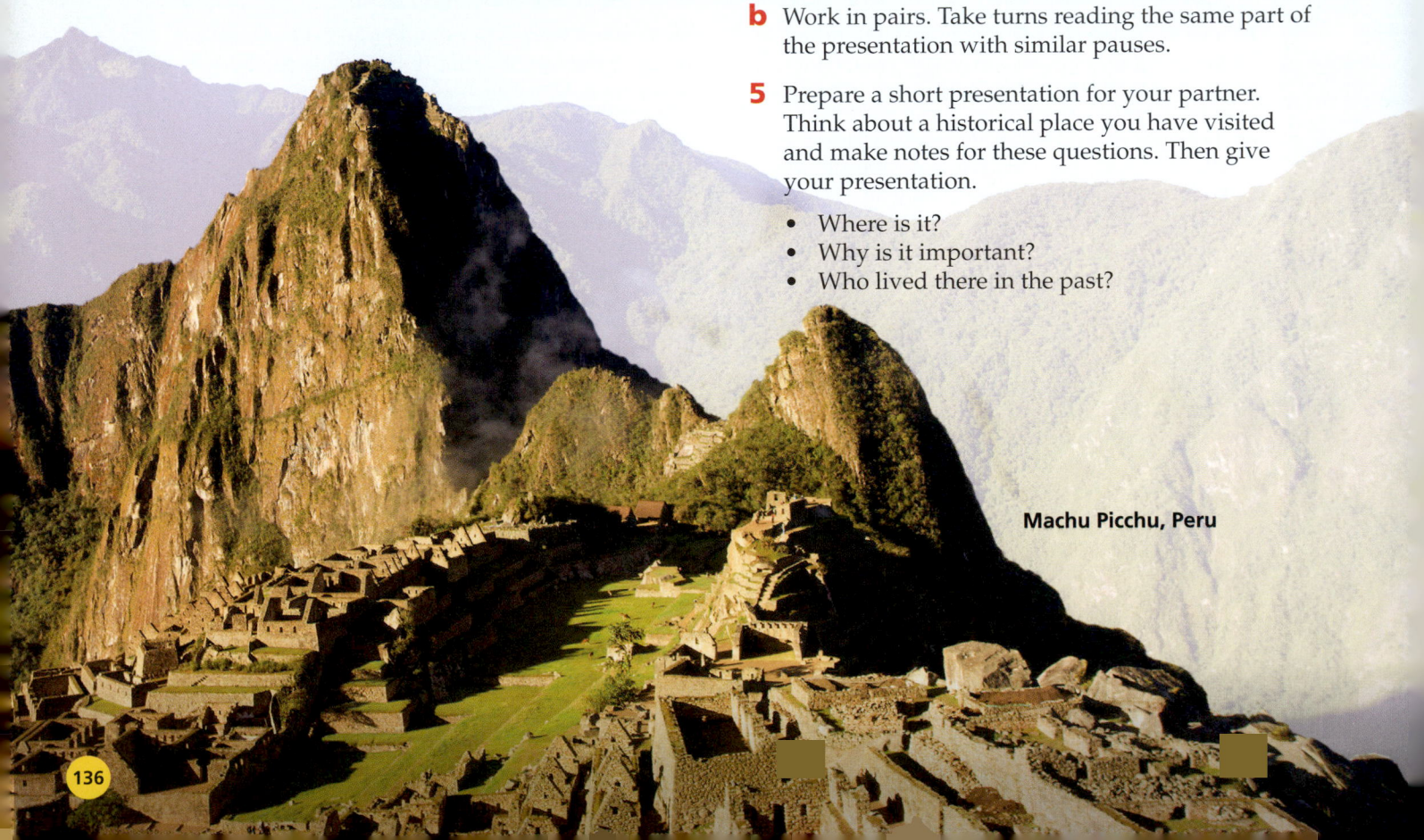

Machu Picchu, Peru

11e The greatest mountaineer

Writing a biography

1 Think of three pieces of information you would expect to find in a biography. Work in pairs and compare your ideas.

2 Read the biography of Reinhold Messner. Does it include your ideas from Exercise 1? Which paragraphs (1–4) mention these topics (a–f)?

a when and where he was born ___
b facts about his childhood and early life ___
c why he became famous ___
d something he said ___
e what other people think or have said about him ___
f what he is doing now ___

3 Writing skill punctuation in direct speech

a The biography of Messner includes direct speech. Underline four examples.

b Work in pairs. Answer these questions (1–4) about punctuation rules for direct speech.

1 Where do you put the two quotation marks?
2 Do you always put a period at the end of the quotation or only if it ends the sentence?
3 Where do you use a comma? What does it separate?
4 Do you always begin a quotation with a capital letter or only if the quotation is a complete sentence?

c Work in pairs. How would you rewrite these sentences with punctuation to show direct speech?

1 My grandfather always told me you should follow your dreams
2 Yes we can said Barack Obama when he campaigned to become the US President
3 Meryl Streep has been described as the greatest actress of her generation
4 Education is the most powerful weapon said Nelson Mandela

4 Write a short biography (100–140 words) about someone famous or someone you admire. Include all the topics in Exercise 2 and use correct punctuation with quotations or direct speech.

5 Exchange your biography with a partner. Use these questions to check your partner's biography.

- Which topics in Exercise 2 has your partner included?
- Is the punctuation in direct speech correct?

The world's greatest mountaineer

1 Reinhold Messner has been described as "the greatest mountaineer in history." He's famous for being one of the first men to climb Mount Everest without oxygen in 1978. He was also the first man to climb all fourteen of the world's mountains over eight thousand meters high.

2 Messner was born in 1944 in a small village in the mountains of northern Italy. When he talks about the area, he still says, "It's the most beautiful place in the world." He started climbing with his father at the age of five. As a teenager, Messner climbed with his younger brother Günther.

3 In their twenties, the two brothers started climbing in the Himalayas, but Günther died in an accident and Reinhold lost six toes. Nevertheless, Reinhold continued climbing and became a legend among other mountaineers. The climber Hans Kammerlander believes Reinhold changed climbing. "Reinhold had so many new ideas," says Kammerlander. "He found new ways, new techniques."

4 Nowadays, Messner spends more time at home with his family, and he has written over sixty books. In 2006 he opened the first Messner Mountain Museum, where people can find out more about the world he loves.

11f The Golden Record

Voyager 1 and the planet Jupiter

Before you watch

1 Key vocabulary

Read the sentences (1–4). The words and phrases in **bold** are used in the video. Write these words and phrases next to their definitions (a–b).

1 The **spacecraft** Voyager 1 was **launched** on August 20th, 1977.
   a sent on a journey (e.g., a boat or a rocket) _____
   b a vehicle used for travel in space _____

2 It is leaving our **solar system** and going farther into **space**.
   a a collection of planets (and their moons) that go around one sun _____
   b the region beyond the Earth's atmosphere _____

3 There's **classical** music from Europe, and **jazz** recordings by Louis Armstrong.
   a type of music written in the eighteenth and nineteenth centuries in Europe _____
   b type of music that originated in African American communities of New Orleans in the early twentieth century _____

4 Voyager carries a message for other **life forms** in the **universe**.
   a all of space and everything in it _____
   b living things or organisms _____

2 Work in pairs. Look at the photo on page 138. Do you think it's important for humans to learn more about space with spacecraft like Voyager 1? Why or why not?

While you watch

3 11.1, 11.2 Watch Parts 1–2 of the video. Work in pairs and answer these questions.

1 Why did Voyager 1 go into space?
2 Where is the Golden Record?
3 What is on the Golden Record?

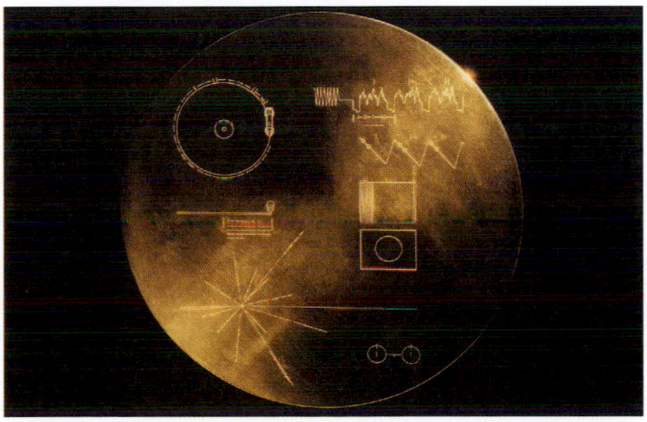

4 11.1 Watch Part 1 of the video again. Are these sentences true (T) or false (F)?

1 A child is speaking on the first message in the video.	T	F
2 Voyager 1's first mission was to photograph Jupiter and Saturn.	T	F
3 The Golden Record has information about the Earth in the year 2000.	T	F
4 A team of six people spent a year deciding what to include on the Golden Record.	T	F

5 11.2 Watch Part 2 of the video again and answer these questions.

1 How many photos are on the Golden Record? _____
2 Number these sounds in the order you hear them (1–5).
   ____ a human heart
   ____ a child crying
   ____ birds and frogs
   ____ wind and rain
   ____ a volcano
3 What language is each message recorded in?
   a "Hello everybody." _____
   b "Hello? How are you?" _____
   c "Greetings to our friends in the stars. We hope that we will meet you someday." _____
   d "Hope everyone's well. We are thinking about you all. Please come here and visit when you have the time." _____

After you watch

6 Vocabulary in context

11.3 Watch the clips from the video. Choose the correct meaning of the words and phrases.

7 Work in groups. Imagine you work for NASA and you are going to send information about the Earth today into space. You can use a memory stick with lots of digital memory. Discuss what to put on the stick.

- What types of photos, videos, sounds, and music will you include?
- What recorded message will you include for other life forms? (e.g., a greeting)
- What else can you include that represents the Earth in the twenty-first century?

8 As a group, present your plans to the rest of the class.

UNIT 11 REVIEW AND MEMORY BOOSTER

Grammar

1 Rewrite the direct speech as reported speech.

1 "I want to fly in space."
He said he _____ .
2 "I'm driving home."
She said she _____ .
3 "He went to the museum."
You said he _____ .
4 "One day I'll visit Rome."
Matt said one day he _____ .

2 Complete the sentences with the correct form of *say* or *tell*.

1 I _____ him to hurry up!
2 Did she _____ what time she was coming?
3 Don't _____ me the answer. I'll figure it out.
4 Who _____ we'd find the tomb here?
5 Did the archeologist _____ who built this house?

3 >> MB Work in pairs. Tell your partner:

- something about the story of this bottle.
- something a news reporter on the TV or radio said recently.
- something your English teacher told you.

I CAN	
use reported speech	☐

Vocabulary

4 Circle the correct options.

In 2010, everyone was talking [1] *on / about* a new video game called Angry Birds. Everyone was playing [2] *in it / it* on their mobile phones because—unlike other types of video games—you didn't have to spend much money [3] *at / on* the app, and you could take it [4] *with / for* you everywhere. For a few months, it was the most popular video game in the world. There were Angry Birds toys and clothes, TV shows, and ads. There is even an Angry Birds theme park in Finland where you can play [5] *about / against* other people using large Angry Birds.

5 Complete the text with these words.

paintings archeologists statues tomb pots

The Inca civilization was the largest civilization in South America in the 13th and 14th centuries. Today, you can visit the huge pyramids that the Incas built, and [1] _____ are still finding Inca objects such as [2] _____ for cooking, or [3] _____ showing pictures from the past. Other items found include [4] _____ , like the one of a llama on the left of the photo. It was found in the [5] _____ of an important person from an ancient Inca city.

I CAN	
use verbs + prepositions	☐
talk about ancient history	☐

Real life

6 Match the beginnings of the sentences (1–5) with their endings (a–e).

1 Good morning everyone ___
2 Today, I'd like to talk ___
3 Let me begin by telling ___
4 Now, let's look ___
5 Before I finish, ___

a you a bit about the city of Pisa.
b and thank you for coming.
c are there any questions?
d about my visit to Italy.
e at my next stop, which was the city of Florence.

7 >> MB Work in pairs. Look at the sentence beginnings (1–5) in Exercise 6. Complete the sentences to make your own presentation.

I CAN	
give a short presentation	☐

Unit 12 Nature

Chasing a tornado in Kansas, USA

FEATURES

142 What if ...?
Discussing the impossible with real science

144 Nature in one cubic foot
Photographing a secret world of animals and plants

146 Living with chimpanzees
The life of Jane Goodall

150 Cambodia animal rescue
A video about the work of an organization that saves animals

1 Work in pairs. Look at the photo and describe what you can see. Use some of these words to help you.

bright	cloud	dark	evening	afternoon
move	rain	light	storm	sun

I think it's the afternoon. There's a tornado and it's moving.

2 ▶ 93 Work in pairs. Listen to part of a documentary about storm chasers and answer the questions.

1 What do most people do when a tornado is coming?
2 What do storm chasers do? Why?
3 What is the most common time of day to see a tornado?
4 Why are tornadoes dangerous?

3 Think about your answers to these questions. Then tell the class.

1 Why do you think people want to be storm chasers?
2 Would you like to be a storm chaser? Why or why not?

12a What if ...?

Vocabulary extreme weather

1 Match these weather words with the photos (a–d).

flood ___	hail ___
snowstorm ___	lightning ___

2 Work in pairs. Discuss these questions.

1 Which parts of the world often have the extreme weather in Exercise 1?
2 Which types of extreme weather do you have in your country? When?
3 What's the weather like today? Is it normal for this time of year?

Reading

3 Read the article. What kind of questions does Randall Monroe answer in his blog?

4 Read the article again and answer these questions with *yes* or *no*.

1 Does Randall work for NASA now? ___
2 Do people send in questions about things that happened to them? ___
3 Does Randall use scientific facts to answer the questions? ___
4 Are you safer from lightning in a boat than in a submarine? ___
5 Can the electricity from lightning move across water? ___
6 Can hail break a car windshield? ___

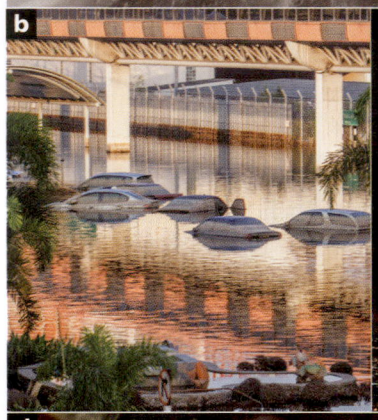

▶ 94

WHAT IF...?

Randall Monroe is a scientist who used to work for NASA. One day, he started a blog called *What if ...?* Every week, people send Randall questions about unlikely or impossible things, and Randall gives scientific answers.

Here are some *What if ...?* questions about weather and nature.

What would happen if lightning hit you in a submarine? What if you were in a boat?
If you were in a submarine, you'd be safe because you'd be underwater. However, lightning usually hits the tallest thing around, so if you were on a flat surface—like in a boat on the ocean—you wouldn't be as safe.

Would I be safe if I was in a swimming pool during a thunderstorm?
You wouldn't be safe if your head was above the water. Lightning might hit you. And if the lightning hit the water near you, the electrical energy would spread outwards across the water.

If it was raining, how fast would you have to drive to break the car windshield?
The rain would break the glass if you drove at the speed of sound. But if you did drive at that speed, the car would take off! Rain won't break the glass if you drive at a normal speed. But in freezing temperatures, hail would break the windshield if you drove fast. In fact, that sometimes happens in some parts of the world.

Grammar second conditional

▶ SECOND CONDITIONAL

***If** you **were** in a submarine, you**'d be** safe.*
***If** you **were** in a boat, you **wouldn't be** as safe.*
*You **wouldn't be** safe **if** your head **was** above the water.*
***Would** I **be** safe **if** I **was** in a swimming pool during a thunderstorm?*
*What **would happen if** lightning **hit** you in a submarine?*

For more information and practice, see page 178.

5 Look at the grammar box. Then circle the correct option (a or b) to complete these sentences.

1 We form the second conditional with ____ .
   a *if* + simple past + *would* + verb
   b *if* + simple present + *will* + verb
2 We use the second conditional to talk about ____ .
   a real situations
   b impossible or unlikely situations
3 The second conditional refers to situations in ____ .
   a the past
   b the present or future
4 A comma separates the two clauses when ____ .
   a the first clause begins with *if*
   b the second clause begins with *if*

6 Work in pairs. Put these words in the correct order to form second conditional sentences. The first word is correct.

1 If / time, / I / had / you / help / I / with / your / 'd / homework / .
2 You / need / help / wouldn't / listened / class / if / you / in / .
3 I / ancient / Rome / 'd / visit / if / time travel / possible / was / .

7 Complete the text about the Gulf Stream with the correct form of the verbs in parentheses.

8 Read the examples and complete the sentences below.

1 It doesn't rain here, so the land is very dry.
   If it ___*rained*___ , the land ___*wouldn't be*___ as dry.
2 The river never floods, so we don't have to leave our homes.
   If the river _____ , we _____ leave our homes.
3 We don't get hot temperatures in my country, so people don't need air conditioning.
   If we _____ hot temperatures in my country, we _____ air conditioning.
4 We don't need to check the weather forecast every day because there are no tornadoes at this time of year.
   If there _____ tornadoes at this time of year, we _____ check the weather forecast every day.

9 Pronunciation *would / wouldn't / 'd*

a ▶ 95 Work in pairs. Listen to a short conversation. How many times do you hear the words *would*, *wouldn't*, and *'d*? Listen again and check.

b Turn to page 189 and practice reading the conversation in track 95 with your partner.

Speaking myLife

10 Work in pairs. Discuss these questions.

1 Would you live in another country if you could? Where would you move to? Why?
2 If you could meet someone famous, who would it be? What would you ask him or her?
3 If you won a lot of money, would you stop working or studying? How would you spend the money?

*If I **won** a lot of money, I'**d buy** a big house.*

What would happen if there wasn't a Gulf Stream?

The Gulf Stream is a stream of warm water that begins in Florida and travels across the Atlantic Ocean. As a result, countries on the west coast of Europe have warmer climates. If the Gulf Stream [1] _____ (stop) flowing, Europe [2] _____ (be) very different. Countries like Great Britain [3] _____ (become) much colder, and spring and summer [4] _____ (not / last) as long. Farmers [5] _____ (not / be able to) grow certain types of food, and heating costs [6] _____ (go up). So if we [7] _____ (not / have) the Gulf Stream, a lot of Europeans [8] _____ (have to) change the way they live.

12b Nature in one cubic foot

Vocabulary nature

1 Work in pairs. Discuss these questions.

1 Do you like taking photos? What kinds of photos do you take?
2 Do you ever take photos of nature? Why or why not?

2 Work in pairs. Look at the photos (A–D). Which of these places (1–8) do you think each photo shows?

1 forest	5 garden
2 mountain	6 ocean
3 field	7 park
4 river	8 desert

3 Work in pairs. Which of the places in Exercise 2 do you:

- see every day?
- see when you go on vacation?
- never see?

Listening

4 ▶ 96 Listen to a documentary about David Liittschwager, the photographer. Why does he take photos of living things in a green metal cube? Discuss with a partner.

5 ▶ 96 Listen to the documentary again. Are these sentences true (T) or false (F)?

1 David Liittschwager wants people to notice the plants and animals near them.	T	F
2 David took his green metal frame to different parts of the world.	T	F
3 He spent three weeks taking photos around the world.	T	F
4 He only photographed living things that were smaller than one millimeter in size.	T	F

Grammar *anywhere, everyone, nobody, something*, etc.

▶ *ANYWHERE, EVERYONE, NOBODY, SOMETHING*, etc.

Affirmative

1 *David Liittschwager wants to show us that everyone can find nature.*
2 *Plants and animals are always somewhere nearby.*

Negative

3 *There's nowhere to enjoy nature.*
4 *You don't think you'll see anybody there except people walking their dogs.*

Question

5 *Did you take pictures of anything interesting?*

For more information and practice, see page 178.

6 Look at the grammar box. Look at the parts of the words highlighted in yellow. Then complete these rules with *-thing*, *-where*, *-body*, or *-one*.

1 We use _____ or _____ to talk about people.
2 We use _____ to talk about places.
3 We use _____ to talk about objects.

7 Look at the parts of the words highlighted in blue in the grammar box. Complete these sentences.

1 _____body loves taking pictures. It's a popular hobby.
2 _____body likes that picture. We all look terrible in it.
3 This picture is too blurry—I don't recognize _____body in it.
4 I know _____body who teaches photography.

8 Read below about the places in the photos (A–D). Circle the correct options.

9 Complete the questions and answers in four different conversations. Use the words highlighted in blue and yellow from the grammar box.

A: Did you go [1] _____where interesting yesterday?
B: No, I stayed in. I wanted to watch [2] _____thing on TV about plants and animals in South Africa.

A: Sorry I'm late. Did [3] _____one call for me?
B: [4] _____body called, but [5] some_____ left this letter at reception.

A: I'm starving. I've had [6] _____thing to eat all day.
B: Well, why don't we go out to eat? There must be a restaurant [7] _____where in this part of town.

A: Have you seen my book? I can't find it. I've searched [8] _____where!
B: No, I haven't. And I didn't move [9] any_____ on your desk when you were out.

Speaking myLife

10 Work in pairs. Complete these questions with words starting with *any-*. Then take turns asking the questions and answering in your own words.

1 Are you going _____ on vacation this year?
2 Did you do _____ interesting last weekend?
3 Have you ever met _____ you know while you were on vacation?

Central Park, New York City

Some people think that there isn't [1] *anywhere / anyone* to see nature in New York City. But Central Park is a quiet place with a forest full of plants and animals. You can always find [2] *somewhere / nowhere* to sit and listen to nature.

Monteverde Reserve, Costa Rica

There's probably [3] *nowhere / nothing* else in the world with so many different plants. There are plants of all sizes and colors [4] *everywhere / somewhere* you look.

Duck River, Tennessee

[5] *Everybody / Somebody* in Tennessee who likes fishing knows about the Duck River. It's one of the best rivers in the USA for different kinds of freshwater animals.

Coral reef, French Polynesia

[6] *Everything / Everybody* looks bright and colorful on a coral reef, and there's always [7] *anything / something* beautiful to look at—from the multi-colored coral to the orange, green, and yellow sea life.

12c Living with chimpanzees

Reading

1 Work in pairs. What are your favorite animals? Explain why.

2 Read the article about Jane Goodall. Which paragraph (1–5) describes:

a Jane's current life and work? ___
b Jane's arrival in Africa? ___
c how Jane became well-known? ___
d Jane's early life studying chimpanzees? ___
e the situation in Gombe in the 1980s? ___

3 Read the article again. Number these events in the order they happened (1–7).

___ The human population in the region increased.
___ Jane became a doctor.
___ A war started in Gombe.
_1_ Jane saw her first chimpanzee.
___ Jane started writing about chimps in a diary.
___ Jane published her first book.
___ Jane left Gombe to travel and give lectures.

4 Match the words and phrases from the article (1–5) with the definitions (a–e).

1 tools (line 17)
2 natural habitat (line 33)
3 survive (line 34)
4 lectures (line 41)
5 conservation (line 47)

a objects for making and doing things ___
b the protection of nature and wildlife ___
c an area where you find a certain type of animal or plant ___
d formal talks on a serious subject given to a group of people ___
e continue to live ___

Critical thinking reading closely

5 Read the article again. Are these sentences true (T) or false (F)? Or is the information not in the article (N)?

1 Jane and her mother didn't arrive in Africa with many possessions.	T	F	N
2 Jane had studied chimpanzees at university before going to Africa.	T	F	N
3 No one knew that chimpanzees ate meat before Jane discovered it.	T	F	N
4 Some scientists didn't believe Jane's research at first.	T	F	N
5 During the seventies and eighties, most of the problems in Gombe were caused by humans.	T	F	N
6 Jane has retired from her work.	T	F	N
7 Jane goes back to Gombe every year.	T	F	N

Word focus *start*

6 Look at the words and phrases in **bold** in these sentences. Match the uses of the word *start* (1–4) to the forms (a–d).

1 Jane Goodall and her mother **started their new lives** in Africa on July 14, 1960.
2 She **started to write** about them in her diary.
3 During the seventies, a war **started**.
4 Jane **started working** with the local people.

a verb + infinitive ___
b verb + *-ing* form ___
c verb + noun phrase ___
d verb (not followed by an object or a verb) ___

7 Match these questions (1–4) with their answers (a–d).

1 Why did you start to learn English?
2 What time does the soccer game start?
3 If you started a new life, what would you do?
4 When did you start working here?

a Two years ago. ___
b I thought it would be useful in the future. ___
c I don't know. Maybe I'd go and work with animals somewhere. ___
d At three o'clock tomorrow. ___

Speaking myLife

8 Work in pairs. Write four interview questions for Jane Goodall using the information in the article.

When did you see a chimpanzee for the first time?

9 Work with another pair and take turns asking and answering your questions from Exercise 8. Imagine you are Jane Goodall when answering.

A: When did you become a doctor?
B: I became a doctor in 1966.

▶ 97

1 Jane Goodall and her mother started their new lives in Africa on July 14, 1960. They arrived on the east shore of Lake Tanganyika in Gombe National Park. A group of men met them and carried their luggage. They didn't have very much: a tent, a few clothes, and a cup. Later the same day, somebody said they had seen a chimpanzee. Right away, Jane started running toward the forest, where she saw a chimpanzee for the first time.

2 Jane had always dreamed of visiting Africa and studying chimpanzees, but she didn't know much about them and she had no scientific qualifications. However, after she arrived in Gombe, she spent many months watching groups of these animals and learning about them. She started to write about them in her diary, and after many months of difficult work, she made three important and new discoveries: Chimpanzees ate meat; they used tools to get food; and they made tools of their own.

3 Jane began to publish articles in journals such as *National Geographic* magazine. After a while, scientists started reading her articles, and she was invited to study at a university. Finally, in 1966, she became Doctor Jane Goodall. Her work also made her famous. There was a film documentary called *Miss Goodall and the Wild Chimpanzees* (1965), and then the first of many books, *My Friends, the Wild Chimpanzees* (1967).

4 During the seventies, there was a war in the region, and Gombe became a dangerous place. Many foreigners left, but Jane stayed. Eventually the war ended, but there was another problem at the start of the 1980s. As the human population increased in Gombe, more trees were cut down. With fewer trees, the chimpanzees lost their natural habitat, and it became difficult for them to survive. By the end of the decade, only about a hundred chimpanzees were living in Gombe. At this time, Jane started working with local people to grow more trees in the region.

5 After 1989, Jane left Gombe and started traveling to other parts of the world. She gave lectures about her work, and she organized safe places for young chimps whose parents had died or been killed. Now in her eighties, she spends about three hundred days a year giving interviews and lectures, meeting with government officials about animal conservation, and raising money for the Jane Goodall Institute—which continues her research. And she still spends part of every year in the forest in Gombe, watching her chimpanzees.

The life of Jane Goodall

12d Discussing issues

Real life finding a solution

1 Work in pairs. Look at the photo of the tiger in a zoo and answer the questions.

1 How do you think the tiger feels? How do you think the girl feels?
2 Do you ever visit zoos? Why or why not?

2 Work in pairs. Read the newspaper article below. What problem does the council need to solve? What would happen to the animals if the zoo closed?

Animals have nowhere to go

The city's zoo is going to close in six months' time if the city council cannot solve the problem of too few visitors and lack of money. The zoo manager is worried about the animals at the zoo. "If the zoo closed, they wouldn't be able to go back into their natural habitat. We'd have to find them a new home."

3 ▶ 98 Listen to a conversation between the leader of the city council and the zoo manager. Are these sentences true (T) or false (F)?

1 The city council doesn't have any money for the zoo.	T	F
2 The zoo manager thinks zoos help some animals to survive.	T	F
3 The zoo manager likes the suggestion about advertising.	T	F
4 The zoo manager likes the suggestion about sponsorship.	T	F

4 ▶ 98 Complete the sentences with these phrases. Then listen again and check.

But if we don't	I'm sorry, but	that isn't
we can't	What if you	why don't you

1 _____ the council doesn't have any more money for the zoo.
2 _____ find a solution soon, then we'll have to close.
3 _____ advertised more?
4 But if we don't have any money, _____ advertise.
5 Well, _____ try sponsorship?
6 Actually, _____ a bad idea.

5 Work in pairs. Match the sentences in Exercise 4 with the correct category of expressions for finding a solution.

▶ FINDING A SOLUTION

Stating and explaining the problem
The problem is that ...

Making suggestions
We could also ... | How about ...

Responding positively
That's a good idea. | You might be right!

Responding negatively
Yes, but ... | No, that won't work.

6 Work in groups of four. Have a meeting between the zoo manager and the employees to discuss the zoo's problems. Try to find a solution(s) that everyone agrees with.

Student A: Turn to page 153.
Student B and Student D: Turn to page 155.
Student C: Turn to page 154.

12e The Eden Project

Writing an article

1 Work in pairs. Read the article about the Eden Project and answer the questions.

1 What can you see at the Eden Project?
2 Why do people visit the Eden Project?

A biome at the Eden Project

The Eden Project

Since it opened in 2001 in the southwest of England, millions of people have visited the Eden Project and learned about the natural world. It is one of England's most important tourist destinations.

As soon as you arrive, you see the huge plastic domes called "biomes." The two biggest biomes are the Rainforest Biome and the Mediterranean Biome. The Rainforest Biome has a warm climate, with plants from parts of Asia, Africa, and South America. The Mediterranean Biome has over 1,000 different plants from countries around the Mediterranean Sea and from California and South Africa.

In addition to the biomes, the Eden Project has outdoor gardens with plants and flowers you can use for medicine, fuel, and food. There are also art exhibitions, theater performances, and outdoor concerts throughout the year. Groups of schoolchildren regularly visit, and there are courses for adults about plants and nature.

So the Eden Project is not just a tourist attraction. It aims to educate people about the importance of plants in our lives, and to protect plants that are in danger of disappearing from the Earth.

2 Writing skill planning an article

a Work in pairs. The writer used the Eden Project website to research and plan this article. Think of three more ways to research an article.

b When you plan an article, it's useful to write questions and organize information using a mind map. Match the questions (a–f) with the information in the mind map (1–6).

a What is the place called? ___
b When and where did it open? ___
c Why is it important? ___
d What's the most interesting thing about the place? ___
e Who visits it? ___
f What else is there? ___

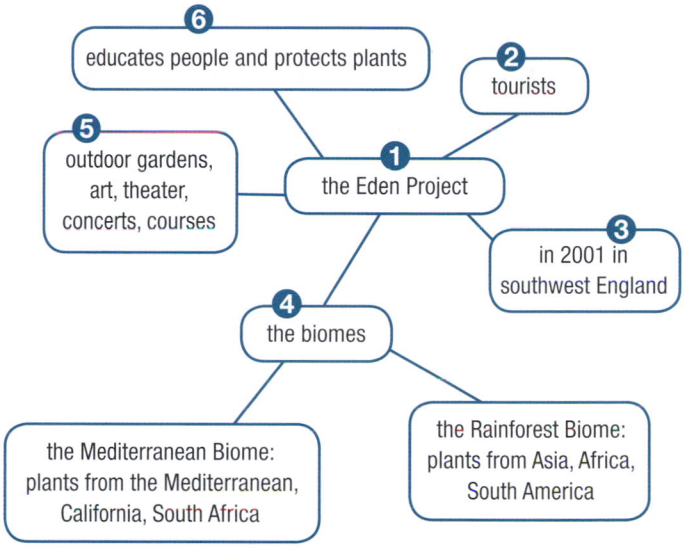

c Work in pairs. Look at the mind map and read the article again. How does the writer organize his information? Match the information in the mind map (1–6) to these parts of the article:

- the introduction (paragraph 1)
- paragraph 2
- paragraph 3
- the conclusion (paragraph 4)

3 Plan and write an article about a place you know or would like to visit. Follow these steps:

1 Decide where you can research the information.
2 Write questions you want to answer, and find the information.
3 Plan the article with a mind map.
4 Decide which information will go in which paragraph.
5 Write the article using the mind map.

12f Cambodia animal rescue

At the Phnom Tamao Rescue Center in Cambodia, there is one thing many of the animals have in common ...

Before you watch

1 Work in pairs. You are going to watch a video about an animal rescue center in Cambodia. Look at the photos and answer these questions.

1 What kinds of animals can you see?
2 What do they have in common?
3 How do you think the rescue center helps them?

2 Key vocabulary

Read these sentences (1–7) from the video. Write the words in **bold** next to their definitions (a–h).

1 Many animals at the center are brought in by a special team called the Wilderness **Protection** Mobile Unit (MU).
2 **Poachers** can make a lot of money.
3 Matt Young works for Wild Aid, a US group that **sponsors** the MU and the rescue center.
4 Once we're sure they're nice and healthy again, we can get them out to Kirirom and **release** them.
5 Dara, and the other animals at the Phnom Tamao Rescue Center, are all **victims** of the **illegal** poaching of wild animals in Cambodia.
6 In some Asian countries, certain parts of the tiger are **ground** into powder.
7 The MU can help stop more wild animals from becoming **endangered**.

a people or animals that are harmed by an unpleasant event _____
b not allowed by law _____
c set someone or something free _____
d at risk of extinction _____
e crushed into very small pieces or particles _____
f the action of keeping someone or something safe _____
g people who kill or capture animals illegally _____
h gives money to _____

While you watch

3 12.1 Watch the video. Check (✓) the animals you see.

☐ tiger ☐ giant panda
☐ rhinoceros ☐ bear
☐ eagle ☐ elephant
☐ gibbon ☐ snake
☐ orangutan ☐ leopard

4 Match the animals (1–5) with the correct phrases from the video (a–e).

1 The tiger
2 The eagles
3 The gibbon
4 The bear
5 The elephants

a was found in a birdcage in a gas station. ____
b is called Mimi and was someone's pet. ____
c need special care and are fed by hand. ____
d are called Lucky and Sima. ____
e is called Dara and loves to play. ____

5 12.1 Work in pairs. Watch the video again and answer the questions.

1 What does the MU do?
2 Why did the family take Mimi to the rescue center?
3 According to the narrator, what would happen to the animals if they weren't at the rescue center?
4 Why are tiger products (e.g., ground powder) popular in some countries?
5 How many animals does the rescue center care for?
6 Can Lucky and Sima be returned to the wild in the future? Why or why not?

After you watch

6 Vocabulary in context

a 12.2 Watch the clips from the video. Choose the correct meaning of the words and phrases.

b Complete this summary of the video using words from Exercise 6a. The first letter is provided.

> The animal rescue center gives special [1]c_____ to many different animals. With [2]s_____ from the government, the center takes care of [3]r_____ animals. Sometimes the animals have been kept as pets that people found too hard to [4]h_____. But many of the animals are also in danger from poaching because parts of their body are in [5]d_____ and are sold for a lot of money.

7 Discuss these questions as a class.

1 Does animal poaching exist in your country? What animals do the poachers catch? Why?
2 Why are places like the Phnom Tamao Rescue Center important? Do you have similar organizations in your country?

UNIT 12 REVIEW AND MEMORY BOOSTER

Grammar

1 Complete the second conditional sentences with the correct form of the verbs in parentheses.

1 If it was hotter, we _____ (go) to the beach.
2 The grass would be much greener if it _____ (rain).
3 We _____ (not / need) air conditioning if we moved to a colder climate.
4 They wouldn't eat my cooking if they _____ (not / like) it!

2 Complete these sentences so they are true for you. Then compare your sentences with a partner.

1 If I had a million dollars, I'd …
2 If I could go anywhere in the world, I'd go to …

3 Complete the sentences with these pairs of words.

anyone + anywhere	everyone + anything
nobody + everybody	someone + somewhere
something + nothing	

1 _____ told me there's a snake _____ in the grass, so be careful.
2 Has _____ seen Michelle? I can't find her _____ .
3 _____ is hungry. Is there _____ in the fridge?
4 I left a message, but _____ called me back. Is _____ on vacation?
5 I'd like _____ special to eat, but _____ on the menu looks very interesting.

4 >> MB Work in pairs. Can you remember why the photographer used this green cube? Complete the sentences.

- The photographer thinks everyone lives near …
- He took pictures of everything …

I CAN	
use the second conditional	☐
use words starting with *any-, every-, no-, some-*	☐

Vocabulary

5 >> MB Work in pairs. Look at these photos from the unit and answer the questions for each photo.

1 What time of day is it?
2 What's the weather like?

6 Work in pairs. Look at these words for places in nature. Compare the two places in each pair and say one similarity and one difference.

forest / park
They both have trees, but a forest has a lot more trees.

river / ocean	field / forest	ocean / desert

I CAN	
talk about the weather	☐
talk about places in nature	☐

Real life

7 Work in pairs. Put these words in the correct order to form sentences for finding a solution.

1 opening / about / how / a new zoo?
2 help? / why / ask for / don't / we
3 won't / we / sell any products / if / advertise / we don't
4 the / that / many people / don't / problem is / recycle plastic
5 but / work / that / I'm sorry, / won't
6 good / a / idea / that's

8 >> MB Work in pairs and look at these problems. Make suggestions to solve the problems.

- Animals have nowhere to go if we close the zoo.
- A school has no money to buy new technology.
- A restaurant doesn't have many customers.

I CAN	
find a solution to a problem	☐

UNIT 1a Exercise 3, page 10

How well do you sleep?

Mostly A answers:
The average human needs around eight hours of sleep per night. You probably get this because you usually sleep very well. You have regular routines, and you are hardly ever tired.

Mostly B answers:
You sleep quite well. Maybe you wake up once or twice a night and that's normal. But you have a busy life, so you need extra hours in bed. Try to go to bed early during the week, and sleep an extra hour over the weekends.

Mostly C answers:
You work hard and get home late, and sometimes work in the evening at home, so you probably don't get the sleep you need. Try to relax in the evening and go to bed early.

UNIT 5b Exercise 12, page 61

Pair A

Write questions for these answers or use your own ideas (e.g., write questions about your own country).

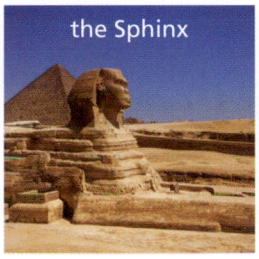

UNIT 5d Exercise 6, page 64

Student A

1 You ordered some clothes online. You received an email from the company. The clothes are not in stock. Call the customer service helpline.

- Say why you are calling.
- Your order number is EI3304A.
- Spell your last name.
- Find out how long you have to wait for the clothes.
- Ask for a refund. The price was $149.50.

2 You are a customer service assistant for a book supplier. Answer the telephone.

- Ask for the customer's order number and the title of the book.
- The book isn't in stock. You don't know when the book will arrive.
- Offer the caller a second-hand copy of the same book. It's $3.50.

UNIT 12d Exercise 6, page 148

Student A

You are the zoo manager and will lead the meeting. Here are two possible suggestions. You can also make your own suggestions.

- Ask companies to sponsor different animals. Their company name will be on a sign near the animal.
- Organize a special day when everyone in the city can visit the zoo for free to learn more about their zoo.

When you are ready to begin the meeting, explain the problem and then discuss each suggestion from your employees. Start your meeting by saying: *Hello, everyone. Thank you for coming. Today we are going to discuss the zoo. The problem is that …*

UNIT 5b Exercise 12, page 61

Pair B

Write questions for these answers or use your own ideas (e.g., write questions about your own country).

UNIT 5d Exercise 6, page 64

Student B

1 You are a customer service representative for a clothing company supplier. Answer the telephone.

- Ask for the customer's order number and his / her last name.
- The clothes aren't in stock, but they will be in two weeks.
- Offer some different clothes at the same price.

2 You ordered a book online called *Learn Spanish in One Week*. You received an email from the company. The book is not in stock. Call the customer service helpline.

- Say why you are calling.
- Your order number is AZE880.
- Find out how long you have to wait for the book.
- Ask for the price of the second-hand copy.
- Buy the second-hand book.

UNIT 12d Exercise 6, page 148

Student C

You work for the zoo. Here are two possible suggestions to make at the meeting. You can also make your own suggestions.

- Start a zoo shop that sells T-shirts, posters, hats, etc.
- Invite newspaper and TV journalists to a special day where you explain the importance of the zoo and its conservation work.

UNIT 9d Exercise 6, page 112

Student B

You work at a tourist information booth. Look at the information about the Caves of Lascaux. Answer the tourist's questions and make suggestions.

The Caves of Lascaux are in the Dordogne region of France. The paintings there are over 17,000 years old.

Hours: Open every day, 9 a.m. to 5 p.m.
Ticket price: Adults: 8 euros, Children: 5 euros
Transportation: Buses leave every 15 minutes from the city center. Taxis also available.
Tours: Free tours are available, but please book in advance.

UNIT 12d Exercise 6, page 148

Student B

You work for the zoo. Here are two possible suggestions to make at the meeting. You can also make your own suggestions.

- Offer special tickets with discounts, such as a "family ticket" or cheaper prices for children.
- Ask people to buy an animal that lives at the zoo.

UNIT 1e Exercise 3b, page 17

1 DOB = Date of birth, No. = number, etc. = et cetera (Latin for "and the rest"), e.g. = for example
2 *Mr.* is used before the name of any man. *Mrs.* is used before the name of a married woman. *Ms.* is used before the name of a woman when we don't know if she is married or single, or if she prefers not to say. *Dr.* means Doctor.
3 Form B: It says "Please use capital letters" at the top.

UNIT 4c Exercise 1, page 50

The riddle: The answer is "your name."
The matchstick puzzle: Move two matches.

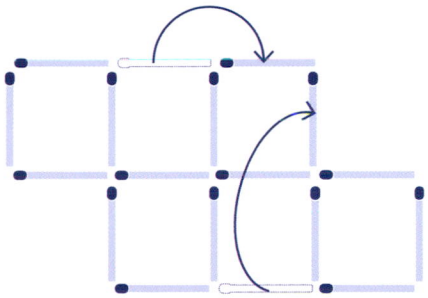

The numbers memory challenge: Most people can remember up to the seven numbers in 7430673, but find it difficult to remember eight numbers or more.

UNIT 12d Exercise 6, page 148

Student D

You work for the zoo. Here are two possible suggestions to make at the meeting. You can also make your own suggestions.

- Contact other zoos and exchange animals, so people will want to come back to look at different animals.
- Have a parade downtown with costumes and food, and some of the animals.

UNIT 5b Exercise 11, page 61

1 the Amazon River
2 the president of the United States
3 the moon
4 Google
5 the Pacific Ocean

UNIT 7a Exercise 1, page 82

According to a report in *Forbes* magazine, these are the jobs employers find most difficult to fill in the US.

1 home health aide
2 physical therapist
3 financial advisor
4 information security analyst
5 medical services manager
6 software engineer
7 registered nurse
8 data scientist
9 general and operations manager
10 truck driver

UNIT 9d Exercise 6, page 112

Student A

You are the tourist. Look at the information about the Caves of Lascaux. Ask questions and complete the missing information.

The Caves of Lascaux are in the Dordogne region of France. The paintings there are over 17,000 years old.

Hours: Open every day, [1]____ a.m. to 5 p.m.
Ticket price: Adults: [2]____ euros,
Children: 5 euros
Transportation: Buses leave every 15 minutes from [3]_____ .
Tours: There are [4]_____ , but please book in advance.

GRAMMAR SUMMARY UNIT 1

Simple present and adverbs of frequency

Use

We use the simple present:

- to talk about habits and routines.
  *I **play** tennis every week.*
- to talk about things that are always true.
  *Sleep **is** really important for health.*

Form

We form the simple present with the base form of the verb. To make negative sentences, we add *don't* before the verb. To make questions, we add *do* before the subject.

After *he, she, it*, etc., we add *-s* to the verb. We use *doesn't* in negative sentences, and *does* in questions.

	+	–	?
I/you/we/they	*I **eat**.*	*You **don't eat**.*	***Do** you **eat**?*
he/she/it	*She **eats**.*	*He **doesn't eat**.*	***Does** he/she/it **eat**?*

The verb *be* is different from other verbs.

	+	–	?
I	*I'm fit.*	*I'm **not** fit.*	***Am** I fit?*
you/we/they	*We're fit.*	*They **aren't** fit.*	***Are** you fit?*
he/she/it	*She's fit.*	*She **isn't** fit.*	***Is** he fit?*

▶ Exercise 1

Adverbs and expressions of frequency

We use adverbs and other expressions in simple present sentences to talk about how often we do things.

*Mike **usually** goes for a run in the evening.*
*I'm **often** late for work.*
*I have a hot drink **five or six times a day**.*
*We go on vacation **two or three times a year**.*

Some common frequency adverbs are:

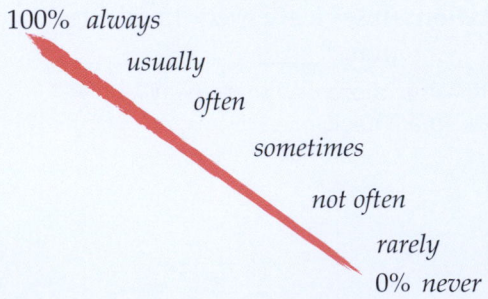

Position

Frequency adverbs and expressions of frequency go in different places in a sentence.

- Adverbs of frequency go before the main verb, but after the verb *be*.
  *They **never** eat out.*
  *She's **always** out on the weekend.*
  *I do**n't often** play sports.*
- Expressions of frequency normally go at the beginning or end of a sentence.
  *I go out with friends **three or four times a week**.*
  ***Once a week**, I go for a run.*

▶ Exercises 2 and 3

Present continuous

Use

We use the simple present to talk about things we do or that happen regularly. We use the present continuous to talk about something in progress in the present. This can be:

- something actually in progress at this moment.
  *I can't answer the phone because I'**m driving**.*
- something happening around now, but not necessarily at this moment.
  *I'**m looking** for a new job.*
- a changing situation.
  *More and more people **are changing** their diet.*

Form

We form the present continuous with *be* + verb + *-ing*.

	+	–	?
I	*I'm **writing**.*	*I'm **not writing**.*	***Am** I **writing**?*
you/we/they	*We're **writing**.*	*They **aren't writing**.*	***Are** you **writing**?*
he/she/it	*He's **writing**.*	*She **isn't writing**.*	***Is** she **writing**?*

Some verbs describe states (for example, *agree, believe, own, hate, know, like, love, prefer, want*). We don't use these verbs with the continuous.

~~*He's **owning** a really nice car.*~~
*He **owns** a really nice car.*

▶ Exercises 4, 5, and 6

Exercises

1 Complete the sentences with the simple present form of the verbs in parentheses.

1 Sam _____ (not live) near me.
2 Sofia _____ (drive) to work.
3 _____ she _____ (speak) any other languages?
4 I _____ (not like) waking up early.
5 _____ they _____ (see) each other on the weekends?
6 We _____ (be) very tired.
7 Some people _____ (not need) a lot of sleep.
8 _____ (be) your bus late?
9 He _____ (have) a big house in the country.

2 Look at the sentences. Find and correct the mistakes with the position of frequency adverbs and time expressions.

1 I often am tired at work.
2 We twice a week eat out in a restaurant.
3 I have two or three times a day a cup of coffee.
4 They don't play often board games.
5 Does usually she take public transportation?

3 Complete the text with words from the boxes. Use an expression from box A and a verb from box B in each pair of blanks.

A ~~always~~ every day often rarely two or three times a month

B eat (x2) ~~get up~~ go meet

I [1] *always* [2] *get up* at about 7:30 a.m. and get ready for work. I [3] _____ [4] _____ breakfast because I don't feel hungry in the mornings. I start work at 9 a.m., and at 12 noon I take a lunch break. I [5] _____ [6] _____ my friend for lunch—normally two or three times a week. At 1:30 I start work again, and I finish at 5:30 p.m. I like to keep fit, so I [7] _____ to the gym [8] _____. I get home at about 8:00 p.m. and make dinner, but I also [9] _____ at restaurants [10] _____. I'm always tired in the evenings, so I go to bed early. And that's my day!

4 Complete the sentences with the present continuous form of these verbs.

become build go not work
talk wait write

1 I _____ for the bus.
2 A: Where _____ you _____?
B: To the supermarket. We need milk!
3 She _____ this week because she's on vacation.
4 A: What are you doing?
B: I _____ an email to my friend.
5 A: Where's Michael?
B: He _____ to someone on the phone.
6 They _____ a new house on my street.
7 More and more people _____ vegetarians.

5 Complete the pairs of sentences with the verbs in parentheses. Use the simple present form in one sentence and the present continuous form in the other.

1 I _____ my lunch very early today. I normally _____ at 1 p.m. (eat)
2 Tina rarely _____ to work. But today she _____ because of the rain. (drive)
3 She _____ to her brother on the phone right now. They _____ at this time every day. (talk)
4 It's 6 p.m. and I _____ hard in the office. I normally _____ only until 5 p.m. (work)
5 I _____ shopping now. I always _____ shopping at this time. (go)

6 Complete the text with the simple present or present continuous form of the verbs in parentheses.

The Mediterranean diet

People in countries like Italy, Spain, France, and Greece [1] _____ (live) longer than people from many other countries. This is probably because of their diet—they [2] _____ (eat) lots of food like vegetables, fruits, nuts, beans, fish, and olive oil. People often [3] _____ (say) that this diet [4] _____ (be) good for your heart. But the traditional Mediterranean diet [5] _____ (change) because more and more people [6] _____ (eat) junk food. So, in the future, the Mediterranean diet might be very different.

GRAMMAR SUMMARY UNIT 2

Modal verbs for rules

Use

To talk about rules, we use the modal verbs *must*, *have to*, and *can*.

- To say that something is obligatory, we use *must* or *have to*.
  *You **have to** train hard to run a marathon.*
  *Runners **must** arrive twenty minutes before the race.*
- To say that something is allowed, we use *can*.
  *Members **can** use the swimming pool for free.*
- To say that something is not obligatory but allowed, we use *don't have to*.
  *You **don't have to** be fit to join the club.*
- To say that something is not allowed, we use *can't* or *must not*.
  *You **can't** touch the ball with your hands or arms in soccer.*
  *You **must not** leave any bags in this area.*

The modal verbs *must* and *have to*, and *can't* and *must not*, have very similar meanings. In general, we prefer to use *have to* and *can't* in spoken English to talk about rules. In formal written English, we prefer to use *must* and *must not*.

*You **have to** pay $40 to be in the race.* (spoken)
*Competitors **must** pay $40 to enter the race.* (formal, written)
*You **can't** go near the pool with shoes on.* (spoken)
*Customers **must not** go near the pool with shoes on.* (formal, written)

But remember that *must not* and *don't have to* have completely different meanings—*mustn't* means "don't do it!," while *don't have to* means "it's not necessary to do it."

Form

We normally use modal verbs before a main verb.
*You **can** borrow my running shoes.*

The modal verbs *must/must not* and *can/can't* don't work like normal verbs. They never change—we use the same form for all persons (*I, you, he/she/it*, etc.). We don't use *do, does*, or *did* to make questions or negatives.

	+	–	?
I/you/we/they	*I **can** swim.*	*I **can't** swim.*	***Can** you swim?*
he/she/it	*She **can** swim.*	*He **can't** swim.*	***Can** he swim?*

The modal verb *have to* works like a normal verb. It changes for *he/she/it* in the simple present, and we form questions and negatives in the past and present using *do, does*, or *did*.

	+	–	?
I/you/we/they	*I **have to** go.*	*I **don't have to** go.*	***Do** you **have to** go?*
he/she/it	*He **has to** go.*	*She **doesn't have to** go.*	***Does** she **have to** go?*

▶ Exercises 1, 2, and 3

-ing form

We use the *-ing* form of a verb after *be* to form the present or past continuous.
*I'm **getting** ready to go out.*
*I was **watching** a movie.*

However, we also use the *-ing* form in some other ways.

-ing form as the subject of a sentence

We can make a verb the subject of a sentence. When we do this, we usually use the *-ing* form.
***Playing** sports is great for your health.*

-ing form after prepositions

When a verb comes after a preposition, it is always in the *-ing* form.
*I'm not very good at **swimming**.*

-ing form after some verbs

We sometimes put two verbs together in a sentence. The form of the second verb depends on the first verb. After the verbs *like, dislike, love, hate, can't stand, enjoy*, and *don't mind*, the second verb is in the *-ing* form.
*Jan loves **watching** sports.*
*I don't mind **running** in the cold.*

▶ Exercises 4 and 5

Exercises

1 Match the rules (1–6) with the meanings (a–c).

a Do this.
b Don't do this.
c This is allowed.

1 You must wear your seat belt in a car. ____
2 You can't hit the ball with your hand in soccer. ____
3 Boxers have to wear special gloves. ____
4 You can walk in a marathon. ____
5 The students can't use their cell phones during the exam. ____
6 We can take photos during the tennis match. ____

2 Circle the correct options to complete the sentences.

1 You *must not / don't have to* kick the ball when you play basketball. You can only use your hands.
2 We *must not / don't have to* go to the football game. We can watch it on television.
3 If the fire alarm rings, you *must / don't have to* go straight outside. It's important to be quick.
4 In many countries, you *must / must not* wait until you are 18 to drive. It's not possible if you're younger.
5 You *don't have to / must not* come tonight. Stay at home if you prefer.

3 Circle the correct options to complete this email.

How are you? I'm doing well. You asked me in your email about the gym I go to, so here's some information for you. You [1] *have to / must* pay for a whole month—you [2] *don't have to / can't* pay for one visit. When you pay, they give you a gym card. You [3] *don't have to / must not* forget this card because you need it to get in the gym.

I like to use the bikes in the gym. I usually ride for about an hour, but when there are a lot of people, you [4] *can't / must not* use the bikes for a long time. I also do a yoga class once or twice a week. You [5] *don't have to / must not* sign up in advance, so I usually decide when I arrive. One last thing—you [6] *must / can't* remember to bring towels with you because the gym doesn't give them to you.

Why don't you come with me to the gym next week? I can show you everything. Let me know!

4 Complete the sentences with the *-ing* form of a verb from the box.

fail	play	help	watch	wake up	read

1 She's really good at _____ the piano.
2 I don't like _____ TV—it's so boring!
3 He hates _____ early on the weekends.
4 I'm worried about _____ my exam.
5 _____ a book is a great way to pass the time on a train.
6 Thank you for _____ me with my work.

5 Circle the correct options to complete the conversation.

A: Why are you [1] *cleaning / clean* the house?
B: It's dirty. Why?
A: It's such a nice day. Why don't we [2] *doing / do* something outside? [3] *Staying / Stay* at home is so boring.
B: OK. What do you think about [4] *go / going* for a run?
A: I hate [5] *run / running*!
B: OK, how about [6] *going / go* for a walk in the mountains?
A: That's a good idea. We could [7] *taking / take* a picnic with us.
B: Great! I love [8] *eat / eating* outside on a sunny day.
A: Good—you can [9] *making / make* the picnic for us, then!

GRAMMAR SUMMARY UNIT 3

Comparatives and superlatives

Form

Adjective	Comparative	Superlative
slow	*slower*	*(the) slowest*
easy	*easier*	*(the) easiest*
difficult	*more difficult*	*(the) most difficult*
good	*better*	*(the) best*

For most **one-syllable adjectives**, we add ***-er*** to form the comparative, and we add ***-est*** to form the superlative.

*fast → fast**er** / fast**est* *old → old**er** / old**est***

For most adjectives that have **two or more syllables**, we use ***more*** + adjective to form the comparative, and we use ***most*** + adjective to form the superlative.

*useful → **more** useful / **most** useful*
*expensive → **more** expensive / **most** expensive*

For **some two-syllable adjectives** (often adjectives that end in *-y*, *-le*, *-ow*, and *-er*), we can use either *-er* or *more* to form the comparative, and *-est* or *most* to form the superlative. We sometimes use one form more than the other (e.g., *narrower* is more common than *more narrow*, whereas *friendlier* and *more friendly* are both common).

friendly → friendlier or *more friendly*
friendliest or *most friendly*
simple → simpler or *more simple*
simplest or *most simple*
narrow → narrower or *more narrow*
narrowest or *most narrow*

Spelling rules

Note the following spelling rules when adding *-er* or *-est* to adjectives.

- For adjectives that end in *-e*, we just add *-r* or *-st*.
  *nice → nice**r** / nice**st***
- For adjectives that end in *-y*, we change the *y* to *i* and add *-er* or *-est*.
  *busy → bus**ier** / bus**iest***
- For one-syllable adjectives that end in consonant-vowel-consonant, we generally double the final consonant.
  *big → big**g**er / big**g**est* *wet → we**tt**er / we**tt**est*
  However, we do not double *w*, *x*, or *y*.
  *slow → slo**w**er / slo**w**est*

Irregular forms

There are three common irregular adjectives.

good → better / best
bad → worse / worst
far → further or *farther / furthest* or *farthest*

Less and *the least*

To make a negative comparison, we use *less* + adjective to form the comparative, and *the least* + adjective to form the superlative.

*fun → **less** fun / **the least** fun*
*popular → **less** popular / **the least** popular*

Use

We use comparative adjectives to compare things. We often use it with *than*.

*A taxi will be **quicker than** a bus.*
*We could get a bus, but a taxi will be **quicker**.*
*This one's **more expensive than** the others.*
*They're **less popular than** they used to be.*

We use superlative adjectives to compare one thing with other things in a group. We usually use *the* before a superlative.

*What's **the easiest** way to get to the center of town?*

We can also use a possessive form (*the company's*, *New York's*, *my*, etc.) and words such as *the second*, *the third*, *the next*, etc., before a superlative.

*Times Square is **New York City's busiest** subway station and Grand Central is **the second busiest**.*

▶ Exercises 1 and 2

as ... as

We use *as* + adjective + *as* to say things are the same.

*Riding a bike there is **as quick as** going by bus.*
*It's **as old as** I am.*

To say things are not the same, we use *not as* + adjective + *as*. The thing we mention first is smaller or less busy / heavy, etc.

*The UK is **not as big as** Italy.*
*The town is**n't as busy as** it used to be.*

▶ Exercises 3 and 4

Comparative modifiers

We use comparative modifiers when we say there is a big or small difference between things that we are comparing.

To say there is a **big difference**, we can use ***a lot*** or ***much***.
To say there is a **small difference**, we can use ***a bit*** or ***a little***.

*Public transportation is **much more expensive** than it used to be.*
*Lucy's house is **a bit closer** than Sue's.*
*We usually fly from Manchester if possible—Heathrow Airport is **a lot less convenient**.*
*Our new car is **a little bigger** than our old one.*

▶ Exercise 5

Exercises

1 Complete the sentences with the comparative or superlative form of the adjectives in **bold**.

1 I've driven lots of **nice** cars, but this one is the _____ .
2 Chicago is pretty **far** from here, but Boston is _____ .
3 Today's lecture was **interesting**, but I think last week's was _____ .
4 I've flown with some **bad** airlines, but SpeedAir has to be the _____ ever!
5 The exhibition is **busy** today, but yesterday was _____ . In fact, I think yesterday was the _____ day so far since it opened.
6 I'm pretty **good** at tennis, but my friend Alex is _____ . Actually, he's probably the _____ player in the club.
7 Peru is a **big** country, but Argentina is _____ . In fact, Argentina is the second _____ country in South America, after Brazil.

2 Complete the transportation facts. Use the comparative or superlative form of the adjectives in parentheses. Add *the* or *than* if you need to.

[1] *The fastest* (fast) time taken to visit all the world's countries by public transportation is 4 years and 31 days.

The world's [2] _____ (long) and [3] _____ (deep) rail tunnel, the Gotthard Tunnel in Switzerland, opened in 2016. It is 57 km long, and is about 3 km [4] _____ (long) the Seikan Tunnel in Japan.

The country with [5] _____ (high) number of train passengers is China with over 17 billion rail journeys per year. This is much [6] _____ (high) India with 8 billion.

3 Write sentences using *as … as* and an adjective from the box.

big	fast	heavy	~~high~~

1 Height: Mount Fuji 3,776 m, Mount Kilimanjaro 5,895 m
Mount Fuji isn't as high as Mount Kilimanjaro.
2 Area: USA 9,833,634 km², Canada 9,984,670 km²
_____
3 Top speed: Kangaroo 71 kmh, Horse 71 kmh
_____
4 Weight: Jumbo Jet 180,000 kg, Dreamliner 120,000 kg
_____

4 Rewrite the sentences using *as … as* so that the meaning is the same.

1 Traveling by car is safer than traveling by motorcycle.
Traveling by motorcycle isn't as safe as traveling by car.
2 Riding a bike and driving are both dangerous. They have the same number of accidents.
_____
_____
3 Heathrow Airport is more convenient for us than Gatwick Airport.
_____
_____
4 Going by car is no quicker than taking the bus.
_____
_____

5 Complete the text about travel in Indonesia. Use the comparative or superlative form of the adjectives in parentheses. Add any other words you need.

[1] _____ (good) way to travel around Indonesia depends on where you are. On major islands, getting around is generally [2] _____ (much / easy). Away from the tourist areas, it can be [3] _____ (bit / difficult).

Buses are [4] _____ (convenient) and popular means of transportation in Indonesia. Between major tourist destinations, air-conditioned buses are available, and these buses are generally [5] _____ (quick). However, prices can be [6] _____ (lot / high) the slower local buses.

Trains run only in Java and in parts of Sumatra. They're [7] _____ (bit / expensive) the bus, but are [8] _____ (much / quick), and it's worth paying extra for a [9] _____ (comfortable) journey.

GRAMMAR SUMMARY UNIT 4

Simple past

Use

We use the simple past to talk about finished actions, events, or situations in the past.

*I **visited** the Taj Mahal last year.*
*We **saw** a great movie over the weekend.*

Form

Simple past forms can be regular or irregular.

- We form the simple past of regular verbs by adding *-ed* to the base form of the verb.
  *want → want**ed* *look → look**ed***
- If the verb ends in *-e*, we just add *-d*.
  *like → like**d*** *hope → hope**d***
- We form the simple past of verbs ending in consonant + *-y* by changing *-y* to *-ied*.
  *study → stud**ied*** *try → tr**ied***
- We don't form the simple past of irregular verbs with *-ed*.
  go → went *hear → heard* *see → saw*

For a list of common irregular simple past forms, see page 180.

To form negatives in the simple past, we use *didn't* + base form of the verb.

	+	–
I/you/we/they	*I **watched**.*	*I **didn't watch**.*
he/she/it	*He **watched**.*	*She **didn't watch**.*

The verb *be* is different from other verbs. Its simple past form is *was* or *were*. We don't use *didn't* to form negatives.

	+	–
I/he/she/it	*I **was** tired.*	*She **wasn't** tired.*
you/we/they	*We **were** tired.*	*You **weren't** tired.*

▶ **Exercises 1 and 2**

Simple past questions

We make questions in the simple past with *did* + base form of the verb.

*Why **did** you **choose** to visit Turkey?*
***Did** she **have** fun on vacation?*

When we make questions in the simple past with the verb *be*, we use *was* or *were*. We do not add *did*.

***Were** you tired after your trip?*
*Where **was** your hotel?*

▶ **Exercise 3**

Past continuous and simple past

Use

We use the past continuous to talk about an action in progress at a moment in the past.

*I **was watching** TV at eight o'clock last night.*
*Tony **was living** in Madrid in 2015.*

Form

We form the past continuous with *was/were* and the *-ing* form of the main verb.

	+	–	?
I/he/she/it	*I **was** reading.*	*He **wasn't** reading.*	***Was** she reading?*
you/we/they	*They **were** reading.*	*We **weren't** reading.*	***Were** you reading?*

We often use the past continuous and the simple past together. We use the past continuous for a longer, continuing activity, and the simple past for a shorter, finished action.

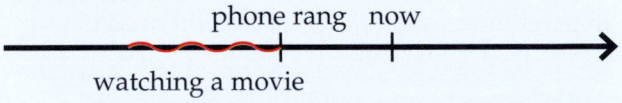

*Jack **was watching** a movie when his phone **rang**.*
*I **met** my husband when I **was traveling** around India.*

We often use *when* and *while* to join the two parts of a sentence with past continuous and simple past together. We use *when* before a simple past or a past continuous verb. We normally only use *while* with a past continuous verb.

*I met Matthew **when** I was living in California.*
*Someone stole my camera **while** I was eating in a restaurant.*

When we use *when* with the simple past, it can also mean "after."

*I called Sylvia **when** I read her message.*

If the part of the sentence with *when* or *while* comes first, we put a comma after it.

***When** I met Matthew, I was living in California.*

Remember that we don't use verbs that describe states (e.g., *believe, like, love, prefer, know*) with a continuous tense.

▶ **Exercises 4, 5, and 6**

Exercises

1 Complete the second sentence in each pair with the simple past form of the verb in **bold**.

1 She **wants** to travel the world.
She _____ to travel the world.
2 It **isn't** easy to get a job.
It _____ easy to get a job.
3 They **don't have** a lot of money.
They _____ a lot of money.
4 He **doesn't like** traveling by plane.
He _____ traveling by plane.
5 They **are** late again.
They _____ late again.
6 I **study** in the school library.
I _____ in the school library.

2 Complete the text with the simple past form of these verbs. One verb is used twice.

hire	be	visit	decide
drive	not know	eat	not want

An island vacation … with a difference

Last summer, my husband and I [1]_____ the island of Sicily in Italy. We love the water, but we [2]_____ to spend every day on the beach. So, we [3]_____ to go to Mount Etna, a live volcano! We [4]_____ to the mountain from our hotel early in the morning. When we arrived, we [5]_____ where to go, so we [6]_____ a guide to help us. She [7]_____ very good and told us about the history of the volcano. When we got near the crater, there was a strong smell, but the views at the top [8]_____ amazing. After that, we went back to the hotel and [9]_____ a delicious lunch there. It was a fantastic experience!

3 Write simple past questions with these words.

1 how / be / your hotel?
_____
2 when / you / get back?
_____
3 they / take the train home?
_____
4 what / be / your / favorite experience?
_____
5 you / call me / this morning?
_____
6 how much / your / plane tickets cost?
_____

4 Complete the sentences with the past continuous form of the verbs in parentheses.

1 We _____ (wait) for the bus.
2 He _____ (not eat) his food.
3 _____ you _____ (talk) to your friend?
4 What _____ those people _____ (say) to each other?
5 It _____ (not rain) when we left the house.
6 Where _____ she _____ (fly) to?

5 Circle the correct options to complete the sentences.

1 Jack *arrived / was arriving* while I *was watching / watched* TV.
2 When the taxi *arrived / was arriving*, we *got / were getting* in.
3 It *was starting / started* snowing while we *climbed / were climbing* the mountain.
4 He *wasn't playing / didn't play* on his computer when I *was seeing / saw* him.
5 *Did she ski / Was she skiing* when she *had / was having* the accident?
6 I *knew / was knowing* he had a problem when I *heard / was hearing* him shout.

6 Complete the text with the simple past or past continuous form of these verbs.

not end	come	eat	look
reach	start	travel	wait

I had an amazing surprise while I [1]_____ around India last year. I [2]_____ dinner in a restaurant in Delhi when someone [3]_____ in and sat at the table next to me. She [4]_____ familiar, but I couldn't remember who she was. We [5]_____ talking, and then I realized—it was Maggie, my best friend from elementary school!

But the story [6]_____ there. When I [7]_____ the airport on the last day of my vacation, who did I see there? Maggie, of course. She [8]_____ for the same flight, and her seat was right in front of mine on the plane!

GRAMMAR SUMMARY UNIT 5

Quantifiers

We use quantifiers with nouns to talk about quantity. The choice of quantifier depends on:

- if the noun is countable or uncountable.
- if we are talking about small or large quantities.

Some nouns are countable. This means they can become plural, for example, *computer, bag, box, magazine*. Other nouns are uncountable. This means they cannot normally become plural, for example, *trash, plastic, paper, metal*.

Quantity	Countable	Uncountable
large quantity	*a lot of / lots of*	*a lot of / lots of*
neutral quantity (not large or small)	*some*	*some*
small quantity	*not many*	*not much*
small quantity	*a few*	*a little*
no quantity (zero)	*not any*	*not any*

We use *a lot of* or *lots of* with countable and uncountable nouns to talk about large quantities.
*There was **a lot of** trash on the streets after the party.*
*We have **lots of** great shops in my neighborhood.*

We use *some* with both countable and uncountable nouns. It does not refer to a specific amount—we use it to talk about quantities that are not large and are not small.
*I found **some** really useful books in the library.*
(= not a lot)

In more formal English, we use *many* + plural noun to talk about large quantities.
*There are **many** interesting places to visit in the city.*

We also use *many* and *much* in questions.
*Are there **many** good shops where you live?*
*Do you have **much** free time?*

We don't normally use *many* and *much* in affirmative sentences in spoken English. We use *a lot of* or *lots of* instead.

We use *not much* and *not many* to talk about small quantities. We use *not much* with uncountable nouns and *not many* with plural countable nouns.
*There were**n't many** people at the party.*
*They do**n't** have **much** money.*

Note that *not* always goes with the verb in the sentence.

We also use *a few* and *a little* to talk about small quantities. We use *a few* with plural countable nouns and *a little* with uncountable nouns.
*I have **a few** really good friends.*
*There's **a little** milk in the container.*

We use *not any* with countable and uncountable nouns to talk about zero quantity (when there is nothing).
*I do**n't** have **any** money.*
*There were**n't any** shops open when we arrived.*

Note that *not* always goes with the verb in the sentence.

We also use *any* with countable and uncountable nouns to ask questions.
*Are there **any** good beaches in the area?*
*Do you have **any** orange juice?*

▶ **Exercises 1, 2, and 3**

Articles (*a/an, the,* or no article)

We use *a/an*:

- to talk about something that isn't specific.
  *Have you got **a** pen?* (not a particular pen)
- the first time we mention something.
  *I saw **an** eagle yesterday.*

We use *the*:

- the second time we mention something.
  A man and a woman were waiting for us at the airport.
  ***The** man helped us with our suitcases.*
- when something is unique.
  ***The** sun looked really beautiful from the top of the mountain.*
- with superlatives.
  *It was **the best** vacation of my life.*
- with the names of some places, such as oceans (e.g., ***the** Atlantic Ocean*), deserts (e.g., ***the** Sahara Desert*), and mountain ranges (e.g., ***the** Himalayas*).

We use no article:

- to talk about plural or uncountable nouns in general.
  I never stay in (–) hotels because they're so expensive.
  (–) Tourism brings a lot of money to the area.
- with the names of most places, for example, the names of continents, countries, cities, and lakes.

▶ **Exercises 4, 5, and 6**

Exercises

1 Choose one quantifier from each pair to complete the sentences.

1 many / much
   a There wasn't _____ cheese in the fridge.
   b There weren't _____ apples left.
2 a little / a few
   a There was _____ space for me on the seat.
   b We have _____ recycling bins outside our house.
3 many / much
   a How _____ tea do you drink in a day?
   b How _____ tourists visit the national park?
4 some / any
   a The parking lot didn't have _____ space for my car.
   b _____ people prefer shopping online.

2 Circle the correct option (a–c).

1 I can't travel this year because I don't have _____ money.
   a much b a lot c few
2 The hotel doesn't have _____ free rooms.
   a some b any c a little
3 I have _____ clothes I don't wear.
   a a lot b lots of c much
4 He made _____ coffee for me.
   a any b many c some
5 There was _____ trash left in the trashcan.
   a a few b a little c little
6 The shop had _____ things that I liked.
   a much b a little c a few

3 Circle the correct options to complete the conversation.

A: Wait! Don't throw your coffee cup in the trash.
B: Why not?
A: Well, if [1] *a lot of / a little* people throw away their coffee cups, it creates [2] *a few / lots of* trash.
B: I only drink [3] *a little / a few* cups of coffee a week. That's not [4] *much / many* coffee cups.
A: Yes, but I read in an article that people throw away 7 million coffee cups every day in the US!
B: Really? That is [5] *a lot of / a little* cups!
A: I know. The article says that [6] *some / any* businesses now have recycling bins for coffee cups.
B: Were there [7] *much / any* recycling bins in the café we were in?
A: Look, here's one! You can recycle your cup here.

4 Circle *a, an, the,* or no article (–) to complete these facts.

Surprising facts about our world

1 Redwood trees are *the* / – tallest trees in the world.
2 – / *The* Lake Superior is the largest lake in the USA.
3 China built *the* / *an* amazing bridge over the Dehang Canyon. *The* / *A* bridge is the highest in the world.
4 Mercury is the closest planet to – / *the* sun.
5 – / *The* honey bees only live for five to six weeks.
6 Until around 4,000 years ago, *the* / – Sahara Desert was green, and animals probably lived there.

5 Circle *a, an, the,* or no article (–) to complete the conversation.

A: I watched [1] *an* / *the* interesting documentary last night about [2] *the* / – flowers.
B: Really?
A: Yeah. [3] *The* / *A* documentary showed where in [4] – / *the* world they grow [5] *the* / *a* flowers and how they arrive here in the US.
B: And what did you learn?
A: Well, they grow the flowers in countries like [6] – / *the* Kenya, and then they ship them around the world.
B: That's not great for [7] *a* / *the* environment. Did you learn anything else?
A: Yeah. Most of our flowers come from [8] *the* / *a* big market in the Netherlands. It's [9] *a* / *the* biggest flower market in the world!

6 Circle *the, a,* or no article (–) in the text below.

In [1] *a* / *the* small town called Rjukan in [2] *the* / – Norway, there is no sunlight for six months a year. People in [3] *the* / – Rjukan live without [4] *the* / *a* sun from September to March. But this is changing, thanks to Martin Andersen—a local man who had the clever idea to use [5] *a* / *the* mirror to bring sunlight to the town. [6] *The* / *A* mirror is on top of a mountain next to the town, and it reflects light from the sun onto [7] *a* / *the* town's main square. [8] *The* / – people love coming to the main square and sitting in the sun.

GRAMMAR SUMMARY UNIT 6

Infinitive forms

An infinitive is defined as *to* + base form of the verb. We use infinitive forms in different situations.

verb + infinitive

Sometimes, two verbs appear together in a sentence. The form of the second verb depends on the first verb. Many verbs (e.g., *decide, help, hope, intend, learn, need, plan, pretend, promise, want, would like*) are followed by infinitives.

*I **need to go** to the store.*
*We **decided to move** abroad.*

adjective + infinitive

When a verb appears after an adjective, it is often in the infinitive form.

*It's **exciting to visit** new places.*
*It's **nice to see** you again.*

▶ Exercise 1

infinitive explaining the purpose of an action

We also use the infinitive form to say why we do something.

*I went to the library **to look** for a book.*
*She's going to Paris **to visit** a friend.*

We don't use *for* + verb to give reasons.

~~*I called Jan **for invite** her to my party.*~~
*I called Jan **to invite** her to my party.*

Note that the negative form of an infinitive is *not to* + base form of the verb.

*I promise **not to do** that again.*
*It's important **not to work** too hard.*

See Unit 2 for when we use the *-ing* form of a verb.

▶ Exercises 2 and 3

Future forms

Present continuous

We use the present continuous to talk about a fixed arrangement in the future, for example, when we have planned something with other people or when we have already spent money. We normally mention a specific time.

*We're **getting** the train at 11:20 a.m.*
*I'm **going** to the theater with Michelle tonight.*

be going to

We use *be going to* + base form of the verb to talk about general plans and intentions.

*I'm **going to travel** around Asia this summer.*
*We're **going to go** to the movies this weekend.*

We form questions and negatives with *going to* in the same way as in the present continuous.

*I'm **not going to have** time to see you.*
*Are you **going to drive** to the party?*

will

We use *will* + base form of the verb when we make a decision while we're speaking.

A: *What can I bring you?*
B: *I'll **have** the tuna salad, please.*

We also use *will* to make promises and offers.

*We'll **meet** you at the train station.*
*I'll **pay** for your ticket.*

▶ Exercises 4, 5, and 6

Exercises

1 Complete the text with the infinitive form of the verbs in the box.

go	complete	pursue	stay

Yesterday was a special day for Michael Sanders. At the age of 75, he finished his college degree. "I always intended [1] _____ to college," says Michael. "But when I finished high school, I decided [2] _____ my career, not study." However, Michael always had his dream, and he didn't give up. He was 70 years old when he started college, and it wasn't easy. "I often found it hard [3] _____ my work on time," he says. "But the other students were great. They helped me a lot." And Michael's not finished—he hopes [4] _____ in college for a few more years and get another degree.

2 Match the beginnings of the sentences (1–5) with the endings (a–e).

1 I'm saving money
2 She went to the university library
3 Let's go to the gym
4 I looked out of the window
5 You need to study hard

a to buy a new car. ____
b to exercise. ____
c to pass your exam. ____
d to see the weather. ____
e to study. ____

3 Circle the correct options to complete the sentences.

1 I can't stand *staying / to stay* inside all day.
2 I think it's easy *learning / to learn* a new language.
3 Jack helped me *to fix / fixing* my car.
4 I would like *to visit / visiting* China one day.
5 I'm not very good at *to paint / painting.*
6 I went to the store *for buying / to buy* some milk.
7 *Eating / To eat* vegetables is good for your health.
8 I was happy *hearing / to hear* about your new job.

4 Complete the sentences with the *be going to* form of these verbs.

come	not get	have	miss
~~watch~~	spend	start	

1 I *'m going to watch* that new crime drama tonight.
2 _____ you _____ to our party tomorrow?
3 Tanja _____ a baby in December.
4 Mathieu _____ six months in Australia later this year.
5 I _____ married until I'm at least 30!
6 _____ we _____ our train?
7 I _____ college in September.

5 Circle the correct options to complete the dialogs.

1 A: This bag's heavy.
B: *I'll help / I'm helping* you to carry it!
2 A: Do you have plans for tonight?
B: *I'm going / I'll go* to the movies. I just bought my ticket.
3 A: There's no more milk!
B: Oh, no! *I'm going / I'll go* to the store and get some.
4 A: I can't wait until the exams are over.
B: I know. *I'm going to take / I'll take* a vacation after my exams.

6 Choose the best explanation (a or b) for each sentence (1–4).

1 I'm meeting my friend John at 4:30 p.m.
a We planned this together.
b This is an idea, but I'm not totally sure.
2 I'm going to travel when I finish college.
a I've already decided where to go, and I've booked some hotels.
b This is my idea, but I haven't booked anything yet.
3 It's raining. I'll take you to the store in my car.
a I just decided this now.
b We organized this earlier.
4 I'm going to join a gym this month.
a I made an appointment at a gym for this Friday at 10 a.m.
b This is my idea, but I haven't organized anything yet.

GRAMMAR SUMMARY UNIT 7

Present perfect and simple past

Present perfect: form

We form the present perfect with *have/has* + past participle.

	+	–	?
I/you/ we/they	***I've arrived.***	*They* ***haven't arrived.***	***Have*** *you* ***arrived?***
he/she/it	*It* ***has arrived.***	*He* ***hasn't arrived.***	***Has*** *he* ***arrived?***

Regular past participles end in *-ed* and are the same as regular simple past forms (e.g., *change → changed, live → lived*).

Many past participles are irregular. Some irregular past participles are the same as the irregular simple past form.
make (base form), *made* (simple past), *made* (past participle)

Other irregular past participles are different from the irregular simple past form.
write (base form), *wrote* (simple past), *written* (past participle)

See page 180 for a list of common irregular simple past and past participle forms.

▶ Exercise 1

Present perfect and simple past: use

We use the **present perfect**:

- when we don't know when something happened, or we don't say because it's not important.
  I've ***visited*** *over fifty countries.*
  He's ***written*** *some really important books.*
- to ask about people's experiences, using *ever*.
  Have *you* ***ever worked*** *in another country?*
- for something that started in the past and continues now.
  I've always ***loved*** *working with numbers.* (= I loved it in the past, and I still love it now.)

We use the **simple past** when we know the exact time something happened in the past.
I ***saw*** *Max* ***this morning****.*
I ***visited*** *our Los Angeles office* ***last year****.*

In conversations, we often start with the present perfect to ask about an experience in general, and then use the simple past to give details.
A: *Have you ever been skiing?*
B: *Yes, I have. I tried it in Colorado last year.*

▶ Exercises 2 and 3

Present perfect with *for* and *since*

We use the present perfect with *for* and *since* to talk about a situation that started in the past and continues now.

We use *for* with a period of time.
I've worked here ***for*** *three years.*

We use *since* with a point in time (when the situation started).
I've known Taylor ***since*** *2005.*

▶ Exercise 4

Prepositions of place and movement

Prepositions can tell us where something or someone is, or the direction something or someone moves.

Prepositions of place

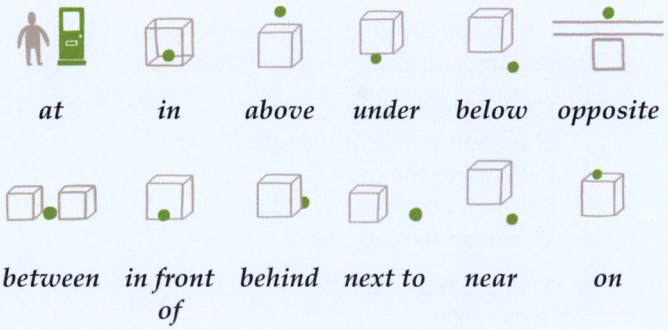

We use *at* to talk about where we work, live, and study.
at *home,* ***at*** *work,* ***at*** *school,* ***at*** *college*
We use *in* with towns, cities, countries, and continents.
in *London,* ***in*** *Mexico,* ***in*** *Asia*
We use *on* to say where on a road places are.
The bank is ***on*** *the left. My house is* ***on*** *the right.*
We also use *on* with floors in a building.
on *the first floor,* ***on*** *the second floor*

▶ Exercise 5

Prepositions of movement

We use prepositions of movement after a verb that describes a movement (e.g., *go, come, walk, climb*).

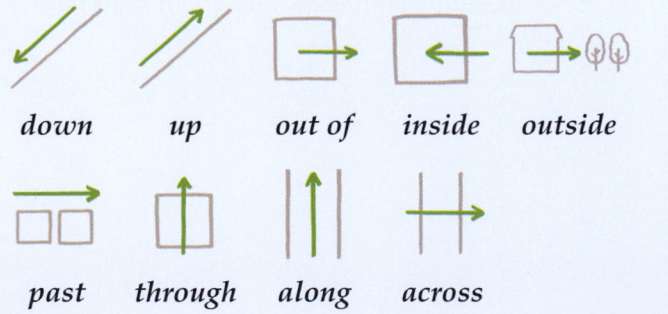

▶ Exercise 6

Exercises

1 Make present perfect sentences using these words.

1 I / see / that movie / five times.
2 you / ever / go / to Australia?
3 They / always / live / in the countryside.
4 she / ever / visit / you?
5 I / not finish / my work.
6 Why / you / apply / for this job?

2 Circle the correct options to complete the sentences.

1 *I've started / I started* my new job last week.
2 *Have you ever gone / Did you ever go* to the USA?
3 *They've always loved / They always loved* playing basketball—they play three times a week now!
4 Jill *has spoken / spoke* to her boss last night.
5 *I worked / I've worked* in a café when I was a student.
6 *I've never gone / I never went* to a concert in my life.

3 Complete the conversations with the present perfect or simple past form of the verbs in the boxes.

finish	have	get

A: [1]_____ you _____ work yet?
B: Yes. I [2]_____ home an hour ago.
A: [3]_____ you _____ a good day?
B: It was OK.

tell	hear	send

A: [4]_____ you _____ about the new job at Max's company?
B: Yes, I [5]_____ already _____ Max my résumé. You?
A: Not yet. Max only [6]_____ me about it this morning.

have	spend	be

A: [7]_____ you ever _____ to Paris?
B: Yes, I [8]_____ a week there last year.
A: [9]_____ you _____ a good time?
B: Yes, it was great.

4 Complete the sentences with *for* or *since*.

1 Have you lived in your apartment _____ a long time?
2 She's worked here _____ 2015.
3 I've studied Spanish _____ two years.
4 He's been a baseball fan _____ he was a child.
5 I've had a cold _____ over a week.

5 Complete the text with these prepositions.

below	between	in	close	on	opposite

I've just moved into my new apartment and I love it! It's [1]_____ a small building with three floors—I'm [2]_____ the top floor. The people in the apartment [3]_____ mine are really friendly, and I've been down to their apartment twice for dinner already. There's a park [4]_____ the building, just on the other side of the road. I often go there for lunch. What else? Oh, my building is [5]_____ two amazing restaurants—on the right, there's a great Greek restaurant, and on the left, there's a really good Mexican place. I'm also really [6]_____ to the subway station, so I can get to work really quickly.

6 Look at the map below and circle the correct prepositions to complete the directions.

Everyone in the office is looking forward to meeting you. Here are the directions you asked for. First, go [1] *out of / down* the station, and then turn right. Go [2] *inside / across* the bridge, and then walk [3] *along / outside* Bridge Street for about three minutes. Go [4] *past / through* the bank and the post office, then turn left and walk [5] *through / along* the park. The building is opposite the park gates. Walk [6] *inside / up* the steps and you've arrived! Call me when you're there, and I'll come [7] *out of / outside* to meet you.

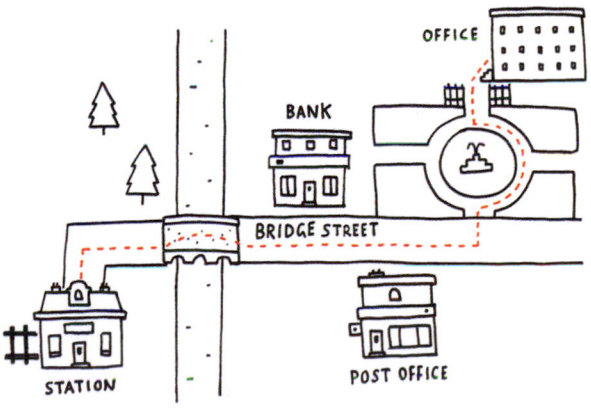

GRAMMAR SUMMARY UNIT 8

Zero and first conditionals

Zero conditional

We use the zero conditional to talk about things that are generally true. The form is:

If + simple present + simple present

***If** there's important news, everyone on Twitter **talks** about it.*

***If** I **get** an email, I **don't** always **read** it right away.*

***If** the weather's bad, **do** you still **walk** to work?*

We can also use *when* instead of *if*. The meaning is the same.

▶ Exercise 1

First conditional

We use the first conditional to talk about a possible future situation. The form is:

If + simple present + *will/won't* + base verb

***If** I **hear** something about the job, I'll **send** you a message.*

***If** you **don't read** my blog, you **won't hear** all my news.*

Note: We never use a future form in the *if* clause.

*If it ~~will rain~~ on the weekend, we'll **stay** at home.*

*If it **rains** on the weekend, we'll **stay** at home.*

Order in conditional sentences

Conditional sentences have two parts: the *if* clause and the main clause. The main clause describes the result of the situation in the *if* clause.

***If** it rains, we'll stay at home.*

IF CLAUSE MAIN CLAUSE

We can put the *if* clause first or the main clause first. When the *if* clause comes first, we put a comma before the main clause. When the *if* clause comes second, we don't need a comma.

*We'll stay at home **if** it rains.*

▶ Exercises 2 and 3

Defining relative clauses

Defining relative clauses give essential information about a person, thing, or place. They say exactly which person, thing, or place we are talking about.

*Look at the box **that's on the table**.* (the relative clause tells us exactly which box)

*He's the scientist **who was on TV yesterday**.* (the relative clause tells us exactly which scientist)

Form

To make a relative clause, we add a relative pronoun after a noun. The choice of relative pronoun depends on the type of noun.

- For a relative clause about a person, use *who*.
  *That's the woman **who we saw yesterday**.*
- For a relative clause about a thing, use *that*.
  *Did you get the message **that I sent you**?*
- For a relative clause about a place, use *where*.
  *This is the place **where they made the first battery**.*

The relative pronouns *who* and *that* can be the subject or the object of a relative clause. If it is the subject, we don't need another subject.

This is an invention that ~~it~~ could change the world!

If it is the object, we don't need another object.

Did I tell you about the movie that I saw ~~it~~ last week?

▶ Exercises 4, 5, and 6

Exercises

1 Match the sentence beginnings (1–4) with the endings (a–d).

1 If I get a text message,
2 If she doesn't sleep well at night,
3 When he has an exam,
4 When it snows,

a he stays up late to study. ____
b she feels tired the next day. ____
c I reply right away. ____
d there are more traffic accidents. ____

2 Make first conditional sentences with the correct form of the verbs in parentheses.

1 If we _____ (finish) the meeting early, we _____ (go out) for a coffee.
2 You _____ (miss) the train if you _____ (not leave) the house now.
3 If the weather _____ (be) bad tomorrow, I _____ (drive) to work.
4 If she _____ (not do) her homework, her teacher _____ (be) angry.
5 I _____ (not answer) my phone if I _____ (be) busy.

3 In each section, match the sentence beginnings (1–4) with the endings (a–d) and complete the sentences with the correct form of the verbs in parentheses.

A Zero conditional

1 When it ___*rains*___ (rain),
2 If I _____ (not sleep) well at night,
3 Plants _____ (die)
4 She _____ (like) to go for a run

a I _____ (drink) strong coffee in the morning. ____
b if you _____ (not give) them water. ____
c when she _____ (wake up). ____
d we ___*prefer*___ (prefer) to stay at home. ___*1*___

B First conditional

1 If she _____ (be) free tomorrow evening,
2 If we _____ (not eat) now,
3 They _____ (not complete) the course
4 I _____ (buy) a new pair of shoes

a we _____ (feel) hungry later. ____
b if I _____ (have) enough money. ____
c I _____ (invite) her to the party. ____
d if they _____ (not finish) the assignment on time. ____

4 Complete the sentences with *who, that,* or *where.*

1 That's the man _____ lives next door to me.
2 This is the book _____ helped me pass the exam.
3 He visited the town _____ his parents were born.
4 We liked the chocolate _____ you bought us.
5 I got this present from the old woman _____ lives on our street.
6 This is the café _____ I first met my wife.
7 Can you see the cat _____ is lying on top of the car?

5 Find and correct the mistakes in these sentences.

1 This is the house that I want to buy it.
2 She bought the car who she saw last week.
3 Look! That's the friend where I was talking about yesterday.
4 Those are the students who they are looking for an apartment.
5 He didn't see the person who he took his wallet.

6 Complete the text with the phrases below (a–e) and *who, that,* or *where.*

a I didn't want to be friends with again
b lived next door to me
c she gave me for my eighth birthday
d we had always played together
e ~~you haven't seen for a long time~~

Facebook is a fantastic way to find old friends [1] ___*who you haven't seen for a long time*___. When I was a small girl, I was best friends with Elena, the girl [2] _____. I still have the doll [3] _____! But then her family moved away, and we lost touch over the years. When I joined Facebook, I wasn't sure about it at first. There were a lot of people [4] _____. But one day, I saw that Elena wanted to be friends with me. We started chatting online, and after a few months we agreed to meet—in the park [5] _____ when we were children. It was so nice to see her and to be friends again. And it's all thanks to Facebook!

GRAMMAR SUMMARY UNIT 9

Past perfect

Form

We form the past perfect with *had* + past participle. See page 180 for a list of common irregular past participles.

	+	–	?
I/you/we/ they	*I* ***had*** *arrived.*	*They* ***hadn't*** *arrived.*	***Had*** *you arrived?*
he/she/it	*He* ***had*** *arrived.*	*She* ***hadn't*** *arrived.*	***Had*** *it arrived?*

In spoken English and informal written English, we use *'d* instead of *had*, especially after pronouns.

*I'**d** already **seen** her.*

Use

We use the past perfect when we need to make it clear that one past action happened before another past action. For the action that happened first, we use the past perfect. For the action that happened second, we use the simple past.

*When we **arrived** at the airport, the plane **had** already **left**.*

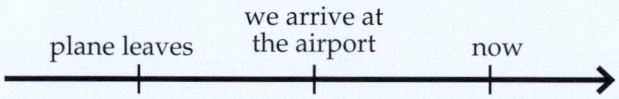

We only use the past perfect when we need to make it clear which action happened first. If the order is obvious, we just use the simple past for all the actions.

*When I **got** to the station, I **bought** a ticket and **waited** for the train.* (all simple past)

We often use linking words and phrases like *but*, *because*, *so*, and *as soon as* to link simple past with past perfect sentences.

*I'd booked the hotel months before, **but** when I got there they said they were full.*
*I was tired **because** I'd been at work all day.*
*It had rained all night, **so** the roads were very wet.*
*The children ran outside **as soon as** the sun had come out.*

▶ **Exercises 1, 2, and 3**

Subject questions

Other questions

We can use questions to ask about different things, for example, time, places, things, or reasons.

When did you visit Brazil? (asking about a time)
Where do you stay? (asking about a place)
How much does it cost? (asking about a thing)
Why didn't you like the hotel? (asking about a reason)

To form most questions, we put an auxiliary verb before the subject. To form simple present questions, we need to add the auxiliary verb *do* or *does*. To form simple past questions, we need to add the auxiliary verb *did*.

Subject questions

We can also use questions to ask about the subject of a sentence.

Who lives here? (Answer: *Katrin lives here.*)
SUBJECT
Who likes the food? (Answer: *We all like the food.*)
SUBJECT

The grammar in subject questions is different from other questions. In subject questions:

- the word order is the same as a statement, and the question word replaces the subject.

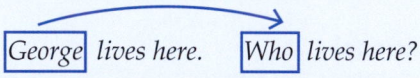

- we do not use the auxiliary verb *do* or *did*.
  Who ~~does want~~ coffee?
  Who wants coffee?

▶ **Exercise 4**

We often ask subject questions using *who*, *which*, *what*, and *how many*.

***Who** put this suitcase here?*
***Which** hotel has the best prices?*
***What** caused the delay?*
***How many** people came to the party?*

▶ **Exercises 5 and 6**

Exercises

1 Match the beginnings of the sentences (1–6) with the endings (a–f).

1 As soon as the rain had stopped,
2 He checked his phone,
3 She was so happy
4 She realized she'd forgotten to bring any money,
5 They told him to get off the train
6 I arrived late at work

a because he hadn't bought a ticket. ____
b because she'd passed her exam. ____
c but the message still hadn't arrived. ____
d because I'd had a problem with my car. ____
e so she needed to go home and get some. ____
f we went for a walk. ____

2 Complete the text with the past perfect form of these verbs.

ask	buy	not check	happen
spend	think	try	

I decided to take a different kind of vacation last summer—I stayed at home for a week! Why? Well, I [1]_____ just _____ my first house, so I didn't have a lot of money. I did lots of different things during my vacation. I went to a museum and learned about the local history—I didn't know that so many interesting things [2]_____ where I live. One evening, some friends came to my new house for a barbecue. I [3]_____ everyone to bring something to eat, and it was lots of fun! Another day, I went to my local swimming pool for the first time. I [4]_____ always _____ it looked kind of old and dirty, but it was really nice inside. Most nights, I ate at local restaurants. There were some excellent places I [5]_____ never _____ before. The only bad day was when I decided to go for a walk in the local park. I [6]_____ the weather, and it rained all day! At the end of the week, I felt really relaxed. And I [7]_____ much less money than I normally do on a vacation. I might even do it again next year!

3 Complete the sentences with these pairs of verbs. Use one simple past form and one past perfect form in each sentence.

call + receive	feel + forget	not go + see
say + help	sleep + feel	study + fail

1 I _____ to the movies with my friends, because I _____ already _____ the movie they wanted to watch.
2 We _____ hungry because we _____ to bring any lunch.
3 I _____ Martin on his mobile as soon as I _____ his message.
4 Lisa _____ thanks to her brother because he _____ her so much.
5 All of us _____ really well, so we _____ great in the morning.
6 Sally _____ hard, but she still _____ the exam.

4 Circle the subject questions.

1 Who wrote this message?
2 Where did you buy this?
3 What did she tell you?
4 How many people live here?
5 Who wrote this song?
6 Why didn't you come?
7 Who called you earlier?
8 When did it happen?

5 Put the words in order to form subject questions.

1 put / bag / here / who / this / ?
2 which / best / computer / works / ?
3 my / broke / glasses / who / ?
4 speaks / French / who / ?
5 work / how / many / people / here / ?
6 the / won / who / race / ?

6 Write questions about the underlined words in each sentence. Some are subject questions.

1 I went <u>to Spain</u> last year.
_____
2 <u>Kate's behavior</u> made me really angry.
_____
3 <u>270 people</u> live in this building.
_____
4 I went outside <u>to get some fresh air</u>.
_____
5 <u>Isabella</u> left her coat here.
_____
6 <u>Julia</u> has spoken to Paolo today.
_____

GRAMMAR SUMMARY UNIT 10

The passive (simple present, simple past)

Active vs. passive

Verbs in English can be active or passive. We normally use the active form when the focus of the sentence is on the "agent"—the person or thing that does the action.

*Apple **produced** the first Macbook in 2006.*
*My father **built** this house in 2004.*

When we use the passive, the sentence isn't about the "agent" anymore.

*The first Macbook **was produced** in 2006.*
*This house **was built** in 2004.*

The focus of the first passive sentence here is "the first Macbook," not the company that produced it. The focus of the second passive sentence is "this house," not the person who built it.

Form

When we use the passive, the object of the active sentence becomes the subject of the passive sentence.

People all over the world love Rihanna's music.
OBJECT

*Rihanna's music **is loved** by people all over the world.*
SUBJECT

We form the passive with the verb *be* and the past participle of the main verb. We can use the passive in affirmative sentences, negative sentences, and in questions. The form of *be* shows the tense.

	Simple present	Simple past
+	*Rihanna's music **is loved** by people all over the world.*	*The Beijing Subway **was used** by over 3.5 billion passengers last year.*
–	*This movie **isn't known** outside of Europe.*	*Bruce Willis **wasn't born** in the USA.*
?	***Is** this product **sold** in Asia?*	*When **was** the first PC **invented**?*

▶ Exercises 1 and 2

Common uses of the passive

We often use the passive voice when it's obvious or not important who does the action.

*Millions of smartphones **are sold** every year.*
(obviously shops sell smartphones)

by

We can use *by* + noun to say who does or did the action in a sentence with a passive verb.

*Facebook **was created by** Mark Zuckerberg.*

When we do this, we make this information sound new or important.

▶ Exercises 3 and 4

used to

Use

We use *used to* to talk about habits or situations in the past that are not true now.

*I **used to** live in California, but now I live in New York.*
*I **used to** go to concerts often, but now I don't have time.*

We don't use *used to* to talk about single actions at a specific time in the past. We use simple past instead.

~~*I **used to hear** a really good song on the radio yesterday.*~~
*I **heard** a really good song on the radio yesterday.*

Form

Used to is always followed by the base form of the verb. We use the same form for all persons (*I, you, he/she/it*, etc.). In negative sentences and questions, we use the form *use to* (not *used to*).

+	*I **used to love** rock music.*
–	*I **didn't use to like** listening to music at work.*
?	***Did** you **use to own** a Walkman?*

There is no present form of *used to*. To talk about habits in the present, we use the simple present with *usually*.

~~*I **use to go** to the gym twice a week.*~~
*I **usually go** to the gym twice a week.*

▶ Exercises 5, 6, and 7

Exercises

1 Read the sentences. Is each one active (A) or passive (P)?

1 Most people recognize the Coca-Cola logo. A P
2 The book was written over fifty years ago. A P
3 The clothes are made in that factory. A P
4 My question wasn't answered. A P
5 I gave him a book for his birthday. A P

2 Complete the sentences with the passive form of the verbs in parentheses. Use the simple present or simple past.

1 The logo _____ (design) fifty years ago.
2 Public transportation _____ (use) a lot in my country.
3 New articles _____ (write) for the website every month.
4 Professional sports stars _____ (recognize) all over the world.

3 Rewrite these sentences in the passive. Include the "agent," using ***by***.

1 Jeff Bezos founded Amazon in 1994.
_____
_____ in 1994.
2 Over one billion viewers watched the 2014 World Cup final.
The 2014 World Cup final _____
_____.
3 Up to four million people visit the Taj Mahal every year.
_____
_____ every year.

4 Circle the correct options to complete the text about tablet computers.

Before 2010, the word "tablet" [1] *was normally used / normally used* to talk about medicine. But that all changed when the first iPad [2] *released / was released*. Not everyone thought the iPad was a good idea, but 300,000 [3] *are sold / were sold* on the first day. Now, hundreds of different tablets [4] *sold / are sold* by different manufacturers, and we [5] *spend / are spent* millions of dollars on apps every year. Most tablets [6] *are bought / are buying* for games, photos, and the internet, but tablets are also [7] *found / find* in schools, universities, and workplaces around the world.

5 Change the simple past verbs in the sentences to a form with ***use(d) to*** + base form of the verb when possible. Circle the sentences that cannot be changed.

1 I took guitar lessons every week when I was younger.
2 Did you see Jack at the concert?
3 I took two really good photos this morning.
4 I didn't like going to the movies when I was young.
5 I didn't enjoy the food last night.
6 Did you like baseball when you were younger?

6 Look at the pictures. Make affirmative and negative sentences about Tony when he was a teenager with a form of ***use(d) to*** and the prompts.

TEENAGER **NOW**

When Tony was a teenager, he …

1 listen / to music / on CDs.
2 have / a smartphone.
3 own / a car.
4 have / a skateboard.

7 Complete the blog post with the correct form of ***use(d) to*** and a verb from the box.

be	~~wake up~~	meet	have	play

Well, it's been six months since I started my job. Life is so different now. When I was in college, I [1] *didn't use to wake up* early—never before 9:30 a.m. Now I have to be at work at 9 a.m.! I [2]_____ my friends a few times a week, but I'm always too tired after work now. I also [3]_____ the saxophone in a band, but I don't have time for that anymore!

Of course, it's not all bad. I [4]_____ much money when I was a student. But now, I can afford a nice car and apartment. What about you? How [5]_____ your life _____ different before you started working?

GRAMMAR SUMMARY UNIT 11

Reported speech

When we want to say what another person said, we can use direct speech. This means we use exactly the words the person said.

Mike said, "I'll see you later."

We can also use reported speech.

Mike said that he'd see me later.

When we use reported speech, we normally change the verb forms.

- Simple present becomes simple past:
  *"I **live** in Seattle." → She said she **lived** in Seattle.*
- Present continuous becomes past continuous:
  *"I'**m waiting** for the bus." →*
  *Julie said she **was waiting** for the bus.*
- Present perfect becomes past perfect:
  *"We'**ve seen** this movie before." →*
  *They said they'**d seen** that movie before.*
- Simple past becomes past perfect:
  *"I **passed** my exam." → He said he'**d passed** his exam.*
- *Will* becomes *would*:
  *"I'**ll** help you." → Mike said he'**d** (= would) help me.*

▶ **Exercise 1**

We often also need to make changes to other words, like pronouns and possessive forms, in reported speech.

*"**I** love **you**."→ He said **he** loved **me**.*
*"This is **my** Xbox." → He said this was **his** Xbox.*
*"**We** live **here**." → They said **they** lived **there**.*
*"It's cold in **this** room." →*
*She said it was cold in **that** room.*
*"**I**'ll see **you tomorrow**." →*
*He said **he**'d see **me the next day**.*

▶ **Exercises 2, 3, and 4**

Reporting verbs (*say* and *tell*)

We use both *say* and *tell* to report another person's words. We normally use *say* and *tell* in the simple past.

With *tell*, we always use an object before the reported speech. The object is often a pronoun.

*Sam **told me** he wanted to come.*
*Clara **told Simon** she would be late.*

With *say*, we never use an object before the reported speech.

*He **said** ~~**me**~~ that he was really happy.*

After both *say* and *tell*, we can use *that*, but it is not necessary.

I said (that) he had won the game.
They told us (that) we needed to leave.

▶ **Exercises 5 and 6**

Exercises

1 Circle the correct options to complete the reported speech.

1 "I'll have the pasta."
She said she *would have / will have* the pasta.
2 "I'm playing a game."
He said he *was playing / had played* a game.
3 "I really don't like this movie."
She said she really *wasn't liking / didn't like* that movie.
4 "I've visited Canada twice."
She said she *visited / had visited* Canada twice.
5 "I lost my phone."
He said *he lost / he'd lost* his phone.

2 Complete the reported speech with these words and phrases.

his	me	the day before	the next day
their	then	there	they

1 "I want to go there tomorrow." → She said she wanted to go there _____ .
2 "It's my new car." → He said it was _____ new car.
3 "We love this restaurant." → They said _____ loved that restaurant.
4 "We live here." → They said they lived _____ .
5 "I'll help you." → He said he'd help _____ .
6 "I'm at home now." → She said she was at home _____ .
7 "We missed our flight." → They said they'd missed _____ flight.
8 "We went there yesterday." → They said they'd gone there _____ .

3 Complete the direct speech.

1 She said Mike had already left.
"Mike _____ already _____ ."
2 Sally said she'd help me with my work.
"I _____ help you with your work."
3 Greta said she didn't speak Portuguese.
"I _____ Portuguese."
4 Martin said it had been cold the day before.
"It _____ cold yesterday."
5 Fatima said she was arriving at 9 p.m.
"I _____ at 9 p.m."

4 Look at these sentences (1–5) and complete the reported speech.

1 "I lost the game."
Jane said _____
2 "I'll see you tomorrow."
She said _____
3 "Your email hasn't arrived."
Mark said _____
4 "I don't want to speak to you."
He said _____
5 "I'm trying to watch the TV."
Luke said _____

5 Three of these sentences contain errors. Correct them by adding or deleting a word.

1 He told that he was really tired.

2 Laura said the food was good.

3 She said me that she needed my help.

4 He said that he would fix my computer.

5 Anna told she was working today.

6 Read the conversation between John and Jack. Then complete the sentences (1–5) with reported speech for each line of the conversation.

John: I've found something interesting.
Jack: You're holding an ancient Greek vase!
John: It's really beautiful.
Jack: It was probably lost in the sea for thousands of years.
John: I'll call the museum right away!

1 John said _____
_____
2 Jack said _____
_____
3 John told _____
_____
4 Jack told _____
_____
5 John said _____
_____

GRAMMAR SUMMARY UNIT 12

Second conditional

We use the second conditional to talk about impossible or unlikely situations in the present or future. The form is:

If + simple past + *would* + base verb
***If** I **had** enough money, I **would love** to visit the USA.*
*What **would** you **do if** you **saw** a tornado?*

In spoken English and informal written English, we use *'d* instead of *would*, especially after pronouns.

Note: We never put *would* in the *if* clause. We always use a past tense.

~~*If I **would have** more time*~~, *I'd go out more.*
*If I **had** more time, I'd go out more.*

When the main clause comes before the *if* clause, we don't add a comma between the two clauses.

▶ **Exercises 1, 2, and 3**

anywhere, everyone, nobody, something, etc.

Words like *anywhere, everyone, nobody,* and *something* are "indefinite pronouns." They can end in *-where, -one, -body,* or *-thing*. We use pronouns ending in:

- *-where* to talk about places.
- *-one* or *-body* to talk about people (there is no difference in meaning).
- *-thing* to talk about objects.

Positive meaning

We use *everywhere, everyone/everybody,* or *everything* to talk about all places, people, or objects.

*I think that **everywhere** in Spain is beautiful.*
***Everybody** can do more to help the environment.*
***Everything** in the shop was really expensive.*

We use *somewhere, someone/somebody,* or *something* to talk about places, people, or objects without being specific.

*We need to find **somewhere** to eat.* (= It's not important where.)
***Somebody** told me about this place.*
*I think **something**'s moving in the forest.*

Negative meaning

We use *nowhere, no one/nobody,* or *nothing* to say there is no place, no people, or no things.

*I found **nowhere** to sit on the train.*
*We saw **nobody** in the mountains all day.*
*There's **nothing** interesting to do in my city.*

We also use *anywhere, anybody/anyone,* or *anything* with a negative verb (e.g., *isn't, haven't, don't want*) for the same meaning.

*I did**n't** find **anywhere** to sit on the train.*
*We did**n't** see **anybody** in the mountains all day.*
*There is**n't anything** interesting to do in my city.*

Note that *anything, anyone/anybody,* and *anywhere* don't have a negative meaning without a negative verb.

Who lives in this old house?
~~*Anybody.*~~ ***Nobody**. It's empty.*

In questions

We use *anywhere, anyone, anybody,* or *anything* to ask general questions.

*Is there **anywhere** to park near here?*
*Can **anybody** help me?*
*Did you see **anything** interesting in the park?*

We use *something, someone, somebody,* or *somewhere* in questions when we make offers.

*Would you like **something** to eat?*
*Do you want me to ask **somebody** to help you?*
*Would you like to go **somewhere** quieter?*

▶ **Exercises 4, 5, and 6**

Exercises

1 Circle the correct options to complete these first and second conditional sentences.

1 If it rains, all the laundry *will* / *would* get wet.
2 If there was a snowstorm, we *will* / *would* be stuck at home.
3 There would be lots of problems if our water supply *becomes* / *became* polluted.
4 If we didn't have air conditioning, it *will* / *would* be impossible to work here.
5 If the world gets hotter, farmers *won't* / *wouldn't* be able to grow certain kinds of food.
6 Sailors would have problems if they *don't* / *didn't* check the weather forecast.

2 Match the beginnings of the second conditional sentences (1–5) with the endings (a–e).

1 If it was hotter here in summer,
2 If he worked harder,
3 You wouldn't need to ask me for money
4 If you didn't drive so fast,
5 If I lived near a train station,

a he'd have a better chance of getting a promotion. ____
b I wouldn't need a car. ____
c if you didn't spend so much. ____
d lots of tourists would come to visit. ____
e you wouldn't get in trouble with the police. ____

3 Complete the second conditional sentences with the correct form of the verbs in parentheses.

1 If I _____ (not be) so tired, I _____ (be able to) work better.
2 If I _____ (have) more money, I _____ (buy) a new car.
3 If Michael _____ (speak) more slowly, everyone _____ (understand) him.
4 I _____ (not tell) you to do this if I _____ (not think) it was important.
5 We _____ (save) lots of water if people _____ (be) more careful.
6 _____ you _____ (come) to visit me if I _____ (pay) for your ticket?

4 Circle the correct options to complete the sentences.

1 I know *somewhere* / *something* really nice to stay in this city.
2 Can I bring you *something* / *nothing* to eat?
3 A: Where are you going now?
B: *Nowhere.* / *Anywhere.* I'm staying here.
4 She didn't speak to *anybody* / *nobody* at the party.
5 *Everywhere* / *Everyone* here has been to college.

5 Complete the text with the words in the box.

anything	everywhere	nobody
nothing	something	somewhere

Ten years ago, I decided I wanted to live [1]_____ different. I was living in a big city, and I was tired of the traffic and pollution [2]_____. So I moved to a small village near the coast. The first few years were a bit difficult. When I moved, there was almost [3]_____ else living here. I enjoyed the peace and quiet, but there was [4]_____ to do in the evenings or on the weekends. But gradually, more and more people have come, and now there's always [5]_____ happening. Now I think it's a perfect place to live—I wouldn't change [6]_____!

6 Rewrite the sentences, using an indefinite pronoun to replace the underlined phrases.

1 Julia lives <u>in a place</u> near here.
_____
_____

2 There was <u>not one person</u> on the beach, so it was really quiet.
_____
_____

3 I've been <u>to all the places</u> in this city, and the park is my favorite place.
_____
_____

4 Mike didn't have <u>any objects</u> with him—he'd left his bag at home.
_____
_____

5 There's <u>a person</u> waiting for you outside.
_____
_____

Irregular verb chart

VERB	SIMPLE PAST	PAST PARTICIPLE
be	was / were	been
become	became	become
begin	began	begun
bring	brought	brought
build	built	built
buy	bought	bought
choose	chose	chosen
come	came	come
cost	cost	cost
do	did	done
drink	drank	drunk
eat	ate	eaten
fall	fell	fallen
feel	felt	felt
find	found	found
fly	flew	flown
forget	forgot	forgotten
get	got	gotten
give	gave	given
go	went	gone
grow	grew	grown
have	had	had
hear	heard	heard
hurt	hurt	hurt
keep	kept	kept
know	knew	known

VERB	SIMPLE PAST	PAST PARTICIPLE
leave	left	left
let	let	let
lose	lost	lost
make	made	made
meet	met	met
pay	paid	paid
put	put	put
read	read	read
run	ran	run
say	said	said
see	saw	seen
sell	sold	sold
send	sent	sent
sit	sat	sat
sleep	slept	slept
speak	spoke	spoken
spend	spent	spent
swim	swam	swum
take	took	taken
teach	taught	taught
tell	told	told
think	thought	thought
understand	understood	understood
wake	woke	woken
wear	wore	worn
write	wrote	written

Unit 1

▶ 1

Normally, national parks are in the countryside. But Bukhansan National Park in South Korea is part of the city of Seoul. It's about forty-five minutes from the city center by subway. About ten million people visit the park every year. People in Seoul go walking there on the weekends. It's a good way to relax.

▶ 5

P = Presenter, D = David McLain

(The words of David McLain are spoken by an actor.)

P: No one knows exactly the reason why some people live longer than others. Why are they so healthy? Is it their diet? Do they go to the gym more than other people? Well, one man is trying to answer these questions—photographer David McLain. He's currently traveling to different places around the world that have large numbers of people over a hundred years old and asking the question: Why are they so healthy? At the moment, he's working on the island of Sardinia in Italy, and he's speaking to us right now on the phone. David, thank you for joining us today.

D: Hello.

P: So, first of all, tell us why you decided to visit Sardinia.

D: Well, Sardinia is an interesting place because men live to the same age as women. That isn't normal for most countries. Men normally die younger.

P: And does anyone know the reason why men live longer in Sardinia?

D: There are different ideas about this. One explanation is that family is so important here. Every Sunday, the whole family eats a big meal together. Research shows that in countries where people live longer, family is important.

P: I see. So, do you think people live longer in traditional societies?

D: That's an interesting question. Sardinia is a very traditional place, but, even here, the younger generation are eating more food like French fries and burgers. Also, young people are moving to the city, so they are exercising less because of their lifestyle. It'll be interesting to see what happens in Sardinia in the next twenty or thirty years.

▶ 8

C = Customer, P = Pharmacist

1

P: Hello, how can I help you?

C: Hello. I have a runny nose and a sore throat. I feel terrible.

P: Do you have a temperature as well?

C: No, it's normal.

P: Well, you should take this medicine three times a day. It's good for a sore throat.

C: Thanks.

P: And try drinking hot water with honey and lemon. That helps.

C: OK, I will.

P: Oh, and why don't you buy some cough drops? They should help. If you still feel sick in a few days, see a doctor.

P = Patient, D = Doctor

2

D: Good morning. What seems to be the problem?

P: I have a backache.

D: OK, how did you hurt it?

P: I was lifting something heavy, and my back suddenly started hurting.

D: I see. Do you feel any pain when I press on it like this?

P: Not too much, but I can't stand or walk for too long.

D: OK, I'll give you something for the pain. Take one tablet twice a day for seven days. Stay in bed and get some rest. If the pain doesn't go away by next week, come back and see me again.

Unit 2

▶ 9

An Ironman competition has three different races. In the swimming race, the competitors swim for 3.86 kilometers. Then they cycle for 180 kilometers, and finally they run a marathon. The world final of the Ironman Championship is held annually in Hawaii, and it's very competitive. Every year, around 1,900 people compete against each other in front of thousands of spectators.

▶ 11

1

Learning to win and lose is important in a child's education because it teaches them about life. So I think competitive sports in schools are good for children. They're also good for physical health, because when children try to win, they work harder and get more exercise. The other good thing about competitive sports is that children learn to work well in teams when they play against another team. Competitions are a great lesson in teamwork.

2

Some children aren't good at sports, so when school sports are competitive, they always lose. That's really bad for the child. The fact is that not all children are the same, and some children don't like sports. I think schools in my country should be more like the schools in Finland. They are successful schools, but they aren't competitive. They don't have competitive sports, either. So when a child can't do a sport very well, that's OK as long as they do their best and try hard at everything they do.

3

We have a sports day at my school and the children love it. Yes, winning is nice for a child, but the whole day is also a lot of fun. So, overall, I don't think there's a problem with having competitive sports in schools—the problem is with some of the parents. Some parents hate losing and get very competitive. When there's a race or a game, some of them shout at their kids. They think it's the Olympic Games or something!

▶ 12

A: What's on TV?
B: Cycling. It's the Tour de France. I love watching it.
A: Oh, no! I think it's boring!
B: I disagree. I really enjoy watching the cyclists ride through the mountains.
A: Sitting in front of the TV all day isn't exciting. I'm tired of doing nothing. Are you any good at tennis? We could play this afternoon.
B: But I want to watch this.
A: What's wrong? Are you afraid of losing?

▶ 13

1 thing
2 win
3 bank
4 sing
5 ran
6 pink

▶ 15

A: Hey! Have you seen this?
B: What?
A: This ad. You're really good at taking photos.
B: I have so much work at the moment. I don't have time for this.
A: But you could win a new camera!
B: I can take nice photos of friends and family, but I'm not really very creative about it.
A: OK. Well, how about joining something else? Er, this one! Are you interested in acting?
B: You're kidding. I hate standing up in front of people. You're more of a performer than I am.
A: Yes, but it's a musical. I'm not very good at singing.
B: Let me see that. But it says here enthusiasm is more important than talent. You should do it. I think you'd enjoy it.
A: Mm, well, maybe. But I think I'd prefer to join this one on Wednesday evenings.
B: What? You? Exercise?
A: What do you mean? Anyway, it looks like fun. Why don't you come too?
B: But I'm so out of shape!
A: That's the whole point. There's a beginner's group. You should do it with me.

Unit 3

▶ 17

This photo was taken on a train in Bangladesh. It was the end of Ramadan, and lots of people travel home at that time of year. Train tickets sell out quickly, so you often see people riding on top of the trains and between the carriages. In this picture, the woman is sitting between the carriages because there isn't space on top of the train. It looks dangerous, but she doesn't look very worried.

▶ 19

A: Sorry I'm late. Eight-thirty in the morning is the worst time for traffic.
B: I know what you mean. My bicycle is faster than your car during rush hour!
A: I'm sure it is, but I travel farther than you. It'd take me hours to get here by bicycle.
B: There's also the cost of gas. It's so expensive!
A: Tell me about it! In fact, last week I went to look at an electric car.
B: Good idea. They're better for the environment.
A: They're better, but they're also more expensive.
B: Really? Well, what about public transportation? Isn't there a bus stop near your house?
A: Yes, but the fastest bus takes over an hour. It has so many stops!

▶ 21

When we talk about transportation, most people think of buses, cars, bicycles, and so on. But in some parts of the world, animal transportation is as popular as these modern vehicles, and sometimes more popular. In fact, at certain times of the year, animals are the only way to travel. Take the desert, for example, with its 50 degrees Celsius temperatures. Yes, you can cross it in the right vehicles, but for long distances, modern vehicles are not as good as camels. A camel can travel over 40 kilometers per day and can go without water for three to five days. Yes, it's slower, and maybe a camel isn't as comfortable as a car. But a camel's big feet make it more reliable in the sand—unlike a car, it doesn't get stuck.

In winter, northern Alaska can be as cold as the North Pole. Temperatures go down to minus 50 degrees Celsius. Engines can freeze, and even if your car starts, snow and ice on the road can make driving impossible. When the weather is as bad as this, the only way to travel is by sled with a team of between six and eight huskies. These famous dogs can pull heavy sleds for hundreds of kilometers. There is even a race for huskies in Alaska called the Iditarod, where large teams of huskies pull sleds over 1,600 kilometers.

▶ 24

J = Javier, D = Driver

1

J: Hello. Are you free?
D: Yes, where are you going?
J: I'd like to go to the station, please.
D: Bus or train?
J: Oh, sorry. The train station.
D: OK. Hop in.

2

D: There is road construction up by the entrance.
J: You can stop here. It's fine. How much is that?
D: Six thirty.
J: Sorry, I only have a twenty-dollar bill. Do you have change?
D: Sure. So, that's thirteen seventy. Do you want a receipt?
J: No, it's OK, thanks. Bye.

S = Shelley, D = Driver

3

S: Hi. Do you stop at the airport?
D: Yes, I do. Which terminal are you going to? North or south?
S: Um. I need to get to the … north terminal.
D: OK. A one-way or round-trip ticket?
S: One way, please.
D: That's two dollars.

J = Javier, T = Ticket office clerk

4

J: A round-trip ticket to the airport, please.
T: OK. The next train leaves in five minutes.
J: Right. That one, please.
T: First or second class?
J: Second.
T: OK. That's fourteen dollars fifty cents.
J: Oh, no! I don't think I have enough cash.
T: Credit card is fine.
J: Great. Here's my card.
T: OK. Here you are.
J: Which platform is it?
T: Um, platform six.

A = Attendant, S = Shelley, J = Javier

5

A: Hello. Can I see your passport?
S: Here you are.
A: Thanks. How many bags are you checking in?
S: None. I only have this carry-on.
A: OK. Window or aisle seat?
S: Err, I don't really care, but can I get a seat next to my friend?
A: Has he already checked in?
S: No, I'm waiting for him.
A: Well, I can't …
J: Shelley!
S: Javier! Where have you been?
J: It's a long story.

Unit 4

▶ 26

My name's Vic, and I live in Tennessee. During the week, I work in a bank. I like my job, but most of the time I'm sitting at a desk, so I need to get some exercise after work and on the weekends. Most people go running or play sports, but I like caving. My co-workers think I'm a little crazy because they say it's dangerous. It's true that sometimes you have to take a risk when you go caving, but I always go with other cavers, and we look out for each other. It's important to work as a team when you go down into a new cave, because every cave gives you a different challenge. The most difficult cave I've explored is Rumbling Falls Cave. You have to use a rope to climb down a hole that's about twenty meters into the ground. At the bottom, you are on your hands and knees for nearly a kilometer, so you need to be physically fit. Then, at the end, you come into the main part of the cave. It's an incredible place, like a huge room. Getting to Rumbling Falls Cave is probably my biggest achievement as a caver so far.

▶ 29

In May 1985, Joe Simpson and Simon Yates climbed the Siula Grande mountain in the Andes. It's a dangerous mountain, but Simpson and Yates were very experienced climbers and felt optimistic about the challenge. The sun was shining when they left their tents on the first day, and everything went well. Three days later, they reached the top of the mountain, but they didn't stay there long. It was snowing, and the weather was getting worse. While they were going down the mountain, Simpson fell and broke his knee. Yates tied a rope between them and slowly lowered Simpson down the mountain with the rope. Sometime later, when they were getting closer to the bottom of the mountain, Simpson slipped and fell over a cliff. For an hour, Yates held the rope while his friend was hanging in the air. But the rope was getting too heavy, and it was pulling Yates off the mountain. Simon Yates had an impossible decision: Either he could hold the rope, but then they might both die, or he could cut the rope and save himself. …

▶ 30

(The first part of the story is repeated from track 29.)
… At the last second, Yates cut the rope. The next day, he looked for his friend, but couldn't find him. Sadly, Yates decided he was dead. But amazingly, Simpson was still alive, and he started to crawl towards their camp. Three days later, Yates was sleeping in his tent. He planned to go home the next morning. But at midnight, he suddenly woke up. Someone was shouting his name. He ran outside and looked everywhere. Finally, he found Simpson on the ground. He wasn't moving, but he was still breathing. Yates carried him to the tent, and Simpson survived. Later, their story became famous as a book and a movie.

▶ 31

1 I was working on my own when a group of people came into my office.
2 We met them when they were living above our apartment.
3 They weren't getting along very well, so the team agreed to have a meeting.
4 The weather was cold this morning, but it wasn't raining.

▶ 33

A: Hi, Mark. How was your camping trip?
B: It was great in the end, but we had a terrible time at the beginning.
A: Why?
B: First, we left the house late, and then after only half an hour, the car broke down.
A: Oh, no! What did you do?
B: Fortunately, there was a garage nearby and the mechanic fixed the problem. But when we arrived at the forest, it was getting dark. After we drove around for about an hour, we finally found the campsite, but it was completely dark by then. And it was raining!
A: Really? So what happened?
B: We found a nice, warm hotel down the road!
A: That was lucky!
B: Yes, it was a great hotel. In the end, we stayed there for the whole weekend.
A: Sounds great!

Unit 5

▶ 35

Every day we throw away objects such as wood, old household appliances, and glass bottles. But an artist from Uruguay called Jaime built a house made from these types of objects. The house is in Brazil, and it has a bedroom, a kitchen, and a bathroom. There are shelves made from trees and old wood, and there's lots of light. That's because Jaime used colored glass from bottles in the walls. When people visit the house, Jaime wants them to think about the environment and about how we recycle and reuse everyday objects.

▶ 37

Nearly thirty percent of the land on Earth is desert. While the ice in the two cold deserts of the Arctic and Antarctica is starting to melt, hot deserts such as the Gobi Desert and the Sahara are getting bigger. Some countries are trying to stop these deserts from expanding.

Take China, for example. People know about the Great Wall of China, but China is planning on building another wall—this time of trees. Known as the Three-North Shelter Forest Program, the project began in 1978. China started planting the wall of trees to stop the Gobi Desert from spreading toward the cities of northern China. Now the wall has about 66 billion trees, and by 2050 it will be 4,500 kilometers long with about 100 billion trees.

There is a similar problem with the Sahara Desert, which is the largest hot desert in the world. Twenty-one countries in Africa are working together to build a "Great Green Wall" against the spread of the Sahara. The wall of trees is meant to improve food security, create jobs, and restore 50 million hectares of land.

▶ 41

V = Recorded voice, C = Customer service representative, J = Jane

V: Thank you for calling Teco Art dot com. Your call is important to us. For information about our latest products, press one. For orders, press two. For problems with your order, press three. … All our customer service representatives are busy. We apologize for the delay. Your call is important to us. One of our customer service representatives will be with you as soon as possible.
C: Good morning. How can I help you?
J: Hi, I'm calling about an order for a Computer Circuit Board Clock from your website. I received an email saying I have to wait seven more days.
C: One moment … Do you have the order number?
J: Yes, it's 8-0-5-3-1-A.
C: Is that A as in America?
J: That's right.
C: Is that Ms. Jane Tan of 90 North Lane?
J: Yes, it is.
C: Hmm. Can I put you on hold for a minute?
J: Sure.
C: Hello?
J: Yes, hello.
C: I'm very sorry, but this product isn't in stock at the moment. We'll have it in seven days.
J: I already know that. But it's my husband's birthday tomorrow.
C: Ah, I see. Well, would you like to order a similar clock? We have an Apple iPod one for thirty-five dollars.
J: Hmm. I really like the one I ordered.
C: Oh, I'm sorry about that. Would you like to cancel the order?
J: Yes, I think so. How does that work?
C: We'll refund the amount of thirty-nine dollars to your credit card.
J: OK. Thanks.
C: And would you like confirmation by email?
J: Yes, please.
C: Let me check. Your email is J Tan at gmail dot com.
J: That's right.
C: Is there anything else I can help you with?
J: No, thanks. That's everything.
C: OK. Goodbye.
J: Bye.

Unit 6

▶ 44

These three people are waiting in a train station in Winterthur, Switzerland. I like the picture because it shows three people at different stages of their lives communicating in different ways. The elderly woman and the middle-aged woman are chatting, and the young woman—she looks like she's in her twenties—is probably texting her friends or using social media.

▶ 46

1 One day, I intend to buy my own house.
2 I'd be happy to live in another country.
3 I want to be good at playing the piano.
4 I want to take a year off to travel overseas.

▶ 48

R = Reporter, L = Lorette

R: It's about six o'clock in the morning here in New Orleans, and the streets are very quiet. But in about six hours, the city is going to have the biggest party in the world, with thousands of visitors from all over. However, Mardi Gras is really about the local communities in the city. So, I've come to the traditional Tremé neighborhood of New Orleans, where there are already some people preparing for the big day. So, I'll try to speak to some of them … Hello? Hello?
L: Hello?
R: Hello. What's your name?
L: Lorette.
R: Hi, Lorette. You're wearing a fantastic costume. Are you going to be in the parade this afternoon?
L: Yes. Everyone is meeting at the float at six-fifteen, and then we're going to ride through the city.
R: As I say, your dress looks amazing. Did you make it?
L: Yes, we all make our own costumes for Mardi Gras.
R: And do you have a mask?
L: Sure. Here it is. I'll put it on.
R: Wow! That's perfect. So tell me—how important is Mardi Gras for the people in Tremé?
L: It's the most important event of the year. It brings people together.
R: Well, good luck this afternoon. You're going to have a great time, I'm sure!

▶ 49

1 One day when I'm older, I'm going to visit Venice.
2 A: Did Jeff email the times of the parade?
B: I don't know. I'll check my inbox right away.
3 A: Have you bought Mark a present for his birthday?
B: Yes, I'm going to give him a tie.
4 A: Hey, this costume would look great on you.
B: Really? I don't think so, but I'll try it on.

▶ 51

I = Ian, A = Abdullah

1

I: Hi, Abdullah. How's it going?
A: Good, thanks, Ian. I've finished all my classes today, so I can relax. I think I'll take it easy this weekend.
I: Why don't you come to my house on Saturday? My family's having a barbecue in the back yard. It'll be fun.
A: Thanks, but I have a few things to do at home. Besides, it's with your family, so you probably don't want other people there …
I: No, really. I'm inviting a few other people from school as well, so you'll know some people there. I'd really like you to come.
A: OK, thanks. That would be great. Is it a special occasion?
I: Well, my oldest sister has a new baby girl, so it's kind of a celebration for that.
A: Oh! So I should bring something then.
I: No, please don't. It isn't like that. There's no need.

J = Joanna, S = Sally

2

J: Hello, Sally. How are you?
S: Fine, thanks, Joanna. It's been a busy week.
J: Yes, I bet. How much longer are you in town for?
S: The conference ends tomorrow, and I'm leaving on Saturday.
J: Oh. Well, what are you doing tonight?
S: Nothing at the moment. I'll probably be in my hotel.
J: Would you like to come out for dinner? Let's go somewhere this evening.
S: Really? I'd love to.
J: Of course. I'd like to take you to my favorite restaurant.
S: That would be wonderful. I'd like that very much.
J: Great. Let's go right after work. I'll meet you downstairs in the lobby.
S: OK. What time?
J: I finish at six. Is that OK for you?
S: Sure. I'll see you then. Bye.

Unit 7

▶ 53

When I graduated from high school at 18, I didn't have a full-time job at first. I worked part-time in a restaurant. I also did some manual work for a construction company. In the end, I applied for a job as a steel worker at our local steel mill. Pennsylvania has a large steel industry, though it doesn't employ as many people nowadays. Anyway, I've been here for about five years now. At first I didn't get paid very much, but I trained a lot and learned new skills, so now my salary is better.

There are eight people on my team—six men and two women—and we all get along really well. It's hard work, and the hours are long. You're indoors most of the day, and you're working with steel at temperatures that can reach three thousand degrees—so it gets pretty hot around here! Sometimes people are surprised when I tell them where I work. I don't think they expect women to work in a place like this, but there are quite a few other women working in this industry. In fact, my supervisor is also a woman.

▶ 55

I = Interviewer, S = Scientist

I: How long have you worked for your company?
S: For five years. Since I graduated from college.
I: Where did you go to college?
S: Boston. I started when I was nineteen, and I graduated about four years later.
I: Have you always wanted to be a scientist?
S: No. I used to think that science was boring. When I was younger, I wanted to be a journalist.
I: What made you change your mind?
S: In high school, I had an amazing science teacher. He showed me how interesting science really is, and encouraged me to pursue it as a career.
I: Have you ever worked overseas?
S: Yes, I have. I worked in a branch office in Dubai, in the Middle East, two years ago.
I: And how does Pennsylvania compare? Has it been easy living here?
S: Yes, it has, overall.

▶ 56

1

A: Hello? Kristina speaking.
B: Hi, Kristina. It's Jeff.
A: Hi, Jeff. Where are you calling from? You haven't come in today.
B: I'm at home, but I'm about to leave for a meeting. Can you help me? I left a list of prices in the office, and I need it for the meeting.
A: Sure. Is it on your desk?
B: I think it's next to my computer.
A: I can't find it.
B: Oh. Maybe it's in the filing cabinet behind your desk. Try the top drawer on the left.
A: Let me look. Yes, there's a folder called "price lists."
B: That's the one! Can you email me a copy of the list with prices for next year?
A: Sure, I'll do that now.

2

C: Hello, Richard Roberts speaking.
D: Hi. I'm here to fix your copy machine. I'm standing at the entrance to the building.
C: OK, great. There are actually two copy machines in the building. You need to come in the entrance and go up to the third floor. Go through the door and you'll see the photocopy room. My office is next to it, so I'll meet you there.
D: OK. See you in a minute.

▶ 59

N = Natalia, M = Manager

M: Have a seat, Natalia.
N: Thanks.
M: I've looked at your résumé, and I see that you're from Argentina. How long have you been in the United States?
N: Two years. I'm studying fashion design here.
M: I see. So why do you want this job?
N: I have some spare time in the evenings after my classes, and I'd like to earn some extra money.
M: OK. And before this, you worked in another restaurant. What did you like about your last job?
N: Helping the customers and trying to give good service.
M: How did you deal with any difficult situations?
N: On the weekends, we were very busy in the evenings, so sometimes customers had to wait a while for their food. But I found that most customers are OK if you are friendly and polite. Also, you need to apologize if the food is late.

...

M: Good. Well, I think that's everything. Do you have any questions for me?
N: Yes, it says in the ad that you provide training. Can you give me more information about that?
M: Well, you already have lots of experience, so you probably won't need very much training. But on your first day, you'll work with another waiter and learn about our menu and the different kinds of pizza we serve.

Unit 8

▶ 60

It's difficult to remember what life was like before the modern technology we have today. Technology solves mathematical problems for us. It sends messages to friends in a second. It even cooks dinner for us. When technology makes a mistake, it's only because a human has given the wrong instructions. So what's the next big step in technology? Robots are common in industries such as car manufacturing, and recently NASA sent the first humanoid robot into space, where it works on the International Space Station. It's called Robonaut 2, or R2, and it does all the simple or repetitive jobs so the astronauts can spend more time doing experiments. Perhaps in a few years' time, every home will have its own robot to do all the boring work around the house.

▶ 62

1 When I go on vacation, I take lots of sunscreen.
2 We'll need a flashlight if we go out late tonight.
3 We always get lost if my brother drives.
4 I can't buy food if the supermarket isn't open.
5 If you have any questions, call this number.
6 If you don't try harder, you won't pass your exam.

▶ 63

More than one billion people in the world need glasses but can't get them, because they live in places where there aren't any opticians. But now there's a scientist who has solved the problem. Joshua Silver has invented glasses that don't need an optician.

Silver's invention looks like a pair of normal glasses, but there is a pump on each side that contains silicone oil. First, you turn a wheel that controls the pump. The pump pushes the silicone oil through a pipe, and the oil moves into the lenses. As the lens fills with silicone oil, the shape of the lens changes, and you turn the wheel until you can see correctly.

Silver had the idea for this invention a few years ago. He did many experiments before he got it right. A man in Ghana was the first person who used the new glasses. This man made clothes for a living, but he had bad eyesight and found it difficult to work. Once he put on the glasses, however, he found it easy to work again. Silver says, "I will not forget that moment."

After that, Silver started an organization called the Center for Vision in the Developing World. In particular, the center works with schools in countries where students can't get glasses easily. Being able to see well can have a big effect on their education. Silver's glasses are cheap to produce, and over one hundred thousand people now wear them.

▶ 68

A: What's the problem?
B: A friend gave me this drone as a present, but I don't understand the instructions.
A: Oh, yes. I have one like this.
B: Can you show me how it works?
A: Sure. It looks complicated, but it's really easy to use. First of all, have you charged the battery?
B: Yes, I've done that.
A: So now, turn on the remote control.
B: How do I turn it on?
A: It's the button on the side.
B: Oh, OK.
A: So, you have two levers—the left and the right. Let's start with the right. If you push it forwards, the propellers go faster and the drone starts to go up. If you pull it back, the propellers slow down and the drone comes back down.
B: And what is this other lever for?
A: When your drone is in the air, you can move this left lever forwards, backwards, right or left, and the drone flies in that direction.
B: OK. And what happens if I press this big button?
A: It takes photos. Or if you hold it for longer, it records a video.
B: Cool. Let's try it.

Unit 9

▶ 69

(The words of Zoltan Takacs are spoken by an actor.)

1

My name's Zoltan, and I spend a lot of time traveling and studying snakes around the world, from the rain forests to the oceans. For me, my work and my vacation is the same thing. When I travel with my family and friends, I often go diving and looking for sea snakes. I've even kept sea snakes in the hotel bathroom. That's what I call a vacation.

2

My name's Greg, and I own a campsite in Maine. Our busiest time for visitors is the summer, so I always take my vacation later in the fall. Because Maine can be cold later in the year, I usually put my tent in the car, drive to Virginia, and go hiking and camping in the mountains. My friends think I'm crazy. They think I should do something different for my vacation, but I love camping.

3

I'm Moira, and I'm a pilot for an international airline. People think my job is a good way to see the world. Sometimes I have a few hours in a city to go sightseeing, but usually I only see the airport and the hotel room. However, the good thing about my job is that I get a discount on flights, so when I have a vacation, I like flying back to some of the interesting cities I've been to and spending more time there. I also prefer to stay in a bed and breakfast instead of a hotel, because I think you meet more of the local people that way.

▶ 71

A: Hey, you're back! How was your vacation?
B: Umm … to be honest, I'm happy to be home.
A: Why? What happened?
B: Well, on the first day, someone stole my bag. I was waiting at reception to check in, and someone just grabbed it.
A: No way! Did you catch the person?
B: No. He'd run off before anyone could stop him. The hotel reported it to the police, but I never got my bag back.
A: That's horrible.
B: Yeah. Luckily, I'd put my passport and money in my pocket before reaching the hotel. So as soon as I checked in, I bought some new clothes and went sightseeing.
A: That's good. How was the rest of the trip?
B: It was OK, but one night, the lights in the hotel suddenly went out and there was no electricity. I looked for the manager, but she'd left for the night.
A: Oh, no! What did you do?
B: Some of the hotel guests had flashlights, so we sat in the lobby and sang songs. That was fun, actually. In fact, that was probably the best night of the trip!

▶ 72

I realized I'd lost my passport as soon as I put my hand in my pocket.

We'd had a wonderful meal, so we gave the waiter a big tip.

▶ 73

I = Interviewer, M = Madelaine

I: So, Madelaine. I know that you're very excited about your new job. What is it exactly?
M: I'm going to be a tour guide for a travel company.
I: OK. Why do you want to be a tour guide?
M: Well, I've always been interested in different countries, and I've done a lot of independent travel. Last year, I spent six months traveling on my own in South America. So I know all about visiting new places.
I: But traveling on your own isn't the same thing as taking groups of tourists around famous cities or taking them from one hotel to another. Aren't you worried that it might be kind of boring for you?
M: Actually, I think it'll be fascinating because the travel company specializes in adventure holidays. My first tour is very exciting. I'll be leading a group to the Galápagos Archipelago, which is a place I've always wanted to visit.
I: That sounds amazing! So who books these types of vacations?
M: They're usually people who are tired of traditional sightseeing and want something a bit different.
I: What can you do on the tours?
M: Well, for example, on day one we walk along the coast and photograph plants and animals. Day two is kayaking. So I have to organize and plan different group activities for every day.
I: I see. How many people go on the tour?
M: Usually eight. People often come on their own and make new friends. And if someone wants a day on their own, that's fine, too. I think the main thing is that they are never bored!
I: No, it doesn't sound like they will be!

▶ 74

1 amazed, amazing
2 bored, boring
3 fascinated, fascinating
4 interested, interesting
5 frightened, frightening
6 worried, worrying
7 annoyed, annoying
8 tired, tiring

▶ 75

Ryan: OK, so what's our budget? How much money do we want to spend?
Maggie: Not too much! How about going to the beach?
Ryan: Good idea. Who wants to go to the beach?
Adriana: I heard that Prainha Beach in Brazil is beautiful.
Maggie: We'll have to fly there, though, and flights are expensive.
Peter: Who has a car? Maybe we can drive somewhere. That's cheaper than flying.
Ryan: Good idea. I can borrow my brother's car. We drove to California last summer, and it was beautiful.
Adriana: Did you go to any beaches there?
Ryan: Yes, we went to the beach in Santa Barbara, but I don't mind going again. It was really fun!
Maggie: Great. How many people agree to go? We can leave on Friday.

▶ 77

TI = Tourist information, T = Tourist

TI: Hello? Can I help you?
T: Hi. I'm interested in visiting the Tarxien Temples. Do you know the opening hours?
TI: Let me check. Tomorrow is Monday, so it might be closed. A lot of places in Malta are closed on Mondays. Oh, wait! The site is open every day.
T: Great! What time does it open?
TI: At ten. It closes at five.
T: OK. Could you tell me the price?
TI: It's six euros. You can book a ticket here if you want. But are you a student?
T: Yes, I am.
TI: Then it's four fifty. Also, how about booking a guided tour?
T: Um, I'm not sure. How much is that?
TI: The guided tour is twenty euros. It's a good tour—it lasts two hours.
T: I think I'll just buy the regular ticket. One more thing—is there any public transportation to the site?
TI: There's a bus every hour from outside this tourist information office. Or another option is to take a taxi. It isn't too expensive.

Unit 10

▶ 79

This man and his family make these baskets in his home in Hung Yen, Vietnam. Local fishermen buy the baskets for catching fish, but some people also use them in their homes for storing food. Every morning, the man puts as many baskets as he can on his bicycle and slowly rides around the area. As he goes, people stop him to look at the baskets and discuss a price. At the end of the day, he hopes to arrive back home with none left.

▶ 82

You may have listened to music on your headphones on your way to school or work this morning. Maybe you downloaded your favorite music onto a device that holds thousands of songs, or played your favorite songs through your phone. These days, listening to music is a personal activity that we all do on our own. But it didn't use to be so easy to get music, or to listen to music on the move. In the seventies, people used to buy music on vinyl records and play them on record players at home.

But in 1979, the Sony Walkman changed the way people listened to music. In the eighties and nineties, you used to see people everywhere with their Sony Walkman, a few cassettes, and a set of headphones. In the end, Sony's product was so successful that other companies copied the idea—but Sony's original Walkman was always the most popular. By 1986, the name "Walkman" was included as a word in the English dictionary.

Looking back, the idea of the Walkman seems so simple, but simplicity was the reason for its success. At the time, some people thought it was a crazy idea. After all, who wanted a music player with no radio, no speakers, no way to record, and small headphones? They were wrong, of course. The Walkman did everything people wanted it to: It was small enough to carry, it played music, and it was personal.

▶ 85

Sergio: Hi, Rachel. How's it going? Did you find out about the website name?
Rachel: Yes, I've checked. No one else has the website name RetakeRecords.com.
Sergio: Great. I think we should buy it today. Oh, and I've also started to design the home page. Let me show you. What do you think?
Rachel: Um, it's OK. But there's a lot of text.
Sergio: Sure. But I think people will want to know about us.
Rachel: I see what you mean, but we can have a photo of the store at the top, and then move this text somewhere else on the website. In my opinion, it's more important that people see the records for sale as soon as they arrive on the home page. Also, we need a search box so customers can find the record they want.
Sergio: Yes, you're right.
Rachel: Lots of other websites have an "About Us" page. Maybe you could put this text there?
Sergio: Good idea. Also, I think we could have a video of the store on the page, with both of us talking about who we are and what we do.
Rachel: Yes, I agree. A video on the "About Us" page would be nice. Customers will like it because it's more personal. Maybe they can also contact us on that page.
Sergio: I'm not sure about that. Regular customers will want to call or email us directly, so I think we need a separate contact page with our details.

Unit 11

▶ 86

Just over a hundred years ago, the British explorer Captain Robert Falcon Scott died with his team of men in the snow and ice of Antarctica. He had reached the South Pole, but never returned to this hut, which was the starting point for his expedition. Now the hut is falling down under the weight of the snow, and we would like to save it—not just because of its connection to Scott, though this of course is important. Actually, we are more interested in what is inside the hut. Because of the freezing temperatures in this part of the world, the hut has become a time capsule. There are items of food—such as butter, biscuits, and tins of meat—that are one hundred years old. The ice has preserved them all. There are even some of Scott's old possessions and equipment, and things like soap and medicine bottles. When you go inside the hut, it's almost as if he only just left it. I think we need to preserve it because it tells us so much about Scott, and also about our own past.

▶ 88

Jack: I need the TV for my game.
Sonia: I'm watching a really interesting show.
Jack: But I want to get to the next level!
Sonia: You're always using the TV. I haven't watched it for ages.
Jack: OK, then. I'll play it later.

▶ 89

Last week, the captain of a Scottish fishing boat pulled an old bottle out of the ocean in one of his fishing nets. He told news reporters that he had been very curious when he'd seen a message inside the bottle. However, the message was a bit disappointing. It wasn't a love letter or a message from someone lost at sea. Instead, the writer said the message needed to be returned to an address.

In fact, the bottle was part of a scientific experiment that had begun 98 years before, when scientists threw 1,900 bottles into the ocean in order to find out more about the movement of the oceans. It took nearly one hundred years for someone to find this bottle. So it's the oldest message in a bottle ever found—it's a world record.

Of course, the history of messages in bottles goes back many hundreds of years. Over two thousand years ago, the ancient Greeks put bottles in the ocean to find out if the Mediterranean Sea and the Atlantic Ocean were connected. And sailors in World War I sent messages home in bottles. For example, one sailor in 1915 wrote a love letter to his wife. The message said that his boat was sinking and that he loved her.

▶ 91

Good morning and thank you all for coming. Today, I'd like to talk about my vacation in Peru, and in particular, about my journey to Machu Picchu. Machu Picchu is sometimes called "The Lost City of the Incas." Let me begin by telling you about the history of the city. It was discovered by the explorer Hiram Bingham in 1911 …

So, that's everything I wanted to say about Hiram Bingham. Now, let's look at the history of the Incas and why they built Machu Picchu. The first Incas lived in the region of Peru around the thirteenth century …

OK. Now, the next part of my presentation is about my own journey through Peru and up to Machu Picchu. For this, I'd like to show you some of my photos. So this first one is a picture of me in the town of Aguas Calientes. You have to catch the bus from here to Machu Picchu …

OK. So, to sum up, Peru—and especially Machu Picchu—is a magical place, and anyone who's interested in history should go there. Are there any questions?

Unit 12

▶ 93

When a tornado is coming, most people drive in the opposite direction. But storm chasers look for tornadoes and drive toward them. Some storm chasers are scientists—they try to learn more about how tornadoes are formed. Other storm chasers are just everyday people who want to get good photos. The most common time of day to see a tornado is between 4 p.m. and 9 p.m., but tornadoes can be very unpredictable. They can change direction at any moment, so they are difficult to follow. This also makes them extremely dangerous. They can destroy trees and houses in seconds, and some storm chasers have died following tornadoes.

▶ 95

A: Would you move to another country if the weather in your country became much hotter?
B: No, I'd love it if the weather became hotter.
A: I'd go and live somewhere else.
B: Would you?
A: Yes, I wouldn't want to stay. I'd find a country with a colder climate.
B: Oh, I wouldn't. I'd stay and spend every day outside by the pool.

▶ 96

If you live in the middle of the city, maybe you think that there's nowhere to enjoy nature. Or if you have a local park, perhaps you don't think you'll see anybody there except people walking their dogs. However, David Liittschwager, the photographer, wants to show us that everyone can find nature. Different species of plants and animals are always somewhere nearby.

David spent five years recording living things in different places around the world. He took a green metal frame that measured one cubic foot to different locations. Then he spent three weeks in each place and photographed everything living inside the green metal cube. This included leaves, animals, plants, fish, even living things that were smaller than one millimeter in size. Some of his photos were taken in places far away from any town—such as the middle of a forest, the side of a mountain, the ocean, or a river—but some photos were taken in parks in the middle of cities.

▶ 98

Z = Zoo manager, C = City council leader

Z: I'm very worried about the situation. The problem is that the zoo will close without the council's help. How about giving us more money?
C: I'm sorry, but the council doesn't have any more money for the zoo.
Z: But if we don't find a solution soon, then we'll have to close. And the zoo is part of the city. It's a tourist attraction.
C: Yes, but that's the point. It just isn't attracting enough tourists. You're going to have to find the money from somewhere else.
Z: It's also an important place for animal conservation. If we didn't have zoos, some of these animals wouldn't survive.
C: I understand that, but we need to find a different solution. What if you advertised more? In the newspaper, on the radio, or online, for example.
Z: But if we don't have any money, we can't advertise.
C: Well, why don't you try sponsorship? You know, ask a company to support the zoo.
Z: Actually, that isn't a bad idea. You might be right!
C: I have the names of some company bosses you could contact …

NATIONAL GEOGRAPHIC
LEARNING

***Life Student's Book 3,* 2nd Edition**
John Hughes, Helen Stephenson, Paul Dummett

Vice President, Editorial Director: John McHugh
Publisher: Andrew Robinson
Senior Development Editor: Derek Mackrell
Associate Development Editor: Yvonne Tan
Director of Global Marketing: Ian Martin
Senior Product Marketing Manager: Caitlin Thomas
Media Researcher: Rebecca Ray, Leila Hishmeh
Senior IP Analyst: Alexandra Ricciardi
IP Project Manager: Carissa Poweleit
Senior Director, Production: Michael Burggren
Production Manager: Daisy Sosa
Content Project Manager: Beth McNally
Manufacturing Planner: Mary Beth Hennebury
Art Director: Brenda Carmichael
Cover Design: Lisa Trager
Text Design: emc design ltd.
Compositor: Doubleodesign Ireland, Ltd
American Adaptation: Kasia McNabb

© 2019 National Geographic Learning, a Cengage Learning Company

ALL RIGHTS RESERVED. No part of this work covered by the copyright herein may be reproduced or distributed in any form or by any means, except as permitted by U.S. copyright law, without the prior written permission of the copyright owner.

"National Geographic", "National Geographic Society" and the Yellow Border Design are registered trademarks of the National Geographic Society ® Marcas Registradas

For product information and technology assistance, contact us at
Cengage Learning Customer & Sales Support, cengage.com/contact

For permission to use material from this text or product, submit all requests online at **cengage.com/permissions**
Further permissions questions can be emailed to
permissionrequest@cengage.com

Student Book + App: 978-1-337-90564-0
Student Book + App + My Life Online: 978-1-337-90570-1

National Geographic Learning
20 Channel Center Street
Boston, MA 02210
USA

National Geographic Learning, a Cengage Learning Company, has a mission to bring the world to the classroom and the classroom to life. With our English language programs, students learn about their world by experiencing it. Through our partnerships with National Geographic and TED Talks, they develop the language and skills they need to be successful global citizens and leaders.

Locate your local office at **international.cengage.com/region**

Visit National Geographic Learning online at **NGL.Cengage.com/ELT**
Visit our corporate website at **www.cengage.com**

CREDITS

Although every effort has been made to contact copyright holders before publication, this has not always been possible. If notified, the publisher will undertake to rectify any errors or omissions at the earliest opportunity.

Text: p10 Adapted from: (from question 2 onwards) http://ngm.nationalgeographic.com/2010/05/sleep/quiz/sleep#/sleep; p11 Adapted from: http://ngm.nationalgeographic.com/2010/05/sleep/max-text; p12 Adapted from: http://ngm.nationalgeographic.com/ngm/0511/feature1/index.html; p13/181 Adapted from: http://ngm.nationalgeographic.com/ngm/0511/sights_n_sounds/index.html; p15 Adapted from: http://www.natgeotraveller.in/web-exclusive/web-exclusive-month/this-is-your-brain-on-nature/; p22 Adapted from: http://americanfestivalsproject.net; p23 Adapted from: http://americanfestivalsproject.net; p24 Quotations, www.brainyquote.com; p27 Adapted from: http://ngm.nationalgeographic.com/2008/09/wrestlers/guillermoprieto-text called "Bolivian Wrestlers"; p34 Adapted from: http://news.nationalgeographic.com/news/energy/2011/11/pictures/111123-amazing-transportation-ideas/; p37 Adapted from: http://news.nationalgeographic.com/news/special-features/2014/08/140808-london-cabbies-knowledge-cabs-hansom-uber-hippocampus-livery/; p39 Adapted from: http://ngm.nationalgeographic.com/2008/04/kolkata-rickshaws/calvin-trillin-text; p44 Adapted from: https://www.itdp.org/2017-sustainable-transport-award-winner/; p46 Adapted from: http://adventure.nationalgeographic.com/adventure/adventurers-of-the-year/2016/vote/pasang-lhamu/; p47 Adapted from: http://www.nationalgeographic.com/field/explorers/reza/; p48/183 Source: Daily Telegraph 22.10.07. http://www.telegraph.co.uk/news/features/3634463/Joe-Simpson-My-journey-back-into-the-void.html; p51 Adapted from: http://solution-dailybrainteaser.blogspot.co.uk/2015/09/classic-matchstick-puzzle.html; p56 Adapted from: http://www.nationalgeographic.com/adventure/adventurers-of-the-year/2015/aleksander-doba/; p58 Adapted from: http://ngm.nationalgeographic.com/2008/01/high-tech-trash/carroll-text/1; p60 Adapted from: http://www.theguardian.com/environment/2016/may/18/portugal-runs-for-four-days-straight-on-renewable-energy-alone; p60/184 Adapted from: http://www.economist.com/news/international/21613334-vast-tree-planting-arid-regions-failing-halt-deserts-march-great-green-wall; p61 Source: BBC Focus, April 2016, page 64; p63 Source: http://ngadventure.typepad.com/blog/plastiki/; p64 Source: http://www.tecoart.com/; p71 Adapted from: http://www.nationalgeographic.com/adventure/photography/adventure-dreams/road-trip/lessons-learned.html; p72 Adapted from:

Printed in China by CTPS
Print Number: 02 Print Year: 2018

Nat Geo Magazine, February 2007, "Culture: World Party"; p75 Adapted from: http://www.bbc.co.uk/nature/humanplanetexplorer/life_events/coming_of_age; p77 Adapted from: http://glimpse.org/a-wedding-story/; p82 "Faces of the Gas Rush", National Geographic Partners, LLC, October 22, 2010. Reprinted by Permission. p82 Marianne Lavelle, "Natural Gas Stirs Hope and Fear in Pennsylvania", National Geographic Partners, LLC, October 30, 2010. Reprinted by Permission. p82 Source: http://www.careercast.com/jobs-rated/toughest-jobs-fill-2017; p87 Source: http://ngm.nationalgeographic.com/2007/12/vaquero/draper-text; p94 Jay Gifford, National Geographic Partners, LLC, July 15, 2010. Reprinted by Permission. p96 Adapted from: "The Eyes Have It" from NG archive, July 2009, page 25; p99 Adapted from: Article on Biomimetics, April 2008 (pg68–90). http://archive.nationalgeographic.com/?iid=52096#folio=70; p105 Zoltan Takacs; p106 Adapted from: "The Tap Dance of Tipping" from NG Traveler, Nov–Dec 2010, page 16, and also at http://travel.nationalgeographic.co.uk/travel/traveler-magazine/real-travel/tipping/; p108 Source at first edition: sources: http://www.nationalgeographicexpeditions.com/natgeoadventures?utm_source=NGdotcom-Adventure&utm_medium=Link&utm_content=TopNav&utm_campaign=Ngdotcom; p111 http://ngm.nationalgeographic.com/2011/02/paris-underground/shea-text; p118 Christina Bonnington, "Former Apple Employee Explains Origins Of Upside-Down Logo", Wired, May 21, 2012. http://www.wired.com/2012/05/upside-down-apple-logo/; p123 "Information on Why Boredom is Good for You" from BBC Focus magazine, April 2016, page 106; p129 Source: http://news.nationalgeographic.com/news/2010/01/photogalleries/100111-100-year-antarctic-hut-scott-pictures#/antarctic-terra-nova-hut-robert-falcon-scott_11856_600x450.jpg; p130 Adapted from: http://tvblogs.nationalgeographic.com/2013/04/16/from-pac-man-to-wow-the-evolution-of-video-games/; p132 Adapted from: http://news.nationalgeographic.com/news/2012/09/120918-oldest-message-in-a-bottle-science-history-messages/; p135 Tom Mueller, "How Tomb Raiders Are Stealing Our History", National Geographic Partners, LLC, June 2016. p137 Adapted from: http://ngm.nationalgeographic.com/2006/11/reinhold-messner/alexander-text; p142 "What If ...?", xkcd. https://what-if.xkcd.com/16/; p144 Adapted from: "Nature in One Cubic Foot", http://ngm.nationalgeographic.com/2010/02/cubic-foot/liittschwager-photography#/explore/; p147 Adapted from: http://ngm.nationalgeographic.com/2010/10/jane-goodall/quammen-text.

Cover: © Handout/Getty Images.

Photos: 6 (t) © Vincent DiFate/National Geographic Creative; 6 (b) © Pablo Corral V/Corbis/VCG/Getty Images; 7 (tl) © Mike Theiss/National Geographic Creative; 7 (tr) © Chris Rainier; 7 (bl) dbimages/Alamy Stock Photo; 7 (br) © Nadia Isakova/Alamy Stock Photo; 8 (tl) © Teerachat paibung/Shutterstock.com; 8 (tm) © Patrick McFeeley/National Geographic Creative; 8 (tr) © Amy Helene Johansson/Kontinent; 8 (mtl) © Stephen Alvarez/National Geographic Creative; 8 (mtm) © Jaime Riccio; 8 (mtr) © Colmar Wocke; 8 (mbl) © Cary Wolinsky/National Geographic Creative; 8 (mbm) © NASA; 8 (mbr) © Zoltan Takacs; 8 (bl) © Ly Hoang Long; 8 (bm) Aurora Photos/Alamy Stock Photo; 8 (br) © Jim Reed/National Geographic Creative; 9 © Teerachat paibung/Shutterstock.com; 10 © Sheli Spring Saldana/Shutterstock.com; 12 © David McLain/Aurora Photos; 15 © BRDG Studios; 18 Marmaduke St. John/Alamy Stock Photo; 20 © Cesare Naldi/National Geographic Creative; 21 © Patrick McFeeley/National Geographic Creative; 22 © Linda Rosier/NY Daily News Archive/Getty Images; 22–23 © AP Photo/Jim Cole/AP Images; 23 © Ross McDermott; 24 (l) © Cameron Spencer/Getty Images; 24 (m) Reuters/Alamy Stock Photo; 24 (r) Xinhua/Alamy Stock Photo; 27 Design Pics Inc/Alamy Stock Photo; 29 blickwinkel/Alamy Stock Photo; 30 © Joel Saget/AFP/Getty Images; 32 James Copeland/Alamy Stock Photo; 33 © Amy Helene Johansson/Kontinent; 34 (t) © andrey_l/Shutterstock.com; 34 (bl) WENN Ltd/Alamy Stock Photo; 34 (br) © Dan Kitwood/Getty Images; 36 (l) Cultura Creative (RF)/Alamy Stock Photo; 36 (r) Martin Harvey/Alamy Stock Photo; 37 © nui7711/Shutterstock.com; 38 Images-USA/Alamy Stock Photo; 39 © Ami Vitale/Getty Images; 40 (l) David R. Frazier Photolibrary, Inc./Alamy Stock Photo; 40 (ml) © Karel Navarro/Bloomberg/Getty Images; 40 (mr) © tateyama/Shutterstock.com; 40 (r) © muratart/Shutterstock.com; 42 dbimages/Alamy Stock Photo; 44 © Pablo Rogat/Shutterstock.com; 45 © Stephen Alvarez/National Geographic Creative; 46 (l) © Aaron Huey/National Geographic Creative; 46 (r) © Shah Marai/AFP/Getty Images; 47 © Reza/National Geographic Creative; 48 © Borge Ousland/National Geographic Creative; 51 © Wachiwit/Shutterstock.com; 53 © VVO/Shutterstock.com; 54 © Val Thoermer/Shutterstock.com; 54 (inset) © Temujin Doran; 55 © Jolanda Aalbers/Shutterstock.com; 56 © Eduardo Munoz Alvarez/AFP/Getty Images; 57 © Jaime Riccio; 58–59 (t) © Peter Essick/National Geographic Creative; 58–59 (b) Andrew McConnell/Alamy Stock Photo; 60 © Forrest Anderson/Getty Images; 61 Courtesy of Sonam Wangchuk; 62 REUTERS/Daniel Munoz/Alamy Stock Photo; 63 © Don Arnold/Stringer/Getty Images; 64 (l, r) © TEcoArt, LLC; 65 Lorenzo Cavoretto/Alamy Stock Photo; 66 epa european pressphoto agency b.v/Alamy Stock Photo; 67 (tl) © Kathie Nichols/Shutterstock.com; 67 (tr) © Amy Walters/Shutterstock.com; 67 (ml) © Gorb Andrii/Shutterstock.com; 67 (mr) © Lisa S./Shutterstock.com; 67 (bl) © Mentos100/Shutterstock.com; 67 (br) Al Kancello/Alamy Stock Photo; 68 (l) epa european pressphoto agency b.v/Alamy Stock Photo; 68 (r) © Forrest Anderson/Getty Images; 69 © Colmar Wocke; 70–71 © Richard Ligato; 72 © Skip Bolen/WireImage/Getty Images; 75 (t) © Erin Patrice O'Brien/Getty Images; 75 (m) © Eric Lafforgue/Art in All of Us/Getty Images; 75 (b) © Koichi Kamoshida/Getty Images; 76 © Hill Street Studios/Getty Images; 77 B.O'Kane/Alamy Stock Photo; 78 © Pablo Corral V/Corbis/VCG/Getty Images; 79 © Lynn Gail/Getty Images; 80 © The Asahi Shimbun/Getty Images; 81 © Cary Wolinsky/National Geographic Creative; 82 (all) © Scott Goldsmith; 84 © X-ray by Nick Veasey; 87 © Ingram Publishing/Getty Images; 90 © Elif Ozturk/Anadolu Agency/Getty Images; 91 (l, r) © Tom, Dick & Debbie Productions Ltd; 92 © Guillermo Garcia/Shutterstock.com; 93 © NASA; 94 © Iridium Communications Inc.; 95 (camera) © Aleksandar Bunevski/Shutterstock.com; 95 (gas stove) © Premier Edition Image Library/Superstock; 95 (cell phone) © 31moonlight31/Shutterstock.com; 95 (hairdryer) © luckypic/Shutterstock.com; 95 (laptop) © Gino Santa Maria/Shutterstock.com; 95 (hat) © kedrov/Shutterstock.com; 95 (matches) © Passakorn sakulphan/Shutterstock.com; 95 (towel) © sergign/Shutterstock.com; 95 (GPS) © Jeff Metzger/Shutterstock.com; 95 (sunscreen) © Konstantin Faraktinov/Shutterstock.com; 95 (flashlight) © SuperStock; 95 (sunglasses, umbrella) © Ingram Publishing/SuperStock; 96 (t) © Joshua Silver/Centre for Vision in the Developing World; 96 (b) © Wong How Man/Centre for Vision in the Developing World; 97 dpa picture alliance/Alamy Stock Photo; 99 (tl, tml, tmr, bl, bmr, br) © Robert Clark/National Geographic Creative; 99 (tm) Stocksnapper/Alamy Stock Photo; 99 (tr) © Greg Dale/National Geographic Creative; 99 (bml) © Honigjp31/Shutterstock.com; 99 (bm) © Flip Nicklin/Minden Pictures; 100 © Buena Vista Images/Getty Images; 101 © mathieukor/iStockphoto; 102 © Chris Rainier; 104 (l) © Silver, Joshua/Centre for Vision in the Developing World; 104 (r) © Buena Vista Images/Getty Images; 105 © Zoltan Takacs; 106–107 Douglas O'Connor/Alamy Stock Photo; 108–109 © Frans Lanting/National Geographic Creative; 111 Hemis/Alamy Stock Photo; 112 © Paul Almasy/Corbis/VCG/Getty Images; 113 © Ralph Lee Hopkins/National Geographic Creative; 114 © Mike Theiss/National Geographic Creative; 116 (l) © Paul Almasy/Corbis/VCG/Getty Images; 116 (r) © RIEGER Bertrand/Getty Images; 117 © Ly Hoang Long; 118 © Al Luckow; 119 (l) Ian Dagnall/Alamy Stock Photo; 119 (r) © GAP; 120–121 Terry Smith Images/Alamy Stock Photo; 121 © Kiyoshi Ota/Bloomberg/Getty Images; 123 © Martin Poole/Getty Images; 125 (all) © Tatiana Popova/Shutterstock.com; 126 Aerial Archives/Alamy Stock Photo; 128 Iain Masterton/Alamy Stock Photo; 129 Aurora Photos/Alamy Stock Photo; 130 Interfoto/Alamy Stock Photo; 132 © Marine Scotland; 132–133 robertharding/Alamy Stock Photo; 134 (l) © robyvannucci/Getty Images; 134 (ml) Peter Horree/Alamy Stock Photo; 134 (mr) © Leemage/Corbis/Getty Images; 134 (r) © DEA/G. DAGLI ORTI/De Agostini/Getty Images; 135 © Javier Jaen/National Geographic Creative; 136 © Alexey Stiop/Shutterstock.com; 137 imageBROKER/Alamy Stock Photo; 138 © Vincent DiFate/National Geographic Creative; 139 © NASA/JPL; 140 (t) Llama, alpaca, and woman, from Lake Titicaca, Bolivia, c.1475–1532 (silver), Incan/American Museum of Natural History, New York, USA/The Bridgeman Art Library; 140 (m) © Marine Scotland; 140 (b) © rvlsoft/Shutterstock.com; 141 © Jim Reed/National Geographic Creative; 142 (t) imageBROKER/Alamy Stock Photo; 142 (ml) © TongFotoman/Shutterstock.com; 142 (mr) Rob Matheson/Alamy Stock Photo; 142 (b) © Salienko Evgenii/Shutterstock.com; 144 (all) © David Liittschwager/National Geographic Creative; 145 © David Liittschwager/National Geographic Creative; 147 © Michael Nichols/National Geographic Creative; 148 © David Cheskin/Press Association Images/AP Images; 149 Marc Hill/Alamy Stock Photo; 150 © Nadia Isakova/Alamy Stock Photo; 150 (inset) © National Geographic Creative/Alamy Stock Photo; 152 (tl) © TongFotoman/Shutterstock.com; 152 (tr) Rob Matheson/Alamy Stock Photo; 152 (b) © David Liittschwager/National Geographic Creative; 153 (l) John Kellerman/Alamy Stock Photo; 153 (ml) © Design Pics Inc/National Geographic Creative; 153 (m) © Richard Nowitz/National Geographic Creative; 153 (mr) © Design Pics Inc/National Geographic Creative; 153 (r) © rvlsoft/Shutterstock.com; 154 (tl) © Happy Together/Shutterstock.com; 154 (tml) © Gordon Wiltsie/National Geographic Creative; 154 (tm) © Sam Abell/National Geographic Creative; 154 (tmr) © Rose Carson/Shutterstock.com; 154 (tr) © Jonathan Irish/National Geographic Creative; 154 (b) © RIEGER Bertrand/Getty Images; 155 © RIEGER Bertrand/Getty Images.

Illustrations: 6–7 DATA SOURCES: Shaded relief and bathymetry: GTOPO30, USGS EROS Data Center, 2000. ETOPO1/Amante and Eakins, 2009. Land cover: Natural Earth. naturalearthdata.com. Population Density: LandScan 2012 Global Population Database. Developed by Oak Ridge National Laboratory (ORNL), July 2013. Distributed by East View Geospatial: geospatial.com and East View Information Services: eastview.com/online/landscan. Original copyright year: 2015; 16, 20 Eric Olsen/Sylvie Poggio Agency; 41, 50, 130, 155 emc design; 48, 175 John Batten/Beehive Illustration; 72, 143 David Russell; 56 Kevin Hopgood; 73 Mark Turner/Beehive Illustration; 100 Laszlo Veres/Beehive Illustration; 168, 169 Matthew Hams.

ACKNOWLEDGEMENTS

The *Life* publishing team would like to thank the following teachers and students who provided invaluable and detailed feedback on the first edition:

Armik Adamians, Colombo Americano, Cali; Carlos Alberto Aguirre, Universidad Madero, Puebla; Anabel Aikin, La Escuela Oficial de Idiomas de Coslada, Madrid, Spain; Pamela Alvarez, Colegio Eccleston, Lanús; Manuel Antonio, CEL – Unicamp, São Paolo; Bob Ashcroft, Shonan Koka University; Linda Azzopardi, Clubclass; Éricka Bauchwitz, Universidad Madero, Puebla, Mexico; Paola Biancolini, Università Cattolica del Sacro Cuore, Milan; Lisa Blazevic, Moraine Valley Community College; Laura Bottiglieri, Universidad Nacional de Salta; Richard Brookes, Brookes Talen, Aalsmeer; Alan Broomhead, Approach International Student Center; Maria Cante, Universidad Madero, Puebla; Carmín Castillo, Universidad Madero, Puebla; Ana Laura Chacón, Universidad Madero, Puebla; Somchao Chatnaridom, Suratthani Rajabhat University, Surat Thani; Adrian Cini, British Study Centres, London; Andrew Clarke, Centre of English Studies, Dublin; Mariano Cordoni, Centro Universitario de Idiomas, Buenos Aires; Kevin Coughlan, Westgate Corporation; Monica Cuellar, Universidad La Gran Colombia, Colombia; Jacqui Davis-Bowen, St Giles International; Maria del Vecchio, Nihon University; Nuria Mendoza Dominguez, Universidad Nebrija, Madrid; Robin Duncan, ITC London; Christine Eade, Libera Università Internazionale degli Studi Sociali Guido Carli, Rome; Colegios de Alto Rendimiento, Ministry of Education of Peru; Leopoldo Pinzon Escobar, Universidad Catolica; Joanne Evans, Linguarama, Berlin; Scott Ferry, UC San Diego ELI; Juan David Figueroa, Colombo Americano, Cali; Emmanuel Flores, Universidad del Valle de Puebla; Bridget Flynn, Centro Colombo Americano Medellin; Sally Fryer, University of Sheffield, Sheffield; Antonio David Berbel García, Escuela Oficial de Idiomas de Almería, Spain; Lia Gargioni, Feltrinelli Secondary School, Milan; Roberta Giugni, Galileo Galilei Secondary School, Legnano; Monica Gomez, Universidad Pontificia Bolivariana; Doctor Erwin Gonzales, Centro de Idiomas Universidad Nacional San Agustin, Peru; Ivonne Gonzalez, Universidad de La Sabana; J Gouman, Pieter Zandt Scholengemeenschap, Kampen; Cherryll Harrison, UNINT, Rome; Lottie Harrison, International House Recoleta; Marjo Heij, CSG Prins Maurits, Middelharnis; María del Pilar Hernández, Universidad Madero, Puebla; Luz Stella Hernandez, Universidad de La Sabana, Colombia; Rogelio Herrera, Colombo Americano, Cali; Amy Huang, Language Canada, Taipei; Huang Huei-Jiun, Pu Tai Senior High School; Carol Humme, Moraine Valley Community College; Nelson Jaramillo, Colombo Americano, Cali; Jacek Kaczmarek, Xiehe YouDe High School, Taipei; Thurgadevi Kalay, Kaplan, Singapore; Noreen Kane, Centre of English Studies, Dublin; Billy Kao, Jinwen University of Science and Technology; Shih-Fan Kao, Jinwen University of Science and Technology, Taipei; Youmay Kao, Mackay Junior College of Medicine, Nursing, and Management, Taipei; Fleur Kelder, Vechtstede College, Weesp; Waseem Khan, YBM; Dr Sarinya Khattiya, Chiang Mai University; Lucy Khoo, Kaplan; Karen Koh, Kaplan, Singapore; Susan Langerfeld, Liceo Scientifico Statale Augusto Righi, Rome; Hilary Lawler, Centre of English Studies, Dublin; Jon Leachtenauer, Ritsumeikan University; Eva Lendi, Kantonsschule Zürich Nord, Zürich; Michael Ryan Lesser, Busan University of Foreign Studies; Evon Lo, Jinwen University of Science and Technology; Peter Loftus, Centre of English Studies, Dublin; José Luiz, Inglês com Tecnologia, Cruzeiro; Christopher MacGuire, UC Language Center, Chile; Eric Maher, Centre of English Studies, Dublin; Nick Malewski, ITC London; Claudia Maribell Loo, Universidad Madero, Puebla; Malcolm Marr, ITC London; Graciela Martin, ICANA (Belgrano); Michael McCollister, Feng Chia University; Erik Meek, CS Vincent van Gogh, Assen; Marlene Merkt, Kantonsschule Zürich Nord, Zürich; Jason Montgomery, YBM; David Moran, Qatar University, Doha; Rosella Morini, Feltrinelli Secondary School, Milan; Christopher Mulligan, Ritsumeikan University; Judith Mundell, Quarenghi Adult Learning Centre, Milan; Cinthya Nestor, Universidad Madero, Puebla; Nguyen Dang Lang, Duong Minh Language School; Peter O'Connor, Musashino University, Tokyo; Cliona O'Neill, Trinity School, Rome; María José Colón Orellana, Escola Oficial d'Idiomes de Terrassa, Barcelona; Viviana Ortega, Universidad Mayor, Santiago; Luc Peeters, Kyoto Sangyo University, Kyoto; Sanja Brekalo Pelin, La Escuela Oficial de Idiomas de Coslada, Madrid; Itzel Carolina Pérez, Universidad Madero, Puebla, Mexico; Sutthima Peung, Rajamangala University of Technology Rattanakosin; Marina Pezzuoli, Liceo Scientifico Amedeo Avogadro, Rome; Andrew Pharis, Aichi Gakuin University, Nagoya; Hugh Podmore, St Giles International, UK; Carolina Porras, Universidad de La Sabana; Brigit Portilla, Colombo Americano, Cali; Soudaben Pradeep, Kaplan; Judith Puertas, Colombo Americano, Cali; Takako Ramsden, Kyoto Sangyo University, Kyoto; Sophie Rebel-Dijkstra, Aeres Hogeschool; Zita Reszler, Nottingham Language Academy, Nottingham; Sophia Rizzo, St Giles International; Gloria Stella Quintero Riveros, Universidad Catolica; Cecilia Rosas, Euroidiomas; Eleonora Salas, IICANA Centro, Córdoba; Victoria Samaniego, La Escuela Oficial de Idiomas de Pozuelo de Alarcón, Madrid; Jeanette Sandre, Universidad Madero, Puebla; Bruno Scafati, ARICANA; Anya Shaw, International House Belgrano, Argentina; Anne Smith, UNINT, Rome & University of Rome Tor Vergata, Italy; Courtney Smith, US Ling Institute; Suzannah Spencer-George, British Study Centres, Bournemouth; Students of Cultura Inglesa, São Paulo; Makiko Takeda, Aichi Gakuin University, Nagoya; Jilly Taylor, British Study Centres, London; Caroline S. Tornatore, Austin Community College; Juliana Trisno, Kaplan, Singapore; Ruey Miin Tsao, National Cheng Kung University, Tainan City; Michelle Uitterhoeve, Vechtstede College, Weesp; Anna Maria Usai, Liceo Spallanzani, Rome; Carolina Valdiri, Colombo Americano, Cali, Colombia; Keith Vargo, Westgate Corporation; Gina Vasquez, Colombo Americano, Cali; Andreas Vikran, NET School of English, Milan; Helen Ward, Oxford, UK; Mimi Watts, Università Cattolica del Sacro Cuore, Milan; Yvonne Wee, Kaplan Higher Education Academy; Christopher Wood, Meijo University; Kevin Wu, Hangzhou No.14 High School; Yanina Zagarrio, ARICANA.